LOOKING
BEYOND
RACE

LOOKING
BEYOND
RACE

The Life of
Otis Milton Smith

✦

Otis Milton Smith and
Mary M. Stolberg

✦

With a Foreword by Vernon E. Jordan, Jr.

 Wayne State University Press • Detroit

Great Lakes Books

*A complete listing of the books in this series
can be found at the back of this volume.*

Philip P. Mason, Editor
Department of History, Wayne State University

Dr. Charles K. Hyde, Associate Editor
Department of History, Wayne State University

Library of Congress Cataloging-in-Publication Data

Smith, Otis Milton, 1922–
Looking beyond race : the life of Otis Milton Smith / Otis Milton Smith and
Mary M. Stolberg; with a foreword by Vernon E. Jordan, Jr.
p. cm.—(Great Lakes books)
Includes bibliographical references and index.
ISBN 0-8143-2939-X (alk. paper)
1. Smith, Otis Milton, 1922– 2. Afro-American judges—Michigan—
Biography. 3. Afro-American politicians—Michigan—
Biography. 4. Michigan. Supreme Court—Biography. 5. United
States—Race relations—History. I. Stolberg, Mary M. II.
Title. III. Series.

KF373.S573 A35 2000
347.774'03534—dc21
[B]
00-038184

For Hamilton Smith
Who made this book possible
in so many different ways
✦

Contents

Foreword

I knew Otis Smith long before he knew me. As a young lawyer in the 1960s, I was eager to know and learn from the best black lawyers in the country. I soon discovered that Otis was both an outstanding attorney and role model. I had come to know him through many conferences of the National Bar Association (a black lawyers group), the NAACP, and other events long before I asked him to join the board of the National Urban League.

The League, founded in 1911 to help rural blacks adjust to the hardships of life in the city, has been engaged in a determined effort to bring all blacks into the nation's economic, political, and social mainstream. As the League's president, I invited Otis to serve on our board because his own remarkable achievements symbolized our organization's greatest hopes and dreams for black Americans. He agreed to serve, not because we were bosom buddies, but because he saw me as a young man who had taken on an enormous responsibility. He wanted to help and he wanted nothing in return. Otis immediately became a public servant to the Urban League and a guide and counsel to me. He brought his strength, experience, and knowledge to those roles. He was an influential trustee.

Perhaps the thing I admired the most about Otis was that he was a very private man. With regard to his personal life, he kept his own counsel. He was uniquely independent and had admirable inner strength. He was a man of ideas and high ideals. Yet he was realistic and pragmatic.

Otis and I shared a background that was short on money and equal opportunity but long on hope, ambition, faith, confidence, hard work, and good, solid values instilled in us by our parents. I grew up in the public housing projects of Atlanta. Otis grew up in the slums of Memphis. The segregated South of our youth was a mean place for blacks. Yet we overcame overwhelming odds with the help of our parents, teachers, and other adults who created a culture of achievement, based on their own accomplishments.

Like many blacks from the South, Otis sought refuge in the North. His stepping stone to success proved to be World War II. He went to work in war industries and then joined the segregated Army Air Corps. Because he was a veteran, he attended college and law school on the GI Bill. None of these achievements came easily, however. He had to work several jobs to get through school. He lacked connections when he graduated. Nevertheless, through sacrifice, determination, intelligence, ability, and integrity, he attained a level of success that was almost unimaginable given the hurdles he faced.

Otis made his mark in Michigan and the nation's politics. From 1957 to 1959 he served as chair of the Public Service Commission, restoring integrity and efficiency to an agency that had been marked by troubles. In 1960 he was elected to be Michigan's auditor general. That election made history because Otis became the first black elected to state-wide office since Reconstruction. He broke another barrier several years later when he joined Michigan's supreme court, becoming the first black to serve on a state supreme court since Reconstruction. In 1967 Otis joined the legal staff of General Motors. By 1977 he had become GM's general counsel. In that capacity he became one of the highest ranking blacks in corporate America.

Otis always regarded these "firsts" with humility. He acknowledged that his success depended largely on the efforts of others who had laid the groundwork for the nation's greater acceptance of black participation at all levels of American society. He believed that being first was not so much a sign of his personal merit, but was the necessary by-product of the belated effort to admit minorities into positions of power. In the greatest tradition of black American leadership, he did his best to help others who came later.

When Otis retired from General Motors in 1984, he received lucrative offers from some of the nation's largest law firms. Rather than accept any of those offers, Otis chose a pioneering, young, struggling black commercial law firm in Detroit, Lewis, White & Clay (now Lewis & Munday). In that era, most black law firms had general practices; it was unclear whether they could generate enough corporate work to be successful. Confident that he could provide leadership and wise counsel, he proudly joined the firm. He invited me to Detroit to speak to his young partners and share my experiences as a senior partner in a major law firm.

Even when his health was poor and his jobs demanding, Otis always found time for public service. He served on many charitable boards and kept up a tiring speaking schedule at black colleges and universities. He took the time to act as a mentor to hundreds of up-and-coming young black executives. Otis was also generous financially, donating to favorite causes and setting up a trust fund to help single mothers in southeastern Michigan.

Herman Melville wrote: "We cannot live for ourselves alone." Otis, more than most men, truly understood and lived the meaning of that phrase.

Vernon E. Jordan, Jr.
New York, February 2000

Illustrations

1
Formative Years

✦ 1 ✦
Growing Up in Memphis

I WAS BORN on February 20, 1922, in a shotgun house on Decatur Street, just off of Jackson Avenue, in the black slums of Memphis, Tennessee. There was considerable debate about what to name me, and I never did find out how I came to be called Otis Milton Smith. My mother was a deeply religious woman and a member of the African Methodist Episcopal Church. At one time, I understand she considered naming me Charles Wesley Smith to go along with my older brother, whom she named John Wesley Smith. In that way, we would have been named for the Wesley brothers of England, who founded the Methodist Church. I do not know why she never followed through. Years later I got my birth certificate and was surprised to discover that it listed my name as Henry Ford Smith. Naming me after the famous car maker would have been in keeping with my mother's great ambitions and hopes for me, even though she could never have guessed back then, in segregated Memphis, that I would become the first black to serve as counsel for a major American corporation when I worked for General Motors. Whatever her hopes or dreams, I always have been known as Otis Milton Smith. I never learned where the Milton came from. I heard later that Otis was the name of a doctor, but I never did know whether it was the man's first or last name. In any case, I was named for him even though he did not deliver me. My mother told me that a female doctor, helped by my Aunt Maggie, attended my birth.

In later years, my mother did not dwell on my birth or talk much about my father. He was white; my mother was black. My birth certificate listed him as "unknown." That was the way they did things back then in the South, when interracial liaisons were illegal. Even

17

though some of my father's relatives and friends may not have known about his relationship to us, we knew who he was. His name was Samuel McCollough Williamson, and he was born in Memphis in 1871. My mother never told me how they met. Even when I was an adult, she refused to discuss it, and when I asked about it, she would just look at me and then pass on to something else. I can only guess that she worked as a domestic in his household, and she formed a secret relationship with him that produced my brother in 1918 and me in 1922.

Given the circumstances, it is not surprising that my mother, Eva Willoughby Smith, was the greater influence in my life. She was born July 25, 1892, in Natchez, Mississippi, the second child and first daughter of Richard James Smith and Maggie W. Smith. As a young woman she followed her brothers north to Memphis to seek better employment and more opportunities than existed in the bowels of Mississippi. My mother was an energetic little lady of high purpose who was very preachy about moral precepts. She was highly religious and very familiar with the Bible. Although she went only through the sixth grade, she had a thirst for knowledge that went far beyond the grade level that she achieved in school. She was very strong-willed and lived until she was eighty-seven years old. I guess I was a mama's boy because we were always drawn to one another. I have always known that my mother was the author of my moral compass, and it was her example that made it fairly easy for me to practice law and operate in high-powered government, judicial, and corporate jobs. I have often said that my mother had more character in her little finger than many of the so-called important people that I later met had in their whole bodies.

It was years later that I learned much about my father. He came from what southerners used to refer to as "good stock." His mother, Delia Talbot, was a member of an old Memphis family that had purchased land from Andrew Jackson. His father, Robert Chapman Williamson, was a lawyer and Confederate war veteran who moved to Memphis from Somerville, Tennessee. My father was brought up Catholic by his mother in Memphis, which like most of the South then was staunchly Protestant. He attended Christian Brothers College, which actually was a Catholic high school in Memphis. He dropped out of school to work as an office boy, but his lack of education did not seem to hurt him. He was a self-made, highly successful businessman. In 1897 he founded one of the largest real estate and banking firms in the city, S. M. Williamson & Company, Incorporated, which covered the entire ground floor of a two-story office building at 115 Monroe Avenue, just off of Main Street, downtown. My father also became a civic leader. He served on the committee that helped build the city auditorium; he served twice as president of the Memphis Insurance Exchange, and he even had a park and a street named for him in 1927.

A year after the stock market crash in October 1929 my father went bankrupt. Many of his company's assets were in cotton plantations, which had been adversely affected first by flooding and later by drought. The resulting decline in cotton prices and drop in the value of agricultural land spelled disaster. He filed for bankruptcy in October 1930, but within three months formed a new, smaller company that specialized in real estate. He reduced his staff and moved into a smaller suite of offices in the Bank of Commerce Building. In a November 1930 article, the *Memphis Commercial Appeal* characterized the rise, failure, and reorganization of my father's fortunes as "one of the most interesting and dramatic business stories of Memphis history."

In any event, I did not know my father well. In the early years, we only saw him when he would bring us our monthly allowance and at Christmastime when he would bring us gold coins. Our monthly stipend was not much. Eighty or ninety dollars. Maybe more sometimes. Before the depression, my father would send two of his trusted associates, P. C. Clarke and Perry Pipkins, to deliver our money. After his bankruptcy, he always brought the cash himself. He would come midmorning, the first day of every month. If my brother and I were at home, we would look out for the small Dodge coupe he drove. He would knock on the door and greet my mother in a civil but somewhat formal way as "Eva." She called him "Mr. Williamson." He would inquire about us, and she would tell him how we were. With very little more than just a short exchange of pleasantries, he would take out his wallet and count the money. The encounter was always brief.

Catching a glimpse of him once a month was not conducive to an intimate father-son relationship. Besides, he was a white man—an important white man—and that in itself at the time was somewhat scary. The way we were brought up in the South, there was always some apprehension when we approached a white man because he had almost unlimited power and we were nervous about what he might do. I was always a little shy and a little fearful of my father. He was a tall man of about six-foot-two who had blue eyes that would pierce right though you. My brother, who was three years older than I was, knew him better, talked to him at times, and admired him. Most of what I know about him, by contrast, is based on things I have read and things I have since been told by my white cousins, whom my brother and I have met and had deep conversations with about the old days back in Memphis when we did not know one another. My cousins are about our ages, and we have had some very pleasant contacts with them. My cousin Ann sent us a small collection of photographs showing my father from the time he was a teenager to about two years before he died. The pictures show a serious person, almost stern, but certainly not harsh.

By all accounts, my father was a person to be reckoned with. Our cousins, his sister's son and daughters, all confirm that my father was addressed by everybody as "Boss." My mother told us about one incident that demonstrated my father's temper. He had a disagreement with a business adversary and became very angry. He struck the man a hard right in the gut, so hard that it snapped the man's belt buckle and his pants dropped. I asked my cousin Sam if he knew about the incident. He did not, but he said he could easily believe that it was true.

My brother tells one story about my father that sums up his and our plight. My brother had a shoe-shine kit and was peddling his services downtown. My father looked at him and did not recognize him at first. Then he took another look. Apparently it was just too much for him—having his son, in his own image, a little black boy running around shining white men's shoes. So my father said to him, "John, is that you? . . . Does your mother know about this?" And, of course, my brother said, "Yes." My father said, "Well, you go home and tell Eva that I don't think you ought to be out here doing this kind of work."

My brother felt that this was an example of a sensitive, caring father. I was a little bit more skeptical. I could never quite forgive my father for putting my brother and me in the position that he did. His wife, Ada Freeman Williamson, was a sickly woman who spent a lot of time in bed, according to my cousin Sam. That, of course, is no excuse for what happened. Still, my parents must have felt a powerful attraction to one another to have engaged in what was then an illegal relationship that went against the strong moral and religious beliefs they both held. I do not know exactly what happened because my parents never talked about it. All I can conclude is that it must have been a strong affinity that went on for some time because my brother and I are more than three years apart in age.

The longer I have lived, the closer I have come to accepting the awkwardness of my parents' situation. I long ago came to appreciate that what sustained me through life was the tradition of achievement inherited from my father and the moral values and work ethic I inherited from my mother. I have also derived some insights about myself and my racial identity. I know who I am, and I know where I come from. I consider myself a quintessential American because my family has many strains of blood: African, European, and Native American. My forebears through my father's line were from England and settled in Maryland during colonial times. They later crossed into Tennessee and were among its original settlers. One of my great-grandmothers, on my mother's side, was a Native American who had children by an African American. It is interesting being part of a family that ranges from jet black to snow white and a few things in between. Assessing where I come from makes me, in my own mind at least, more comfortable with who I am. Mine may not have been the kindest and gentlest way to be born, but we do not have any control over who our parents are. Whoever and whatever they are is just part of our inheritance.

There were definitely drawbacks in my case. Growing up as I did, I developed a high anxiety about situations. I was always fearful of being hungry and fearful of being exposed as the bastard child of a white father. Even as an adult, I have lived my life on an anxious edge. Still, to me the strengths outweigh the weaknesses. I appreciate the fact that I inherited very little in the way of weakness from my parents. After having been the cause of two bastard children, my parents did fairly well by us. Neither one was a weakling or so lacking in character that they dumped us off onto somebody else. Considering the helplessness of children, anybody is damned lucky who gets parents who will look after them until they grow up and are able to go out on their own.

Despite my mixed feelings about my father, I did cry at his funeral, which I attended in a manner of speaking. My father was a daily communicant at St. Peter's Catholic Church at Third and Adams in Memphis. When he died, I rode my bicycle down to the church. I watched from across the street and wept from a distance as the pallbearers brought out his body in the casket.

Luckily, I always had my older brother to look after me. He was born on November 26, 1918, about two weeks after the Armistice was signed ending World War I. My mother named him John Wesley Smith, and he bore that name until he was about fifteen or sixteen years old when he decided that it was far too common. After experimenting with several names like J. Wesley Smith, Wesley Yardon Douglas Smith, and Johnson Smith, he named himself J. Hamilton after Professor G. P. Hamilton, a prominent black educator and author in Memphis. For the past twenty-five or thirty years, he has been known simply as Hamilton Smith. My brother has always been my best friend. I often said if I had to invent an older brother, he would most likely meet the description of Hamilton, who was wise beyond his years and matured at an early age. He seemed absolutely grown at fifteen, helped me over several major hurdles, and was my principal cheerleader.

Even with our father's financial help, we never lived that well. We always resided in the poorest section of town and moved around like gypsies. In seventeen years, I think we moved eleven or twelve times from Decatur Street to Jackson Avenue to Hasting Street to Fourth Street to Mosby Avenue to Robeson Avenue to Delmar Avenue to Overton Park Avenue to Peach Avenue, all in North Memphis, just north of Poplar Avenue, between Poplar and Jackson. We moved often because of my mother's sense of embarrassment about our complicated family situation. We probably lived longest on Fourth Street, next to St. James A.M.E. Church, which we attended regularly when the Reverend James S. Kelly was pastor.

Invariably we lived in little shotgun houses, so-called because they used to say that you could shoot through the front door and the bullet would go right through the back door. There were just three straight rooms: the front room, the middle room, and a kitchen. They were double tenements, two houses joined by a common wall. There was no basement. The houses sat up on brick or concrete pilings. We never had hot water or central heating. We used wood stoves and heaters. The toilet stool was usually on the back porch, in an enclosed area, or in the backyard. Several houses that we lived in did have bathrooms, and on a couple of occasions we lived in four-room houses. We did not have electric lights until the Tennessee Valley Authority (TVA) came through and made it quite cheap to have electricity around 1940. So, for the early part of my life, we used kerosene lamps.

People now would call the neighborhoods we lived in black ghettos, although there were often poor whites living in the same block. My brother observed that as boys in Memphis we were more integrated than in the Washington, D.C., neighborhood where he raised his children decades later. Even though we were poor and black, we always thought we were middle class. It is kind of a joke we have in the family. We thought the way people were supposed to think as members of the middle class. We were ambitious. We were God-fearing and law-abiding. We always respected learning. Most of our neighbors were the same. Although we lived in a poor neighborhood during the Great Depression, there was very little crime. About the worst thing we heard of was someone stealing chickens from backyard coops.

My family was goal-oriented, and I nursed my first ambition in 1927 when I was five years old. I remember 1927 very clearly because that was the year that Charles A. Lindbergh flew the Atlantic Ocean alone in his plane. After his triumphant landing in Paris, he came back and toured the United States. He was a St. Louis boy and got down as far as Memphis, where the city fathers threw a great celebration for him. He flew the silver *Spirit of St. Louis* low over the city and dipped the plane's wings for us as we were looking up at him. I decided at that moment that I would become an aviator when I grew up, and I am sure that was why I joined the Army Air Corps during World War II.

The next memorable year of my life was 1930 because my brother and I got to visit our mother's kin in rural Mississippi. As a result of my father's financial troubles, he dropped the amount of our monthly allowance from eighty or ninety dollars to fifty dollars, which changed our lifestyle considerably. My mother responded by trying to find us a stepfather. While she looked, she sent my brother and me away for two months, down to her ancestral home very close to Natchez, in a little town called Rodney. It was where my mother's grandmother, Frances McAllen, lived on a small farm that is still there after all of these years. The farm is not too far from the Mississippi River, and the water used to come very close to flooding the place, although it never got up quite that far during my boyhood.

What an event it was to meet our great-grandmother, who told us about slavery firsthand! She had been a member of a small family with one or two sisters. She was sold away from her home in Virginia in the slave market and ended up in Mississippi. Unfortunately, I was not bright enough at the age of eight to ask her questions about slavery, although she did tell us how excited she was on what she called "Manumation" Day, January 1, 1863, when Abraham Lincoln issued the Emancipation Proclamation. In any case, I am not sure whether she was sold directly to my great-grandfather, John McAllen, but she wound up in his possession. He was an Irishman who had come to Mississippi from Texas seeking a better life. He was a carpenter and single-handedly built a little Catholic church in the center of Rodney. At first, he owned my great-grandmother. After the Civil War, he married her and they had three children. His picture always graced the walls of her little shack.

By the time I knew my great-grandmother, she was in her eighties. She was a little woman, feisty as she could be, and honored and revered by everyone around her. She would go out in the hot sun and take water to the field hands working on the farm. It was a very small farm, probably less than forty acres. My Aunt Udoxie was the oldest child, then came my Grandmother Maggie, and then my Uncle Frank, who was the youngest. Uncle Frank was married to my Aunt Ada, who was a schoolteacher. They had two children, Bud and Darling, as we called them. Bud was really named John after my great-grandfather. Anyway, they lived in the other shack on my great-grandmother's property. Uncle Frank was crippled and could not do much except help out a little with the farming.

Rodney was an interesting town because most of the people had been there for a long time, so the black-white relations were not typical of the South. Instead, there was an understanding of some closeness or kinship or something. Maybe not blood kinship but close friendship. The next-door neighbors on one side, Charlie and John Pape, were white. They were very kind to us and let us ride their horse. On the other side was a black family. Across the dusty road, there was a little grocery store owned by the Hecklers, who also were white. During that summer we got to know the neighbors and got to work around the farm. We helped take care of the animals. Occasionally, we took treks down the road to bring water from the spring, probably a quarter of a mile away. Sometimes, we would go up to the little business district, which had a couple of stores, the post office, and the church that my great-grandfather built.

In 1984 or 1985 when my brother and I made one of our nostalgic trips back South, we met in Memphis and drove down the Natchez Trace. We stopped along the way to see what was left of Rodney. The little stores had gone. The Catholic church was gone. We were told by our cousin Bud that the church had been moved by the Natchez Historical Society from Rodney to Grand Gulf State Park, which is about twenty-five miles away. We drove to the park to see this little church that my great-grandfather was supposed to have built. I did not think it was the same church that I saw back in 1930, which was primitive wood and unpainted with very crude stations of the cross. The church we saw at Grand Gulf State Park was about the same size, but it was more professionally done. My brother wants to give my great-grand-father credit for it, but I am not sure we can. Anyway, we know that he built a church of some kind.

In the fall of 1930, not too long after we got back to Memphis from visiting our kinfolks in Mississippi, my mother introduced us to Paul Jefferson Grant, a gentleman of color who worked at an auto factory in Memphis. He was a nice, quiet man—a tall fellow. I guess he would have been the appropriate kind of a stepfather for my brother and me, but I never had much chance to find out. Unfortunately, my mother's marriage to Mr. Grant did not last very long, maybe a matter of months. I never knew what their problem was, but Mr. Grant just moved out, and I never knew what happened to him. Nevertheless, from then until her death in 1979, my mother was known as Mrs. Eva Smith Grant.

During the marriage we lived on Seventh Street, near Auction Avenue, across from Grant School, which I attended for five years. I started school there a little bit early because I was five years old in September 1927 and did not turn six until February 1928. There was no such thing in Memphis as kindergarten then; it was just right into the first grade. I was so afraid. Our mother sent me to school with my brother, and I sat with him in class. I sat with him all day a couple of times, and when my time came to stay in my own class I got up and ran out with him whenever he would leave. Finally, my first-grade teacher, Mary D. King, told me to sit, and I sat and cried for almost half the day, as I remember it. Occasionally, I peeked up to look at the kids around me as I was sniffling and blowing my nose. At noon they all got up and went out to lunch, and I finally got up and looked out the windows and cautiously crept outside and found it was not so bad. I came back in, took my place, and discovered that I liked school.

I was a good student, usually getting all A's or close to it. I arrived in the fifth grade, and after a few weeks, the teacher said there was not much more I could learn, so the principal promoted me to the sixth grade. We moved and I attended Carnes Grammar School. I was salutatorian of the eighth grade graduating class at Carnes and was a champion speller, coming in second as the school's representative in the citywide spelling bee for Memphis's sixty black schools. This was no surprise really. My mother read quite a bit, the Bible mostly, and instilled in us a love of words and spelling. She used to hold the spelling book and have us spell the words and make us look up the words we did not know. My brother was a champion speller before me. I was just following in his footsteps.

Like every other period in life, there was good and bad, usually occurring at the same time. While I progressed in grammar school, I was haunted by my very light skin color. It was not unique. There were always a handful of kids around school who were very light, reflective of what somebody euphemistically called "midnight social equality in Dixie." Still, some kids used to harass those of us who were light-skinned. They would call us "white folks," and that would be the most embarrassing thing that could happen. I remember one occasion vividly. A couple of bullies took exception to me—a little yellow boy with gold and bronze curls—and punched me in the face. I was humiliated by my black eye and went home to get it fixed so I could return to school and participate in the third grade Christmas play.

All of the time I was growing up, I was conscious that there were a few light-skinned children who seemed to like themselves, but they were not in the majority. Later, when I was older, I heard about so-called blue-vein societies in places like Memphis and Washington, D.C., where there were light-skinned people who were the result of the "selective inbreeding" of light skin marrying light skin. But that was not part of the way I was raised. It has been a long-standing tradition in my family that color has no place whatsoever in the value system. Although my father was white and I am close to him in color, my brother is a shade or two darker. My mother was medium brown. In our extended family, my grandmother was light because her father was white, but her mother was black. My aunts and cousins are every color of the rainbow, and I am glad that in my family, color never was equated with worthiness.

As I got older, I would do almost anything to avoid being called white by my classmates. I would not fight about it, but I would try to avoid it happening by trying to make special friends out of the people who were likely to taunt me. Years later, when I was the only black working in a world of whites, I developed this habit into what I called "the ten percent rule." I reasoned if I had ten percent in common with anyone, I could discuss those things we shared, eventually building on that common ground either to become friends or, at the very least, to forge a working relationship.

Some of my attitudes about getting along with others came from reading Dale Carnegie's *How to Win Friends and Influence People*. When we were young, my brother and I decided to pool our resources to buy the book as part of our self-improvement agenda. We also bought books on physical training and how to conduct oneself. In any case, we learned every darn thing in Carnegie's book. I still remember things like "A man's name to him is the sweetest and most important word in the English language" and "A man convinced against his will is of the same opinion still. Don't argue." My brother and I memorized all this stuff and used to practice it on each other. We eventually realized that our efforts were artificial, and we decided the best way to employ Carnegie's suggestions was to use them only in an earnest way at appropriate times. Our desire to get along with people was always strong because we were both outgoing and made friends easily. Not everybody, of course, because there will always be people who reject you because of skin color and other arbitrary things. But most people we found were easy to make friends with. So we did.

I found another source of self-esteem by joining the Boy Scouts when I was eleven years old. I was too young to join by two months when I showed up for my first meeting, but Charles Chatman, the scoutmaster, felt sorry for me and let me stay on condition that I be a good Boy Scout. I always tried to keep my promise to him. Troop 107 met in the basement of St. Stephen's Baptist Church on First Street, in North Memphis, not far from downtown. It was not in the neighborhood where I lived. In fact, hardly any members of the troop lived there. Mr. Chatman came from South Memphis, the other side of town. None of us had cars or bicycles, so we had to walk three or four miles to our weekly meetings. Our patrol leader, Monroe Bolden, or the assistant scoutmaster, Earl Withers, would collect me and other boys along the way. Other older scouts and Mr. Chatman would pick up boys from whatever direction they were coming. Once or twice we had citywide jamborees in which all of the black scout troops (not the white, of course) took part. These jamborees involved a lot of events like knot-tying, first-aid practice, signaling, fire building, water boiling, and the great, final event—chariot racing. Each troop built a chariot and put the smallest kid in it and had the biggest kid pull it. My favorite activity was building a fire without matches. In fact, a fellow scout and I took the record for it. All of these things held a larger significance because Mr. Chatman always reminded us about former Boy Scouts who took part in such activities and then went on to enjoy great success as educators or doctors.

In addition to providing role models and character training, the Boy Scouts allowed me the chance to develop other skills, including leadership. In those days every troop was supposed to have four patrols, each with eight boys. We had only three patrols, and after I had been a scout for about a year, I suggested we form the Silver Fox Patrol. Mr. Chatman gave his permission, and I became the patrol leader and junior assistant scoutmaster. After Troop 107 was rolling along pretty well under his leadership, Mr. Chatman had the vision that we ought to have a drum and bugle corps to march in the annual Armistice Day Parade and to participate in other functions. Our parents could not afford to buy the equipment. Most of them had a hard time just putting food on the table. Mr. Chatman thought we could raise the money—or most of it—by selling penny boxes of matches on the streets of Memphis. And so we did. We built a twenty-one-piece drum and bugle corps. I still have a photograph of me leading the troop down Main Street during the Armistice Day parade in 1937 or somewhere along in there. I never did understand how Mr. Chatman accomplished so much with our troop. What faith! The Bible says "faith can move mountains." Charles Chatman had such faith, and he imparted it to his boys.

I kept up with Mr. Chatman until his death, at age ninety-four, in 1989. In 1978, when I returned to Memphis to help raise money for Fisk University, which had set up a scholarship fund in my name, Mr. Chatman spoke about me. Eight years later, I went back to Memphis on Scout Sunday to establish a trust fund to help youth in his name. He once asked me why I was so solicitous of him. I said, "You were like a father to me, the father I didn't have. And you don't know how much it meant to have someone in my corner, someone who believed in me." I guess next to my mother and brother, he had the greatest impact on me as a child.

Someone has said that all history is biography. That is, you can understand history in terms of the great men who have marched across time in seven-league boots, who have charted the seas and made the great discoveries, and so on. I take nothing away from them, but it is my firm conviction that over the centuries the people who have held the world together are people like Charles Chatman, common people who through their uncommon kindness, their uncommon generosity, their uncommon moral character have held

Being a Boy Scout was a major influence in Smith's life. He is pictured in the center of the first row. His six-foot-four-inch height earned him the nickname "Too Tall" Smith in high school.

neighborhoods together, and cities together, and nations together, and through these the world.

Mr. Chatman went no further than the eighth or ninth grade in school, but he was a great success in helping to mold the lives of young boys, including me. No boy who went through his troop was ever the same, so great was his impact on their characters. He was a man of enormous faith—faith in God, faith in his country, faith in the scouting movement. He believed there was no such thing as a bad boy, only bad habits, and he had a way of changing habits and bringing out the best in boys. He was serious without being stuffy, and he was friendly with none of that palsy-walsy stuff that comes with trying to pretend he was one of the boys. He was a man—a real man—not a muscle-flexing jock, but a sober, consistent man with a vision of developing boys individually. I remember one incident in which several of us threw rocks at an old, abandoned building as we were walking home from a scout meeting. The first order of business at the next meeting, after the opening ceremonies, was to convene a board of inquiry with the final result being that we all came to understand that even old buildings were owned by somebody and that we were bound to respect the rights of property owners.

By trade, Mr. Chatman was a porter and a sometime elevator operator, who put all of his spare time in teaching boys in such a way that they would never forget the elements of character and good citizenship. His boys are spread out all over the country, and many are doctors, lawyers, teachers, soldiers, and policemen. In my opinion, he was a far greater success than many people I have known with far loftier occupations. He personified the belief—which my mother also held—that hardly a day goes by when we do not have the opportunity to exhibit faith, to demonstrate hope, and to practice charity. We can all search our memories for the unforgettable persons who have passed in and out of our lives but whose impressions are indelibly left. Mr. Chatman always comes to mind for me. Although he had no children of his own, he had a way with boys. Born a humble man, working on a humble job, working in a humble troop, in a humble church, in a humble neighborhood, his accomplishments were rivaled by few men that I ever met.

Mr. Chatman, like my mother, was a great believer in inspirational quotations. He and his wife operated a little florist business, and every day Mr. Chatman would place a sign in the window on which he had laboriously printed a "thought for the day." One day he might go with the Boy Scout motto, "Be Prepared." On other days, he might use a quote from Benjamin Franklin's *Poor Richard's Almanac,* such as "God Helps Them that Helps Themselves." I remember others that appeared in his window: "A Man is Known by the Company He Keeps" and "As the Twig is Bent so is the Tree Inclined", or as my mother would have put it, "If you keep leaning toward sin, you are going to become sinful." As I get older, I am surprised at how much these old sayings, which contain so much wisdom but seem so trite, really are part of many admirable people's value systems. One of the sayings that stuck with me seemed to appear with regularity in Mr. Chatman's window. It read, "What I am to be I am now becoming." Mr. Chatman used to say that you could not be a habitual liar as a boy and grow up to be a truthful man. "Cheat in little things; cheat in big things," he would warn us. Over the years, I have noticed that the guys I grew up with in school and in the Army who liked to flaunt the rules usually wound up in serious trouble later on. And whiners and complainers who could only find fault in the other guy seemed to become the malcontents who moved from job to job unless there was a major overhaul in their character.

In 1934, the same year that I graduated from grammar school, my mother's brother, John T. Smith, and his wife, Josie, made their biannual pilgrimage to the South from their home in Flint, Michigan. Josie was from West Memphis and Uncle John had spent some time in Memphis, and they came back to see kinfolks. They invited my brother to stay with them in Flint, where they promised they would put him through school and send him to the University of Michigan. When he was away that year, things were pretty rough. My mother had begun working again as a domestic, and she worked the usual hours for that job in those days. She would leave about six or six-thirty in the morning and come home about the same time in the evening. Most often she walked to work—a mile or two each way. She worked six days a week with half a day off on Thursday and half a day off on Sunday. In those days, domestics did everything. My mother worked for middle-class whites, and she would cook breakfast for them, then clean house, then prepare dinner and serve it.

With my brother away and my mother at work, I began to "climb fool's hill." I did not negotiate the transition from grammar to high school well. The larger classes, the looseness of it, and the lack of time from my mother and guidance from my brother added up to trouble. I got very sloppy in schoolwork, made poor grades, and played truant with my buddies. On a spring day, instead of going to school, we found it more enticing to go out to the railroad tracks and wander around. Sometimes we would go to the back of Sears and Roebuck on Watkins Street to see if there was anything of value to pick out of the trash. Sometimes we would head the other way and go across the shaky, wooden Harahan Bridge that spanned the Mississippi River from Memphis to West Memphis, Arkansas. We were not looking for any excitement. We did not steal anything or get into any trouble. All we were looking for was something that was beyond our neighborhood. I do not know why we did not get picked up by the truant officer. Anyway, it was a sorry year. The ninth grade was not too bad, but the tenth

31

grade was disastrous. To make matters even harder, I developed severe acne that got worse and worse. My height—I was six-feet-two-inches by then—was another source of embarrassment. Classmates called me "Too Tall" Smith. For all of these reasons, I decided to drop out of school.

That did not mean that I enjoyed days of leisure. I went to work full-time. One aspect of my family's middle-class outlook was our belief in work. I had begun helping my brother sell newspapers when I was seven. We would go up and down the streets on Sunday yelling, "Paper, paper, Sunday morning *Commercial*," referring to the *Memphis Commercial Appeal*. We went from that to selling weekly black newspapers: the *Pittsburgh Courier*, the *Chicago Defender*, and the *Memphis World*. From the time I was eight until I turned eleven, I worked on weekends for a woman who had a severe hearing impairment and owned a small grocery store. During the summers, I would hire out as a free-lance house cleaner—scrubbing floors, taking out bedding, and beating rugs. Sometimes my brother and I would buy turnip and mustard greens from the Front Street Market. Then, using a wagon drawn by a billy goat, we would sell them on the streets. Other times we would hire out to men who owned trucks or wagons and sold all kinds of vegetables. We walked alongside and were available to housewives who would signal that they wanted to inspect the tomatoes or the green peppers or whatever else the vendors were carrying. Occasionally, some of the vendors would refuse to pay me and the other boys after we had spent a full day working in the hot sun helping them. We had no recourse, except to look for more scrupulous employers the next time.

I also worked as a delivery boy for a woodman. We had horses and wagons that carried kindling for coal wood stoves. When I dropped out of school, I began working full-time as a milkman's helper. It was a very trying job for a fourteen-year-old. I got up at two o'clock in the morning. My dear mother would get up with me to cook me some hot oatmeal and milk, and I would take off to meet the milkman at 2:45 A.M. I would work until 12:30 or 1 P.M., seven days a week, for a little bit over four dollars a week. It was in this job that I experienced one of the most frightening incidents of my youth.

◆ 2 ◆
Propelled by Ambition

O
NE MORNING I was on my way to meet the milkman and
the cops stopped me. They stopped me because I had
been running in great fright. I had passed in front of
an abandoned house on Poplar Street, just east of Dunlap Street. It
was all overgrown with weeds, and I heard a rustling in the bushes. It
sounded like a human being in there, and it scared the hell out of me,
so I took off running as fast as I could down Poplar Street, which was
one of the main streets in North Memphis.

The cops saw me running, and they overtook me in their squad
car and stopped me and got out and shined their flashlights in my
face. One of them asked me where I lived and I told them, then the
other asked me, "What are you? Are you white or colored?" When I
told him "colored," he became verbally abusive. Before that he was
sort of neutral, but when I said "colored," he said, "Nigger son of a
bitch, get in the back of the car." I pleaded to be taken to the all-night
restaurant, where I waited every night for the milkman, so that the
owner could identify me. However, the police took me off to a home
where somebody apparently had tried to break in through a door. I
had never been on that street in my life. Nevertheless, the old couple
who lived there identified me as the culprit.

So the cops had something to go on, but I pleaded for further
identification. I begged them again to take me to the all-night restaurant, but they refused and we headed downtown to the police station.
I had heard all kinds of stories about the police beating confessions
out of people with rubber hoses, and I was afraid. Over and over, I
pleaded to be taken to the restaurant. I even told them that I was a
Boy Scout. Then the good cop asked me, "Well do you know the scout

oath and law?" Well, I gave them the oath and law, the slogan, the motto, everything. I would have given him the history of scouting if he had wanted it. Anyway, I persuaded the good cop that I probably was not too bad of a fellow, and he convinced the bad cop to turn around and drive me to the restaurant. They took me in the entrance for blacks and asked the Greek fellow who ran the restaurant, "Do you know this boy?" He said, "Oh yeah, a good boy. He comes here every morning and works with Mr. Peeler the milkman." They turned me loose and said, "We think you did it, boy. You stay away from those doors." They stopped me a couple of times thereafter, recognizing me on the way to work, and asked me nagging questions like, "You been around those doors?" I told my mother about it, and she thought it was just too dangerous. She insisted that I quit my job, and I did.

That run-in with the police was the most frightening, but it was just one of many examples of racism that I experienced growing up in Memphis. The first time I knew I was black was when the poor white kids from across the street, when we lived on Fourth Street, had their baby urinate in a pot, then they came over and poured it on our porch. My mother, who at that time obviously was far more sophisticated than I was at five years old, thought the kids resented us because even though we were black we had more toys than they did. When I was ten or eleven, a friend and I were taking a shortcut home from school behind an abandoned cemetery. Three or four white boys jumped out, taunted us, and made us say, "White folks are smarter than niggers." They pelted us with stones as we ran away. When I got home and told my brother, he was so enraged that he grabbed me and said, "Let's go find them." I was not very eager at the prospect. By the time we got there, the group had split up. Still, my brother found the principal miscreant and gave him a pretty good beating.

There were so many little things like that. Once, when we were carrying newspapers and selling them to the black porters and messengers who worked downtown, the white boss came out and asked what I was selling. I told him the black weekly newspapers, the *Chicago Defender* and the *Pittsburgh Courier*. He said, "You can't sell that *Chicago Defender* in here. It's too radical." So, he let me sell the *Courier* to his "colored" help but not the *Defender*.

Perhaps the worst aspect of racism back then was the school system. The so-called separate-but-equal schools that the state of Tennessee and the city of Memphis provided somehow did not turn out that way. The despicable thing was that even in high school we were sitting two to a seat in many classes because of the overcrowded conditions. We had, as I remember, about 2,200 students in my high school and an inappropriately low number of teachers—maybe forty or fifty. Sometimes the teacher-student ratio was one to fifty. I also remember how the white superintendent of schools used to come to our high school and address our principal, Professor Blair T. Hunt Jr., a man of great learning and dignity, by his first name. Some kids were so angered that they would quietly hiss.

One of the great mysteries to me is why some American white men, particularly southerners, have felt it necessary to so thoroughly humiliate black men over the centuries. There was no ultimate ability for blacks to exercise force effectively. There were very few uprisings. Even when President Abraham Lincoln issued the Emancipation Proclamation on January 1, 1863, few southern blacks revolted. After the Civil War, there remained the mathematical disparity of blacks being about one in ten in the population, no more. Whites overwhelmed blacks numerically, as well as in terms of money, weapons, and governmental power. They always dominated. So why all the effort to humiliate? Since whites had the power and controlled blacks in every way, it seems that they could at least have respected the individual dignity of a fellow human being without the need to belittle him at every turn. I never understood that meanness, and I still do not.

Speaking of humiliation, there cannot be a black person alive in the United States who has not experienced his or her share of humiliation by some whites. Thank God I do not dwell on such incidents. There have been a number of them over the years, and it takes some effort to remember them all. I cannot, even with effort, recall most of them. When I was young we countered the racism by looking up to inspirational role models from the black community.

Close to home there were our teachers, Mr. Chatman, doctors, and businessmen. I remember J. C. Oats, who had a funeral home close to where we lived in North Memphis. Oats had three or four sons who were dashing figures and who took some part in the business. On the other side of town were the Hayeses. T. H. Hayes & Sons Funeral Home, Incorporated, was the oldest continuously operating black business in Memphis. The Hayes sons were good-looking and cut quite a figure because they could afford cars. I guess if my brother and I had been looking for something to do back then we would have thought about becoming undertakers.

The most striking figure for both of us, however, was Professor

Hunt, who was the son of slaves. He attended LeMoyne Normal Institute (now LeMoyne-Owen College) in Memphis and graduated from Morehouse College. He was one of only three blacks in Memphis with a teaching degree in 1913, when he began his career. Later, he took a chaplain's course at Harvard and served as a lieutenant with the 340th Service Battalion in World War I. In addition to his job as principal of Booker T. Washington, Hunt was the longtime pastor of Mississippi Boulevard Christian Church. The city's black newspaper, the *Memphis World,* used to publish his sermons. He had piercing eyes and flawless diction.

We also kept up with role models beyond Memphis. There were no black magazines to speak of then except for the National Association for the Advancement of Colored People's *The Crisis,* which we would see occasionally. But even without such magazines as *Ebony, Jet, Essence,* and all of the others that have proliferated in modern times, we managed to keep up with things through the very limited black press. We learned what other people of color were doing in the United States and the world through the black newspapers, principally the *Pittsburgh Courier* and the *Chicago Defender.* There was only one black daily at that time, the *Atlanta Daily News,* which was owned by the Scott newspaper syndicate that also owned the weekly newspaper in Memphis. The white dailies carried almost no news about black people. The criminals got ink, but people who were doing constructive things got no mention. Anyway, in the black press we read about such outstanding leaders as Walter White of the National Association for the Advancement of Colored People (NAACP) and Lester Granger of the National Urban League. The papers focused on college presidents like Dr. Mordecai Johnson, a Memphis boy who had been educated at the University of Chicago and was improving Howard University as its first African-American president.

We also learned a lot about the people who had come up before—not so much from the black press but during Negro History Week, which was founded by Dr. Carter G. Woodson, the famous historian at Howard University. During that one week in February, in the Negro schools, we paid a lot of attention to famous blacks. We learned about Frederick Douglass, George Washington Carver, and others. We read Booker T. Washington's autobiography, *Up from Slavery.* The rest of the year we learned about everyone else—the great white explorers, the white political leaders, and the white founding fathers of the country. We did not have a separatist mentality. As a matter of fact, it was our great desire to become part of the mainstream and to have the mainstream know about us.

We followed sports figures, including players in the famous black baseball leagues. As kids, we heard about Jack Johnson, Joe Gans, and a few other prominent black boxers. But nobody inspired us like Joe Louis, whom I met years later. He came along in the middle of the terrible depression decade. He was a handsome young man with an appealing modesty about his considerable talents. Joe was our hero and not just because he was beating up on such white men as Max Schmeling. Joe became our symbol for the African-American drive for equality because he was performing in the mainstream, taking on all comers and winning. There were, of course, a lot of other good black boxers who came along after Joe—John Lewis, Henry Armstrong, and Sugar Ray Robinson, to cite a few—but nobody was like Joe.

I am always puzzled today when I hear people say that there are not enough black role models represented in the media. Compared to when I was coming up, there is so much news about black achievers that I sometimes wonder where people's eyes and ears are. In many cities, including Detroit where I live, it appears at times that the white press does a better job covering the black community than the black newspapers do. It is amazing when I think about it. When I was growing up, we kept up with a very small number of role models despite the media. Now, the number of role models has increased a thousandfold and people complain that the media do not cover them. What shocks me even more is when I talk to black kids who have never even heard of the people whom we considered to be extraordinarily important to the uplifting of the African-American community.

In addition to reading and telling us about black leaders, my mother provided a good role model for dealing with racism. She never let it stop her, and she instilled in us the idea that hard work and effort would ultimately prevail. When I quit working for the milkman I quickly found another job, working in a Kroger store on Poplar delivering groceries on a bicycle. I carried heavy baskets over the front and back wheels. It was tough work, particularly for a young boy who was not too strong. Decades later, when I told the chairman of Kroger, on whose board I served, that that was one of my first full-time jobs, he looked a little incredulous. I was a delivery boy at Overton Park Pharmacy, and I eventually wound up working for Alvin Winkler, who owned a bakery. Winkler and his wife were German immigrants, and the two of them, along with a little Dutchman by the name of Oelrich, produced the baked goods and I delivered them. Later, I worked as a busboy in the dining room of the famous Peabody Hotel and then the Claridge Hotel, where my brother was head waiter. When I was sixteen, I drove a truck for a wholesale meat market. I also parked and washed cars in the Sterick Building garage. On a good Saturday, I would wash seven or eight cars, even in the winter. On my busiest days, I could make a dollar fifty and then stop by the Wonder Bakery on the way home to pick up day-old bread and cupcakes. When that happened, I always felt it was a lucky day.

Those early years set a pattern. I have always had a compulsion to be employed. Somehow, I figure that if you want a job, you can get a job because there are always things to do. My philosophy from the earliest age has been that any job is better than no job. Take whatever is available and, if it is not what you want, look for a better job while you work. That is what I have always tried to do, and it has been effective for me.

After a year my brother came home from Michigan. A stubborn fellow, he refused to be pushed around by Aunt Josie, who was a very tough lady, God bless her soul. They did not get along, and my brother returned to Memphis to finish high school at Booker T. Washington, from which he graduated in 1937. He made it a project to get me back in school. I will never forget one conversation we had in the summer of 1937. We were sitting on the steps of the place where we then lived, 753 Robeson, and as usual my brother was giving me the pitch that he calculated was most suitable for me. He always accentuated the positive. He repeated time and time again how much ability I had and why that could not be lost. He persuaded me to go back and transfer from Manassas High School, on the city's North Side, which I was attending when I dropped out, to Washington, the city's other black school, which was on the South Side.

After it was decided that I was going back to school, my brother began advising me about extracurricular activities. I entered Booker T. Washington in the fall of 1937 with a new lease on life. I was determined to be a good student, and I was even more excited about pursuing other opportunities. Somewhere along the line I read that it was through such endeavors that one really found what one wanted to do, so I plunged in with enthusiasm. I joined the Senior Glee Club. I joined the Motor Club. I joined the staff of the *Washingtonian,* the school newspaper. Most important, I decided to run for president of the junior class. I was the new guy on the block, but my brother had left a reputation. To have been Hamilton Smith's brother at Booker T. Washington during that era meant being stamped with a certain kind of approval because people assumed you were a serious-minded student, an all-around guy, and an astute leader.

From that point on, I was well on my way. I had a new focus on life. My god was achievement, and I was bent upon achieving all that I could. I had always read voraciously, even during the year I dropped out of school. As a child I read adventure stories and westerns by Zane Grey. In high school, I began reading philosophy, history, and political science. I was very busy in the next two years, the eleventh and twelfth grades. My brother was working and, because of our stringent economic circumstances, we helped each other. I had helped my brother a bit earlier when I was working and he was in school. After he graduated and I went back to school, he returned the favor. He put me on a budget, contributing a little bit, a dollar or so a week, to my spendable income so that I could participate in many activities.

In the twelfth grade I added football to my other endeavors and won a letter as a tackle. Our team claimed the West Tennessee championship that year. As I look back on it, my senior year was an exercise in ego. I held almost every office there was. I was president of the senior class. I was editor of the high school newspaper, the *Washingtonian*. I was editor of the first class annual that was published at Washington High School by students. I still belonged to the Motor Club, the Glee Club, and the debating team. The debate issue that year was "Resolved That the Several States Should Adopt a Unicameral System of Legislature" patterned after the system used in Nebraska.

A lot of people now think that anyone who attended a black segregated school during the 1930s and 1940s could not have received a good education. But we were not necessarily deprived of everything. We did learn from teachers who introduced us to a world of literature and music. We started with Shelley and Keats, then studied Longfellow and Whittier. In fact, I always kept in mind one line from Longfellow's "Psalm of Life" that goes: "Lives of great men all remind us we can make our lives sublime and departing leave behind us footprints on the sands of time." I was introduced to so much, and it stayed with me, waiting to be developed. It made me want to find out about the larger world.

Our high school principal and teachers encouraged our ambitions, no matter how ridiculous they may have seemed at the time. Based on the fact that I had served as both junior and senior class

Smith in 1939 at the time of his graduation from Booker T. Washington, one of Memphis's two black high schools. He dropped out of high school to work for a year. After he returned to school, Smith made his mark academically and as president of his class, editor of the school newspaper, and a member of the debating and football teams.

president, I got the idea that I might be headed for elective office. So, I happened on the idea of becoming a United States senator. You have to remember that I was living in Memphis, Tennessee, then. I had no realistic chance of becoming a senator from that state. Anyway, there was a tradition at our high school that one day during our senior year, called "Class Day," we would all declare our ambitions and wear clothes that indicated what our dreams were. Something must have overcome me because I stopped Professor Hunt and asked him, "Do you think I could become president?" He looked at me and said, "President of what, son?" I said, "Of the United States." He looked at me, mumbled something encouraging, and walked away, probably thinking, "This boy is crazy." But the point is he encouraged me.

I must have been hallucinating a little bit to think of myself as president, but my experiences at Booker T. Washington High School and my ambition were not at all unusual. People do not really understand the African-American southern culture of my generation and before. It had an unusual focus—a boundless optimism about what could be done if you were really qualified. We used to say that you had to be twice as good as the white person to get the same job. Often we did not know realistically what lay ahead. We just thought we had to be good at whatever we did. We used to say, "We want to be somebody." The distinction between being good for nothing, on one hand, and being somebody was a generalization applied to people with college degrees who were schoolteachers or lawyers or doctors or dentists. It also included folks who worked for the post office, not the modern post office, but the post office when it really used to provide service. To be a railway mail clerk, for example, was a real accomplishment. One of that culture's motivating sayings was, "Shoot for the stars, at least you'll land someplace in the sky." I must have heard that at least a hundred times when I was growing up. If you look at the people who came out of that milieu, they may not all have been as lucky as I have been, but they certainly had a lot on the ball.

Anyway, when my brother graduated from high school in June 1937, he decided to go to Tuskegee—Tuskegee Institute as it was then known. It had been founded by Booker T. Washington. The great George Washington Carver and the famous choir were there, and my brother was attracted by all of that, and he wanted to go. Of course, we had no money. My brother, after consulting my mother, decided to talk to my father about his college plans. Sometime during the summer my brother laid out his goals and what would be required to achieve them. My father provided the money that my brother needed to enter Tuskegee. My brother did not ask for enough, however, for he ran out fairly soon and had to cut back his class hours and work more in order to be able to survive the year. It did not help when our father died a few months later.

My father left no trail of us with anybody. He died and we were cut off. He made no provision for us. We were plunged into the lowest rung of poverty. My mother turned in her small life insurance polices for cash surrender values. I sold my bike. We never asked for welfare assistance, and there was no Social Security. We gutted it out. We missed my brother's help. My mother and I just lived to pay the rent, keep a roof over our heads, and buy food when we were able. My mother continued to work as a domestic, toiling six days a week for four and a half or five dollars a week. I worked weekends at any job I could find.

I even came up with a harebrained scheme to try and support us by going into the restaurant business. I was working as a delivery boy and saw a huge commercial gas range put to one side at a meat market. I asked the owner if he wanted to get rid of it. He said yes and offered it to me for five dollars. It was heavy cast iron with six burners. Somehow I loaded it onto the delivery truck during my lunch hour and took it home and got it onto the back porch, where I cleaned off years of accumulated grease. I searched around and found an old top-loading ice box and put it in the living room. There was an open field across the street—there were no parks for blacks in those days in Memphis—where guys played ball on Sundays. I supplied food and drinks for a couple of weekends until the competition down the block complained. A city official came to the house and asked, "Are you conducting a business here?" Ever ready to serve, I said, "Oh yes, what would you like?" He asked if I had a license. I had not even thought about that. He told me to shut down immediately, which I did. That was the end of my home restaurant business. It was back to the same old grind.

Any number of days I went to school hungry, literally without a crust of bread or anything in the house to eat. Often, I did not have any food until the noon recess when I worked in the cafeteria to get a free meal. After everybody else had eaten, I was able to eat my lunch from whatever was left, and it seemed that what was left most often was watery spaghetti, so I filled up on that.

It is hard now to describe what it was like to be poor during the depression. Poor was completely running out of food and buying a loaf of half-price, day-old bread, which with water made a meal. Poor was having just enough money to go to the store and buy five pounds of cornmeal to make mush to take up the empty space in your stomach. Poor was waking up in the morning without a crust of bread in the house and putting on your clothes and going to school hungry. Poor was wearing out your shoes and not being able to afford to take them to a shoe repairman and have them half-soled. You did not even worry about the heels, just the soles to keep your feet off the ground. You went to the store and bought some puttylike material, black stuff that stuck to the shoes, and spread it over the hole in the shoe to keep your feet from hitting the ground. Being poor was turning the collar on your shirt, which was already worn out, and using flour and water instead of starch to make it very stiff so that you could press it in a way to hide the worn parts.

The most difficult thing to deal with was that there was nothing you could do about it. There was no work. Grown men and women

42

with families were out of work. Everybody was damned poor, and we were all in the same boat. You just had to look for little things to do, like going out knocking on doors after school in middle-class neighborhoods and asking if you could clean homes or do other odd jobs. Anything that was honest we would do.

I do not know why so many people did not just give up and turn to a life of crime. Of course, given the way my mother raised my brother and me, it would never have occurred to us to steal anything. I suspect that if we had found a lot of money, we would have returned it to the owners. We believed that honest was honest and dishonest was dishonest, and there was nothing in between. I do not think we were unique in that regard.

We had a built-in optimism about what could be done in America. We believed that if we just kept on going, somehow things would be a little bit better the next day. We did not think very far ahead except to dream that sometime we would be able to eat a nourishing dinner or get some clothes that were not ragged. Maybe it was the kind of people we lived with and the times we lived in. Everybody was just making it, just trying to survive. There is nothing really heroic about being poor, despite the efforts of some writers to make it appear that way. We just hung on, believing in that old adage, "And this too shall pass away." And it did.

Even when times were at their hardest, I never thought about dropping out of school again or about abandoning the ambition to make something out of myself. "Hope springs eternal." It certainly did in my case, and with a little bit of luck and a lot of hard work it turned out reasonably well. What I am saying is not that I was superior in surviving, but that they were tough times for many people. Those of us who lived through them developed a strong feeling that no matter what happened, we could survive. I suppose I have what is often called the "Depression mentality"—the belief that you should never get too free with money because of a deep-seated fear that you could lose everything and might be forced back to those days when you were hungry. For example, I could never bring myself to drive a Cadillac even when I worked for General Motors; I could never bring myself around to the idea of consuming so conspicuously.

Sometimes I am asked about current welfare problems. One interviewer even asked if I thought the standards to qualify for payments were too high because my mother and I would have felt that we were on top of the world if we had received the help provided to many folks today. I have thought a lot about that, and I have come to the conclusion that poverty is too relative to draw broad conclusions. There is, after all, a tendency to be too subjective about things based on one's own experiences. What we endured in the 1930s is different from what people endure today because almost everyone back then was having a hard time. There were people who had food to eat and nothing else. Then there were folks like me who had shelter and a loving family and little food. I sometimes used to go by the homes of kinfolk just to get something to eat. My Aunt Laura, bless her heart, was married to a man who worked at a meat market, so they always had plenty of food. They lived almost as poorly as we did, except they had food. They had a terrible-looking house and lots of kids. I would stop by regularly and inquire about the health of my aunt, her husband, and my cousins— one, two, three, four, five, and six. My aunt was on to me, and she would say, "Boy, you look hungry. Sit down and have some food." And I would say, "I just came by to say 'Hello.' " And she would insist that I sit down and eat anyway. I was most appreciative. A lot of people did things like that. There was a sense of generosity because we basically were all in the same boat.

During those hard years in the middle of the depression, I developed an abiding respect for my mother. I never detected any weakness in her. She was very strong and resourceful. She was the last person to think in terms of calling on welfare, the government, or anybody for anything. It was her self-reliance and example, more than anything else, that brought us through tough times. We did not have electrical appliances. We did not even have electricity most of the time. She had to do everything the hard way—the cooking by fire, the laundry by hand, and the traveling by foot.

Perhaps what I liked best about her was that she lived her convictions. She did not like hypocrisy, and she was not a hypocrite. What she believed in she lived. She believed in truth, and, therefore, she was truthful. She was honest to a fault and very hardworking. One story demonstrates my mother's character. Mrs. Florence Siegwart, a sixty-year-old German immigrant, owned a little store on North Fourth Street, a block or two from where we lived. We traded there for such simple necessities as flour, sugar, meal, canned goods, and milk. During the depression we used to run up a bill with Mrs. Siegwart, as a lot of people did, because she granted credit liberally. We were usually able to pay two or three dollars a week, but we bought five or six dollars in groceries. Our bill kept growing, and she agreed to hire me to work all day Saturday and half a day on Sunday, waiting on people in the store, running errands for her, and doing other odd jobs. Even after I left Memphis, we still had a substantial bill, well over one hundred dollars, which was a lot of money then. Yet even after Mrs. Siegwart had closed her store and moved to the suburbs, my mother would get on the bus and make payments on the bill that we had accrued ten or fifteen years earlier.

My mother was very religious. When I was young we went to church, all day practically. I was baptized at St. James A.M.E. Church and our lives were focused on the weekly rhythm of preparing for the Sunday services from 9:30 Sunday School, to the 11 o'clock service, then the 3 o'clock service and, after a brief break, back to the young people's church at 6 or 6:30. As if this were not enough, we were occasionally required to attend the 8 P.M. service, which was primarily conducted for those who for some reason could not attend the principal service at 11 A.M.

I still remember the gentle and sedate hymns from the old Cokesbury hymnbooks. We would sing "God is our refuge and our strength," which, of course, was true.

When my mother resumed work as a domestic and I began working in Mrs. Siegwart's store, we were no longer free to attend church on Sunday mornings. Still, we showed great respect for the Lord's Day. We always put on nice clothes. We never listened to jazz. We observed Sunday in respectful silence and recollection of faith. My mother always had an absolute trust in God. Late at night, when I would wake up sometimes, I could hear her praying earnestly, especially during the middle of the depression when things were so bleak. We had no rent money, no food money, no clothing money, no nothing: just faith. When I would hear her speaking to God, it always seemed to me that He was sitting quietly over in the corner with his face focused on Mother, listening to her because that was the way she spoke to Him. Even in her later years, Mother had no time for such worldly things as movies. She used to say, "I am in the world but not of the world," and that was essentially true, even though she was very pragmatic about getting along in life.

Mother would always regale us with quotes from the Bible, *Poor Richard's Almanac,* anonymous authors, or anybody else she thought could get the point across in some wise saying. When we were growing up, she liked to remind us that the Bible commanded: "Spare the rod and spoil the child." She was never cruel, but when we got out of line

45

she would get a tree branch and administer a little corporal punishment. She always liked to say, "God helps those who help themselves." Lord knows that is true. And one of her favorites was "Cleanliness is next to godliness." She would say that many times to remind us that we had to keep clean in mind, body, and house.

By the time I left home, I was so well drilled in fundamental morality by my mother that I, with some occasional lapses, never found it difficult to find my moral compass. My mother had laid everything out before me, and I could never forget the things she had taught me. Nor did I want to forget them. I did not want to do anything wrong, first, because I did not want to feel guilty about it, and, second, because I would remember how my mother had struggled so hard to take care of us, to keep us alive, to keep us well, and to keep our feet on the straight and narrow path. Even later in life, I never wanted to do anything that would embarrass my mother.

That was part of the reason I rejected a suggestion from my high school football coach, Julian Bell. He was a man of dark brown skin color, and because we were fairly close, he realized that I was an atypical football player who valued my mental attributes more than my physical strengths. In his own quiet way, he could be a very blunt man. One day during my last year at school, he said out of the blue, "Smith, why don't you just pick up your things and go North and turn white and avoid all of this mess?" I was shocked and sputtered that I did not think I would like doing that. He said, "Well, I just thought about it. You could pass for white. A lot of people do. And if you can pass, why in the hell take all of this mess when you can get out of it?" His remarks did one thing. They crystallized my thinking. I had never really thought about the matter before, but I realized that I would never try to pass. It would be a denial of my mother, my other relatives, and all of the good people I knew who were clearly black. Besides, it would have been a fraud, so I never thought about doing it. Years later, after I had served on the Michigan Supreme Court, I ran into Mr. Bell in the lobby of an Atlanta hotel. He jokingly said, "I've been reading about your accomplishments, and I see you did it the hard way."

Looking back over my lifetime, I am still glad I never tried to pass. I would not have wanted to miss all of the experiences that I have had, and I certainly would not have wanted the headaches that go with trying to be two different people. More important, I have been edified by the enriching experiences I have had by being in a slightly ambiguous position. I have enjoyed the ability to stretch across racial lines, to be clearly a part of both the minority and majority, and to be able to understand things that affect the psyche of both groups. I think I have had a fuller life than I would have had otherwise, and as a result of the dichotomy, I have had more chances to do more things.

Rather than going North after I graduated from high school, I joined my brother at the Memphis Furniture Factory, where he worked that summer. I had received a full tuition scholarship to Morehouse College in Atlanta, and I probably would have gone down there and become part of that legend except for my brother's experience at Tuskegee. I remembered what a rough time he had endured, eventually cutting his hours in half just to survive. So, I thought rather than go off and be subjected to the burden of trying to study and support myself, I would work a few years to save money. My job in the furniture factory was one of those jobs typical of the 1930s—ten hours a day, six days a week. I think we made about twelve dollars a week. It was hard work, but I had done hard work before so that was nothing new.

Then my life took a dramatic turn. Within a couple of weeks after I began at the furniture factory, Professor Hunt came to our house at 312 Decatur. Neither of us boys was home. But my mother was, and Professor Hunt said that he had the authority to choose one of us for a job working as a messenger and janitor for the state government in Nashville. The Democratic Party machine, headed by Memphis political boss Edward Hull Crump, arranged for a certain number of such patronage jobs every year, and Hunt acted as the Crump machine's conduit to the African-American community. My brother had first refusal and chose not to leave. He was courting the woman who later became his wife, Ruth Lumpkin, so the choice came to me. Hunt sent me to see the head of the black Democratic Party in Memphis, who sent me to the sheriff who ran the Shelby County party for the Crump machine. He arranged for me to work for the Game and Fish Division of the state Department of Conservation. I readily accepted and left Memphis, never to live there again.

✦ 3 ✦
Spreading Wings

ALK ABOUT spreading one's wings! At age seventeen I was moving out on my own in a new city, joining the adult work world, and participating in all kinds of exciting activities. It was a heady time in which I was exposed to new people and new ideas. I joined and became active in the adult branch of the NAACP. Through an experimental theater, I met left-wing radicals and came to consider myself a socialist. I learned more about social and racial problems as a reporter for the city's black weekly newspaper, the *Nashville Globe-Independent.* I took my first trip North, tasting a kind of freedom unknown to blacks in the South then. After two years of working and scrimping, I was finally able to begin my higher education at Fisk University. Then, I decided to seek my fortune on more hospitable ground. I took advantage of the booming World War II industries, moved to Philadelphia, worked, and eventually joined the Army.

When I first arrived in Nashville in July 1939, I lived at the colored YMCA and worked five and a half days a week as a porter and messenger for the state Department of Conservation. I was assigned to the Game and Fish Division, an administrative unit that distributed hunting and fishing licenses to vendors. My job consisted of mailing licenses, answering general correspondence, maintaining the machinery, operating a mimeograph machine, cleaning all of the offices, and running errands around the capitol. I learned a lot about human nature and state government, knowledge that would serve me well years later when I became active in Michigan politics.

Soon after arriving in Nashville, I rejected the notion of going to Tennessee Agricultural and Industrial State College (now Tennessee

State University) because its reputation at that time was not very good. It was known as a "big high school" that was underfunded and not very challenging. Instead, I set my sights on Fisk University, which was a fine African-American liberal arts school with a small student body and a strong reputation. Unfortunately, it was a private school and cost more money. So, in addition to working for the state, I picked up odd jobs to supplement my savings. For example, I worked as a waiter for a black woman who catered parties for Nashville's white elite. It took me two years to earn enough money to finally enroll at Fisk. In the meantime, I kept busy with all kinds of other activities.

I continued my drive for social and cultural self-improvement. There was no one leading me. I figured I had to pull myself forward. I tried to read such serious books as Will Durant's *Story of Philosophy* and works by Kant, Nietzsche, Schopenhauer, and Voltaire. I did not understand much of it, but I read it. I also thought I ought to learn more about classical music, having been first introduced to it in high school. On Saturday afternoons, I would rush home to my room at the YMCA to listen to the Metropolitan Opera broadcasts on the radio with the great Milton Cross as the commentator. I bought a book called *The Story of One Hundred Operas,* which I read before the operas were played. I am not sure I enjoyed it. It was more of an intellectual exercise rather than anything to which I was emotionally attached. I got far more enjoyment from the jazz bands of Duke Ellington, Count Basie, Jimmie Lunceford, Andy Kirk and his Twelve Clouds of Joy, Don Redman, and the Henderson Brothers—Fletcher and Horace.

I also tried to learn more about drama. Alfred Lunt and Lynn Fontanne came to Nashville and performed at the Ryman Auditorium, which was famous as the home of the Grand Ole Opry. The stage was transformed for a presentation of Shakespeare's *The Taming of the Shrew.* Nashville was segregated then, and I do not remember if I broke the rules and sat in the white seats or went to the segregated section, if there was one. All I remember is that I bought a ticket and found it somewhat interesting. It would have been better had I read the play and understood it before I saw it performed. But I was stretching out to see what was in the mainstream, something I have done ever since.

As a condition of my employment through the Crump machine, I was required to participate in local and state politics. Boss Crump came from Memphis, but his real political base was in Nashville, from which he controlled most of the state, except the remote eastern parts. Even though I was not yet old enough to vote, the machine drafted me to write campaign material aimed at African Americans. The machine also demanded that I return to Memphis to take part in elections. I tried to avoid this because of my great dislike for Crump's political power and tactics. I owed my job to his machine, but I did not have any loyalty to it because of its heavy-handedness, especially in delicate problems of race. Among his other failings, Crump fought a long and hard battle to keep the state of Tennessee from repealing the poll tax that kept many blacks and poor whites from voting. *The Crisis* declared that Memphis under Crump's leadership was "as un-American as any dictator-ridden country in Europe" because "its citizens have everything but the right to vote and talk as they please."[1]

In 1940, when Franklin Roosevelt was seeking his third term as president, a group of black Republicans in Memphis tried to mount a campaign for Wendell Wilkie. There was a great debate across the nation about Roosevelt's unprecedented run for a third term because it violated the unwritten rule that no president should serve more than twice. Two terms had been enough for George Washington, and many people thought that ought to be good enough for every other president. Black Republicans in Memphis hoped they could capitalize on the controversy, while members of the Crump machine feared the dispute might weaken their position.

Crump and his minions met with George Lee, who headed the local black Republican Party, and other such leading party members as Elmer Atkinson and the Martin brothers, John B., B. B., and William S., and ordered them not to campaign for Wilkie. They refused to capitulate, which was not surprising because all were prominent in Memphis's African-American community. Lee, who later became known as the "Sage of Beale Street" because of the many books he wrote about Memphis history, was a well-known businessman. Atkinson owned a lunch stand on Beale Street, as well as a pool hall and a taxi service. B. B. Martin was a dentist, William Martin was a physician, and John Martin was a dentist and owned a drugstore and funeral parlor. The Martin brothers also owned the city's black baseball club, the Memphis Red Sox. But their high standing in the African-Ameri-

---

1. Thomas F. Doyle, "Gestapo in Memphis," *The Crisis* 48, no. 5 (May 1941): 152.

can community did not protect Atkinson and the Martins from the Crump machine.

J. B. Martin refused to call off a Republican rally scheduled ten days before the election, and Crump responded by ordering police to put the Martins' offices and Atkinson's restaurant under twenty-four-hour surveillance. The police searched everyone who went in and everybody who came out under the pretext that they were drug dealers and that Atkinson was using Martin's drugstore to fence stolen goods. Those caught in the dragnet included children entering the drugstore to buy ice cream and a Franciscan priest who was pastor of a black Catholic church. Police did not want to search the friar's cassock, so they made him take off his shoes instead.

The trumped up charges were preposterous to anyone who knew these honorable men, but they could not do a damned thing about it. J. B. Martin left Memphis for Chicago and never returned. When black leaders complained about the violation of civil liberties, Police Commissioner Joseph Boyle declared: "This is a white man's country," implying that whites were responsible for everything good and blacks were responsible for all of the nation's ills. He explained that because blacks in Memphis paid only 5 percent of the city's taxes and, therefore, did not even begin to pay their share for the services they received, they had no right to complain about the police department or any other part of municipal government. Crump joined in by defending Boyle and accusing George Lee and other Republican leaders of being Communist agitators trying to stir up racial hatred.

Years later, I was reminiscing with Estes Kefauver, the Democratic senator from Tennessee, about the Crump machine. We were attending a meeting of railroad and utilities commissioners at White Sulphur Springs, West Virginia, a few months before Kefauver's death in 1963. Nothing seemed to be beyond the purview of my fellow Tennessean. He had a lifelong suspicion of concentrated power, which explains why he took on Crump in the 1940s, organized crime in the 1950s, and big business throughout his career. He investigated the drug industry, big steel, and large bakeries. At the time of the conference, he was just beginning to challenge the upcoming Penn Central merger.

He said to me, ruefully, that he thought he had lost his constituency and indicated that he had grown somewhat tired of fighting what had become unpopular battles. It was a sad admission from a man who had been a political hero in Tennessee. During our conversation,

Kefauver reminded me how he happened to adopt that famous trademark of his, the coonskin hat, when he was running against a Crump candidate. Kefauver first entered Congress in 1939 and quickly earned a reputation as the most liberal congressman from the South. In 1948, he tired of the House and decided to run for the Senate against the lackluster incumbent. Crump disliked Kefauver's support for enlightened causes and tried to portray him as pro-Communist. Kefauver, of course, denied that he was a radical. Crump responded with one of the most famous quotes in Tennessee politics. He compared Kefauver to "the pet coon that puts its foot in an open drawer in your room, but invariably turns its head while its foot is feeling around in the drawer. The coon hopes, through its cunning by turning its head, he will deceive any onlookers as to where his foot is and what it is into."[2] Kefauver responded by donning a coonskin cap, and it became his trademark.

The election became a referendum on whether Crump would maintain his hold over Tennessee politics. On election day, Kefauver voted in his home district of Chattanooga, then flew to Memphis to campaign. He hoped his presence in Shelby County would inspire some voters to break with machine politics. Kefauver scored a stunning victory. Shelby County voters gave Kefauver most of his winning margin, and he ended up carrying twenty-two city and four county precincts in Crump's home bastion. Some of those votes came from blacks who supported Kefauver's courageous stand against the poll tax. That is how Kefauver became the first politician in memory to beat Crump. It was one of his better achievements in my estimation and I think also in his.

Long before Kefauver, many African Americans in Tennessee saw through Crump's feeble efforts to court the black community through patronage jobs and other meager political handouts. Many of us fought back by joining and becoming active in the NAACP. An interviewer once asked if I felt personally put upon, growing up poor in the segregated South. I answered honestly that I never had taken my hardships personally, although I did feel very strongly about a system that denied us first-class citizenship. I suspect that is what most African Americans in the region would have answered. At least most of

---

2. Joseph Bruce Gorman, *Kefauver: A Political Biography* (New York: Oxford University Press, 1971), 47.

the people I got to know in the NAACP. When I arrived in Nashville, I did not go into the NAACP as a youth member. Instead, I joined and became very active in the senior branch. I think because of my height and appearance everybody accepted me as an adult. I became chairman of the downtown recruitment campaign even though I was only eighteen years old and not really eligible, and I spent my only week of vacation in 1939 or 1940 trying to get people to sign up for membership.

There were so many racial incidents unfolding back then that I will recount only the most egregious. I remember quite vividly going to an emergency meeting of the Nashville chapter of the NAACP in late June 1940. Walter White, the national executive secretary, came from New York to hear a report about the murder of an NAACP member in Brownsville, Haywood County, northeast of Memphis. Inspired by the NAACP's national campaign to secure voting rights, a half dozen blacks led by thirty-three-year-old Elbert Williams went to the courthouse and asked to be registered so they could vote in the upcoming election. County officials responded that they did not register black people to vote and had not ever done so. Their history was accurate. Since Reconstruction no blacks had ever been registered to vote in Haywood County. The Brownsville NAACP met, and its officers decided to return to the courthouse to try and convince county officials to reconsider. The county officials refused, and Williams was lynched. His body was fished from a river a few days later. A white mob, including at least two law officers, drove the rest of the Negroes involved in the voting campaign from Brownsville. Elisha Davis, who owned a gas station, was forced to leave his pregnant wife and seven children and hide in a neighboring town. Another of those forced out was a preacher, Buster Walker. Brownsville police were posted on all of the highways leading into town so they could keep "troublemakers" out and turn away any other blacks who did not live there.

All of the Brownsville NAACP leaders were hard-working taxpayers. None had criminal records, and none were known as "radicals." Their only crime had been trying to vote. Reverend Walker later appeared at the NAACP national conference in Philadelphia and raised money for a defense fund. Davis also appealed for money to help his wife and children until he could return home. The NAACP sent the names of the white mob leaders to the White House. The FBI promised to investigate the incident and protect voters who tried to register for the primary in September. Despite FBI assurances, none of Williams's murderers ever were brought to justice and no blacks were registered to vote in Brownsville until 1960.

Twenty years later, believe it or not, I was telling this story one Sunday afternoon in a black church in Niles, Michigan, during my election campaign in 1960 for state auditor general. I was trying to illustrate the importance of voting, and my punch line was, "If people will threaten you and even kill you to keep you from voting, it must be important." There was a man in one of the front rows who was wagging his head vigorously, and I thought he was mentally disturbed. I had told this story about Brownsville before without incident, so I did not know what to think except that the man was a little off. When I finished, I found out why he had been emotional. He came up to me and said, "Everything you said was true because I was there. I'm one of the Davis brothers." His was certainly one of the more sadly true stories about blacks in their efforts to win the right to vote. No wonder we had to pass the Voting Rights Act in 1965 and put federal registrars in many places in the South in order to make certain that African Americans secured this most basic of all rights in a democracy.

These kinds of incidents, commonplace in the South of my youth, were damnably inexcusable, and I worked hard in all kinds of organizations to do my little bit to change the system. In addition to the NAACP, I also volunteered for the Southern Negro Youth Conference (SNYC), which had been founded in 1937. SNYC leaders realized that not all Negroes would or could move North, so they hoped to raise the consciousness of black youths living in the South so that we could find ways to improve our lives in that region. The SNYC had local councils in various cities, including Nashville, which sponsored dramas and concerts to heighten our appreciation of African-American cultural and artistic achievements. The SNYC also promoted forums in which we could learn about and discuss the economic and social issues facing us in the South. The ultimate goal was to inspire black youths and develop our leadership skills to fight for civil rights.

As if that were not controversial enough in the segregated South, the SNYC waged protests against discrimination. Its political agenda had only limited success in those difficult times. Years later, I found out that the SNYC was on the U.S. Attorney General's list of subversive organizations because many of its members were also left-leaning labor organizers. To my mind, however, the designation was ridiculous because the SNYC shared essentially the same civil rights platform as such other unlisted organizations as the NAACP. Its major goals, as far as I was concerned, included lobbying for federal laws to outlaw lynching and to bar payment of a poll tax as a prerequisite for voting. I felt that if wanting to vote without restrictions or wanting to prevent people from killing others with impunity was subversive, then I was honored to be listed that way. I thought I must have been in good company.

I also did a lot of reporting for the *Nashville Globe-Independent,* which was a local black weekly. I volunteered because the paper had no money to pay me. I got books about how to write, and I bought a camera to take pictures to go along with my stories. I also used to give myself tests to improve my powers of observation. I would walk around the block, try to notice everything, come back to my room, write everything down, and then go back and compare what I remembered with what was really there.

Working for the *Globe-Independent* was an interesting experience. I wrote a sports column. I reported on a strike waged by the hotel workers' union against the major hotels in Nashville. Occasionally, I was even sent to racial programs that were held at white colleges because with my complexion I could go undetected and just sit and listen. Nothing spectacular happened at those meetings to promote what was then called "racial tolerance." They were programs at which few, if any, black people took part, so it was a special experience for me to learn about open-mindedness on the white side of the fence.

I wrote all of these articles under the by-line of S. Russwurm Vann. S was for Smith. Russwurm was for John Brown Russwurm, the first noted black journalist in the nation. A graduate of Harvard, Russwurm founded *Freedom's Journal* in New York City in 1827. Vann was for Robert L. Vann, who was the editor and publisher of the *Pittsburgh Courier,* which, at that time, was the nation's most influential black weekly and circulated all over the country. I used the nom de plume because I figured that if any state government officials ever took time to read Nashville's black newspaper, they might not appreciate some of the things I wrote if Otis Smith was the byline. This was especially true when I covered the hotel workers' strike. I had not fully learned about objective journalism at that time, so I walked along the picket lines and talked with the strike leaders and sympathetically reported their demands. I did not want to be detected by the State of Tennessee serving with people trying to organize a union. Most officials I knew thought all union members were Communists or, at the very least, dangerous radicals.

I also joined something called the Nashville Suitcase Theater, which specialized in protest plays. It was modeled after the famous Harlem Suitcase Theater, which had been founded by Langston Hughes and others in 1938 as a "proletariat" theater to give voice to the black masses. The name stemmed from the theater's reliance on simple sets and equipment, the joke being that all of the theater's belongings could fit into one suitcase.

One of the plays in which I performed was written by Thomas Richardson, the executive director of the Harlem Suitcase Theater. The piece, *Place: America,* was a "living newspaper" play, a kind of drama that was made popular during the depression by the Federal Theater Project (FTP) of the Works Progress Administration (WPA). The FTP provided money for unemployed actors, playwrights, and other theater people to stage productions across the nation. Some of the plays were "living newspapers"—stories based on contemporary news events—which were written to draw attention to pressing social and political issues. The plays all followed the same formula. They began with a recent, sensational news event that presented a problem and the need for a solution. The protagonist, his or her curiosity aroused, began researching the problem and its origins. Once the cause was established, the main characters considered various solutions, weighing the advantages and disadvantages of each proposal until only one remained, which they then advocated eloquently. *Place: America* used that formula by drawing on events from the NAACP's history to dramatize the struggle for citizenship and political rights in both the North and the South.

I met a lot of nice people through the theater. Bill Hale was the son of the president of Tennessee State. Paul Walker was a political activist at Fisk who became a prominent Baptist minister in Detroit. Peter Price was the son of a black banker in Nashville. I cannot claim that I was close with them because they were older than I was, but they did influence me.

Through the theater I became interested in socialism. I attended meetings and broadened my horizons by looking at things from the socialist and communist partisan points of view. The people at the meetings, black and white, all seemed to be very smart, very dedicated, and very American. I began reading a good bit of socialist material. I read Karl Marx's *The Communist Manifesto* and started *Das Kapital,* although I never finished it because it was too abstract. I began to think of myself as a socialist or, at the very least, a fellow traveler because the socialists I met were the only white people who seemed to be genuinely interested in absolute freedom and pure equality for African Americans. The thought of a classless society in which race did not matter was very appealing. Of course, I know a lot more about socialism now than I did in the late 1930s and early 1940s. And I think there is a lot of truth in the saying, "A man who is not a Socialist at twenty has no heart, but one who is a Socialist at forty has no head."

Probably the most significant experience I had with the radicals was a trip I made with three other young people to the Emergency Peace Mobilization (EPM), which was held in a Chicago stadium in 1940 or 1941. This was memorable because it was my first trip out of the South. We drove from Nashville through the northern half of Tennessee, up through Kentucky, and on into Indiana. We traveled to Chicago by way of Terre Haute through Hammond, and once we arrived I felt an incomparable joy at the sense of being free. I could use all public facilities, and that made me feel like a first-class citizen. People who had gathered by the thousands for this mobilization were of all races and colors, and there was a true sense of fraternity that was impressive. It was eye-opening for me that these white people seemed to sincerely regard African Americans as equals. It was very dramatic, something I have never forgotten because it was the first experience of that kind I had ever had.

It also taught me a valuable lesson. I came to realize that the fight for civil rights was never simply a matter of black against white. I recognized that freedom would not have happened had it not been for a lot of sincere and thoughtful white people, beginning with the abolitionists. It is a fact that whites outnumber blacks nine to one in the United States, and if all whites were racists we could never have made any progress. The fight for equality has always required courageous, energetic, enlightened whites to join the cause.

In the past twenty to twenty-five years, with the growing of black awareness, there has been a kind of verbal thrashing of white liberals for not going further and for failing to subscribe to the entire black agenda, as blacks have seen it. I have never agreed with this. It is indeed the rare white person who has the insights or the courage to be a total supporter of African-American causes. In fact, I believe it is impossible because of differences in experience and outlook. When I hear such criticism of white liberals, I reply that nobody, black or white, is 100 percent for black causes. Even Martin Luther King Jr., at his best, spent 75 percent of his time fighting for civil rights and the remaining 25 percent of his time pursuing his own ambitions and goals. No black is 100 percent for group ambition over personal goals, so why should we hold white liberals to such a high purity level? If somebody white is only 10 percent in our corner, he is going to get a small smile and a modest "thank you" from me. If he is as much as a 25 percenter, he is going to get a very hearty handshake. If he happens to come in close to 50 percent, then he is going to get a hug and a testimonial. I just do not think that it is easy for people to understand what is required, then agree upon what should be done, and then have the courage to do it.

This does not mean that I am fatalistic about racial understanding. I just think that it points to the fact that no one can do anything alone. Equality has never been a matter of black versus white. The issue has always been essentially one of good versus evil, and you fight evil with goodness, which comes in many forms. Never, almost never, is there perfect goodness. There are various degrees of goodness, and so people of goodwill, of all kinds, are simply wise enough to form coalitions around the things that they consider to be worthy of support. Blacks are constrained, like other people are on other issues, to seek support from people who are only with us part of the time. In other words, people may be in favor of what you are for, but there is a limit to their support. I would never reject support simply because it has limits. We all have to live with the reality that almost nobody supports a cause totally, and we should enlist help to the extent people can offer it.

I do not, by any of this, brush off the impact of racial segregation and discrimination. In my own case and in the case of just about everybody else I know who is of African-American descent, there are scars left from the heavy-handedness of segregation and discrimination, particularly for those of us who grew up in the South before the 1950s and 1960s when so many laws and attitudes changed. I came out of the South with a hell of an inferiority complex. I thought that whites were always better and things that were black were just not as good. It took some time to change my thinking. Now it is clear that some things white are awfully good and some things black are awfully good, just as some things white are awfully bad and some things black are awfully bad. All of it comes down to seeing the big picture and realizing where we stand in the world. It is just a fact that there is nobody else like me in the world, and I am just me with my whole set of inheritances, good and bad. In that regard, I claim kinship to every other human being in the world, whether they know it or like it or not. I am part of the human race, and that is where it starts. Before I am black, or male, I am a person.

In any event, I had determined to go to Fisk University and was saving money. I skimped in every way I could, including on food. One of my most frequent diets, which I would hold to for as long as a week sometimes, was to buy a quart of milk, a loaf of rye bread, and a head of lettuce every day and split it three ways and eat a third for breakfast, a third for lunch, and the last third for dinner. It was awfully boring. I figured with that diet I got virtually all the nutrients that I required to maintain health. I would go off the diet sometimes and eat at a bargain restaurant. I saved about $350 over the two-year period, which was a lot of money considering the fact that I earned $15 weekly at first and later $17.50, and had to pay all of my living expenses.

I enrolled at Fisk in September 1941. I went to a moving and storage company and found a very large, old theatrical trunk. It had room on one side for hanging up clothes, and on the other side it had little drawers for storage. I cleaned it vigorously, aired it out, and then put everything I owned in it and moved onto the campus at Fisk. I did not have the money to stay in the men's dormitory, Livingstone Hall, but I had been able to work out an arrangement with the coach and athletic director, Henderson A. Johnson, known familiarly by many people as "Tubby." I was allowed to take a cot in the basement of the old Fisk gymnasium, and, in return for that, I was secretary to the coach. While working for the state government, I had bought a typewriter and had taught myself to type reasonably well. I also worked as a janitor in the gymnasium and waited tables at Ann's Tea Room for breakfast, lunch, and dinner for my meals. I read to a blind student for about five or six dollars a month and was paid by the state of Connecticut, where he was from.

A few weeks into my first term at Fisk I had an experience that haunted me for years afterward. I was living in the basement of the gym, which had been built in the nineteenth century. So it was a fairly old building by 1941. For the first couple of weeks, great big two-inch roaches and rats would get into bed with me. I woke up one night with a giant rat on my chest, its tail agitating my nose. I flung the covers back, and it hit the floor. For fifteen or twenty years after that I would wake up with a start of terror just remembering that rat. After I had lived in the basement for a while, the animals and insects accommodated themselves to the human there. I guess they did not like my smell because they did not trouble me after that night.

Coach Johnson insisted that I go out for football. It quickly became clear to me that I could not do all my jobs, play football, and excel with my classwork. Considering the fact that I had been out of school for a couple of years, I had lost touch with serious study. The professors at Fisk were very demanding. So I asked Coach Johnson to allow me to quit football. He seemed disappointed, but I guess he knew I would not make his team anyway, so he allowed me to drop off the squad. He let me keep my cot in the basement, and I kept my jobs as his secretary and as janitor in the gymnasium.

I got to know some interesting fellows while I was working at the gym. One was Homer Harris, a nice-looking, strapping guy with broad shoulders who had been an end and the captain of the football team at the University of Iowa. He was the first black captain in the Big Ten. He was in his first year at Meharry Medical College and would come over to play basketball. Clinton Canady was a native of Detroit who played basketball at Wayne University before it became Wayne State. He was in his first year at Meharry's dental school. When Homer, Clinton, and the other Meharry fellows needed a fill-in, I would play. Clinton later became my dentist in Lansing.

I worked awfully hard to learn. I kept up with my interest in classical music and theater. I found a fellow at Fisk who was a music major from Boston. I would go with him and listen to him practice the organ and piano. He did a lot of work on Bach fugues. I would sit there and listen, and this brought me a little closer to classical music from an emotional point of view. I became attached to some of the great melodies. Fisk was also a good place for theater. The head of the drama department, John M. Ross, was the first African American to receive a master of fine arts degree from the Yale School of Drama. An acting group, the Fisk Stagecrafters, used to perform some of the most interesting dramas. I remember seeing *Mary, Queen of Scots* and enjoying it immensely.

Fisk had able teachers, every one of them. I was particularly impressed by the artist Aaron Douglas, who taught art history as no one else possibly could. I learned about Titian, Tintoretto, and Rubens, along with African and African-American artists. His instruction gave me a lifelong appreciation for art that served me well years later when I sat on the board of the Detroit Art Institute. I had many other fine teachers, but so much of what I was learning seemed to take a back seat to the drama of current events. The big event of 1941, of course, was the Japanese attack on Pearl Harbor, prompting the United States to enter the war. I finished up the year at Fisk and, along with five or six other fellows from the school, went to Pennsylvania to work in war industries. It would change my life.

✦ 4 ✦
Moving North

EVER SINCE that trip to Chicago, when I experienced my first taste of relative freedom, I had planned to go North. But in the summer of 1942, when I headed to Philadelphia to work, I had every intention of returning to Fisk for the fall term. I had no idea that events would propel me in a far different direction. Instead of going back South, I ended up taking a four-year respite from higher education—first living and working in Philadelphia, then entering the Army Air Corps. By the time World War II ended, I had decided to pursue my dreams far from Tennessee.

My first detour began when I arrived in Philadelphia. William J. Faulkner, who was Fisk's minister and dean of men, had procured jobs for several students, including me, at Sun Ship Building and Dry Dock. I made the mistake of going home to Memphis for a few days before leaving for Pennsylvania. I think we all may have made that mistake because we had the wrong idea about when we were supposed to report for work. When I arrived in Philadelphia, I found that the person whom Dean Faulkner had contacted at Sun Ship Building had reserved one day for the Fisk men. That day had been the previous week; therefore, my fellow students and I had no jobs. It was nail-biting time again.

I went to the local employment office and was able to hire in as a helper and handyman for a small traveling circus that was in town for part of the summer. I set up the Ferris wheel and did other things there for a week or two while trying to find a more permanent job. I finally was referred to the Baldwin Locomotive Works in Eddystone, about fifteen miles south of Philadelphia near Chester. Baldwin was an old company that made all sizes of locomotives. By the time I began working there, it had received defense contracts to build armored plating for Sherman tanks and locomotives for military application. Working at Baldwin was probably the worst job I ever held. I do not think there is any way to describe what it was like working in a boiler shop. It was a mean place—sweltering, dirty, loud, and smoky—or at least this one was. The shop had very hot, oil-driven, blast ovens. There were two or three smaller ones and one very large one that was used to heat steel plates. At first I worked as a helper around the ovens, and, God, they were hot! They would heat up to around 1,700 degrees Fahrenheit. The place was bad enough when the oven doors were closed, but when they opened, it was unbearable.

I worked on a team that took circular metal pieces, put them in the oven, and heated them to 1,600 degrees. The pieces were then put on a press that pushed down the edge to turn them into a cup shape. After they were cooled and drilled properly, the pieces were used to hold steam pipes in place on locomotives. My first job required me to don an apron and attach what they called a "dog." When the hot steel pieces came out of the oven, our squad leader would point out spots that were bent, and I would attach the "dog"—a square piece on a pole. Men wielding twelve-pound sledgehammers then pounded the "dog" until the metal underneath was straightened.

Even though it was hard work, I kept at it. I was promoted to sledgeman and then to flanger, a key step to becoming a blacksmith, which was one of the highest jobs in that shop. I was promoted to become leader of a very small group and was offered a job in management if I would stay there and not go into the military. Baldwin needed people and could get them exemptions from the draft because its operations were considered a critical defense industry. I refused the offer, having made up my mind to go into the service. The foreman and superintendent were puzzled by my decision, but I had no regrets.

I felt that I ought to be in there helping to defend the United States from Nazi aggression, the fascism of Mussolini, and the danger posed by Japan. In later years some people asked me why I, as a black man, would feel obligated to go to war for a country that discriminated against me. One reason was that I wanted to defend all of the good people of the United States, and that was most of them, black and white. A second reason was that even though I am an African American, I have always felt as American as any WASP who was born in Connecticut or Boston. I have never felt estranged from the land in which I was born. I have always recognized that I am descended not only from slaves who were brought here but also from white people who came here in the early days of the nation. I am also descended from Native Americans who were already here. I do not think I am being romantic about patriotism simply because I am descended from these three bloodlines.

Most of my life I have felt very deeply about this country. I guess I am emotional about it. After all, my ancestors' blood has gone to nourish the earth here because many of them have died one way or another in the fight for freedom. So I am not an African American who looks to someplace else as home. I am not even sure where I would start in Africa to look for my ancestors. For that matter, I am not really sure where I would look in Europe for my white ancestors or on this continent for my Native American forebears who were, of course, here before the coming of whites or blacks. As for me, my genetic memory goes no further back than these shores, this land, and I have always felt very deeply about it, which is why I enlisted.

How did I come to have such feelings? I am not really sure. I think it had something to do with being in the Boy Scouts for four and a half years and having recited the Pledge of Allegiance and all of the things that are in the Scout program: respect for the flag and the nation and one's obligations to them. I have always felt a part of this country. I have built on that my entire life. I am touched very deeply every time I hear "America the Beautiful." I cannot sing it without choking up. The images of the land, the mountains, the lakes, the North, the South, the East, the West, and the Midwest are all very dear to me.

Even when I was growing up in Memphis, when things were at their segregated worst and when discrimination was at its harshest, I found some way to have hope in what America could be for me and for people like me. I know there are a lot of people in this country, black and white and yellow and every other brown, who are not possessed with the values that I believe represent the essence of America, but I believe most people are. These values come down to an elemental sense of fairness, a feeling of live-and-let-live, and an understanding that all people are equal in the eyes of the law. Not all of us have equal abilities. However, we are all entitled to basic respect as human beings. I believe most Americans share my respect for the Constitution—especially the Bill of Rights—as the foundation of our national values because it protects all of us, rich and poor, all nationalities and races. Fundamentally, most of us share the same ideals, and that is what makes the United States a great place to live. There may be other great places to live, but I would not want to live anyplace but here.

I was not alone in my patriotism or in my desire to serve my country. There were lots of black men eager to join the military, and African-American leaders waged a long, hard struggle so that we would receive opportunities that had been denied us during World War I, when most black soldiers had been assigned to service and infantry units. In retrospect, it was a strange and contradictory time. The American world was much smaller, and some of our attitudes matched it. Here our country was engaged in an all-out war against the tyrannies of fascism and Nazism, yet it was denying able-bodied, skilled men and women the chance to contribute to the war effort simply because of their race.

The discrimination became readily apparent in the fall of 1940 when the draft began. After only a short time, it was clear that draft boards were not calling Negro men to serve in proportion to their numbers in the population. Black leaders—especially Walter White, executive director of the NAACP—protested vigorously to President Roosevelt and others, asking them to end discrimination in the Selective Service System. In response, the federal government established a policy directing local draft boards to induct more blacks. We went into the quartermaster corps, the combat engineers, and the infantry. African-American leaders then pointed out that we had other skills that should be utilized in the service of our country. The *Pittsburgh Courier* and the *Chicago Defender* waged a vigorous campaign to expand opportunities in the military. One battleground became the Army Air Corps. Many white officers did not believe that blacks had the capacity to become pilots. Under steady political pressures, the Army finally agreed to build a training field at Tuskegee, Alabama, and the "Negro Air Force," as it was affectionately called, got its start. These historic events all had a profound impact on my career in the Army and its Air Corps.

Once I decided to enlist, I thought it would be best if I first got some training. I considered it carefully. I decided that if I went into the military simply as an untrained volunteer, then I would probably wind up like many other black soldiers in one of the service outfits like the Combat Engineers or the Quartermaster Corps, driving a truck. Being a laborer in the Army did not excite me from the standpoint of wanting to be a real soldier. I wanted to get into something more technical, so I got into radio.

I had been interested in radio from the time I was a kid, about twelve or thirteen years old. I read a lot of books and knew a lot about it. Picking up stuff out of trash cans behind Sears, Roebuck and other places, I started out with a crystal detector set and worked up to building four-tube battery sets. I could also repair radios and did. I was still quite fascinated by the whole business in 1942, and so I decided to enroll in a radio school in Philadelphia.

I could have taken free radio classes at Temple University, but I was suspicious about whether anything free could be very good. I opted, instead, to attend a private radio school, which was part of the Chamberlain Aircraft Corporation. Clarence Chamberlain was one of the nation's most famous and colorful aviators. Two weeks after Lindbergh crossed the Atlantic, Chamberlain became the first pilot to cross the Atlantic with a paying passenger—Charles A. Levine, a wealthy New York junk dealer who financed the trip. Soon after, Chamberlain became the first aerial photographer, snapping pictures of fires, accidents, and the opening game of the World Series. During the 1930s he crisscrossed the nation lecturing high school students by day and civic groups by night about the glories of aviation. He also served as a consultant for airport construction. When the war came along, he opened a "training division," which quickly became larger than all of his other operations. He had several schools, and I attended the one on North Broad Street in Philadelphia. The course in radiotelegraphy ran for about eight months, from September until May. Chamberlain, like many others who ran technical schools across the country then, had worked out an arrangement with the military. His students enlisted in the reserves, he trained them, then they entered the regular Army. So, on October 1, 1942, I enrolled in the United States Army Signal Corps Enlisted Reserve.

Chamberlain's school served another purpose in my life; my experience as a student there played a key role in developing my self-esteem. I had come out of the South with a tremendous inferiority complex. At Chamberlain's school I quickly learned that I was well able to compete with the other two or three hundred people in my class, most all of whom were white. I came out third or fourth in the class, and that opened my eyes and convinced me that I could absorb training like anybody else.

When I began radio school, I moved into Philadelphia and roomed with a buddy of mine from Baldwin, Frederick Clinton Branch, who later became the first African American to be commissioned in the

Marine Corps. Fred had a great smile and a quarter-miler's gait from his days on his high school track team in Mamaroneck, New York. Fred was one of seven brothers and had been born in Hamlet, North Carolina, where his father was a Methodist minister. Later, his father became the pastor of black churches in Connecticut and New York. Fred returned South to attend college at Johnson C. Smith University in Charlotte. Like me, he had come to Philadelphia for a summer job, then decided to stay. Fred and I roomed with a fine family on North Van Pelt in Philadelphia. He went into the Marine Corps, and I went into the Army in May 1943. He later became a science teacher in Philadelphia.[1]

In those eight months until I went into the regular Army, I had a hectic schedule. I attended school five days a week from noon until about 3 o'clock. Then I rushed by subway to the transfer station in downtown Philadelphia to get the Pennsylvania Railroad train out to Eddystone. I worked second shift, 4 P.M. to 1 A.M., six days a week. Still, I managed to find time to squeeze in extracurricular activities. I played semi-pro football for part of the season after I met a fellow at Baldwin by the name of Lloyd White. He had been a Negro All-American at Talladega College and was captain of the New York Brown Bombers. He invited me to play because they needed a tackle, a role I took on until one of my front teeth got kicked out. I also continued trying to improve myself. I kept up with my reading program, and I pursued informal studies of classical music by attending concerts of the Philadelphia Symphony Orchestra at the Academy of Music. One Saturday night that I will never forget, Maestro Eugene Ormandy conducted an all-Schubert concert, and the music was so beautiful that I felt transfixed. I thought heaven must surely be somewhat like this.

When it finally came time to join the regular Army, I had a decision to make. It brought to mind the occasion when my high school football coach had urged me to "try and pass." Now I was up in Philadelphia, far away from home and family. Coach Bell's suggestion came back to me, briefly. I decided again that I could not live a lie. Several fellows I knew in Philadelphia did pass when they entered the military.

---

1. On July 9, 1995, the Marine Corps named its education building at Officers Candidate School at Quantico, Virginia, after Branch, who was released from active service in 1952. Branch remained in the Reserves and was promoted to captain in 1954. He resigned his commission the following year.

I remember one in particular. We attended radio school together and met on the way to the induction center at Thirty-fourth and Lancaster. He went into the part marked for whites, and I went in the part marked for blacks, and I never saw or heard from him after that.

From the induction center, the Army sent me to Fort George G. Meade, Maryland. After about a week, I was transferred from the Signal Corps Enlisted Reserve to the Air Corps, which needed radiomen. From Fort Meade I attended basic training at Kearns, Utah, which was outside of Salt Lake City on a high, windy plain about four thousand feet above sea level. I arrived there in the early part of June. Snow was still on the ground, although it was not that cold. Kearns was segregated. Blacks and whites lived in separate areas of the camp. Each area had its own barracks and mess halls, although we shared some movies and training sessions. All of our drill instructors were white.

The thirteen weeks of basic training were rigorous, and I enjoyed them. I was a gung-ho soldier and took everything seriously. I worked hard to be the best soldier I could, figuring that if I tried to cheat by not doing the push-ups and not really working, then I was only fooling myself because the day could come in combat when I might need every ounce of strength and endurance to survive. There were a significant number of men who tried to goof off, although I think most of us took the training seriously.

Interestingly enough, among the black soldiers that I knew in this particular training unit, there were a large number of college men, a higher percentage than among white soldiers. I am not sure how to account for that, except for the fact that the military held blacks to much higher standards. In any case, I know that in my group of forty or so, more than half had been to college at least one year. Some had been in school longer, and others had already graduated. These men were headed for technical training after basic training. The technical training in the Army Air Corps was usually in airplane mechanics, radio, and weapons systems.

After finishing basic training in the fall of 1943, I had a short furlough and visited my mother and brother in Memphis. When I returned to Utah, there was no room at the radio school at Salt Lake City Air Base. This kind of delay was not unusual for African Americans in the Air Corps because the Army never created enough slots for all of the black men who wanted to serve. In any case, the Army sent nine of us to Blythe Army Air Base, a godforsaken place in the desert country of southeastern California. Blythe was a B-24 training base for white airmen. We spent a couple of awful months out there doing menial service work until there were openings in technical school. We had guard duty, we worked as cooks around the bachelor officer quarters, and we drove trucks. Finally, we were transferred to Scott Field in Illinois for a five-month training course in radio.

It was an interesting class. I think there were between three and four hundred men in it. Of those, about fifty of us were African Americans. The rest were white, including about fifty Free French soldiers. We were in class together, although we did not live in the same areas. The barracks and mess halls were segregated. To my great pleasure, when the class graduated, six out of the ten top spots were earned by African Americans, one of whom made a perfect score on the four-hour final examination. That person happened to be me. I never had done anything before and I have never done anything since then that was perfect. It was apparently the one time in my life that I did something exactly right. I harbored no illusions that I was brilliant, but it provided more evidence in my growing awakening that God had given me a good mind. There was a ceremony at the end of graduation and my name was inscribed on the permanent honor roll at Scott Field. Years later that would play a part in my getting into law school.

After a short furlough at the end of the training session, I was assigned to the 477th Bombardment Group, which had been organized at Selfridge Field, thirty miles outside of Detroit. The Army organized the 477th in late 1943 to serve in the Pacific. It followed in the footsteps of the better-known 332nd Fighter Group that was on its way to Europe and North Africa. The 332nd was comprised of the 99th Pursuit Squadron—the original famous Tuskegee Airmen—and three other black squadrons. The 332nd compiled an admirable record and became renowned for never losing a single plane to enemy action. The 477th never achieved such success. According to combat instructors I interviewed as our group's assistant historian, the 477th was mishandled from the beginning. How else could you account for the fact that many of the white combat instructors who were sent to prepare us for combat had significantly fewer hours in the air than the trainees? They could not understand it and neither could we.

The 477th's troubled history pointed up all of the problems that stemmed from the prejudice and segregation that plagued the Army Air Corps. Because there were so few top-level African-American officers, and most of those had shipped out with the 332nd, the Army assigned whites, some of whom were not sympathetic to the idea of racial equality, to command the 477th. The base commander, Colonel William L. Boyd, for example, ignored Army regulations and refused to admit blacks to the officers club. He also assigned armed escorts to whites in the Women's Army Corps when they were on base to protect them from possible molestation by black soldiers.

Problems began soon after the group began training at Selfridge Field. On January 1, 1944, three black officers were refused admission to the officers club. Tensions continued to mount, and Army investigators blamed the base's racial problems on its proximity to Detroit. They feared that racial activists and the black press in the city were fomenting trouble that spilled over to Selfridge. Instead of dealing with the root cause of the problem, the racism of its own policies and officers, the Army tried a geographic fix by moving the unit to Godman Field, Kentucky. Officially, the military attributed the move to the need for better weather conditions, but that was just an excuse. The weather there was not that much better, and besides, Godman was a poor choice for many reasons, including the fact that its terrain was not suitable for night flying and its runway was too weak for bombers. Because of Godman's liabilities, several squadrons trained at other locations, and at one point the entire group moved to Freeman Field, Indiana.

It was there that the 477th's officers staged a well-publicized mutiny to protest segregation. Changes of locale had done nothing to improve racial tensions. The new base commander, Colonel Robert R. Selway Jr., proposed the same kind of segregation of facilities that had existed at Selfridge, although he tried to cloak his purposes by not mentioning race. Instead, he set up two clubs—one for instructors and a second for trainees—supposedly based on rank and experience. Under his plan, the instructors, all of whom were white, met in one place, and the trainees, all of whom were black, met in another. Selway's compromise grated on black officers, especially those who had been transferred from the 332nd to help form the core of the 477th, because many had more flying time than their white instructors. On April 1, 1945, thirty-six black officers staged a sit-in at the white officers club. After they ignored an order to leave, military police arrested them. The next day twenty-one more black officers went to the club and were placed under barracks arrest.

Selway closed the club and waited for legal experts from headquarters to investigate. The Air Corps came up with a solution it hoped would ease the problem. The military lawyers helped Selway draft another, "clearer" order about who could use what facilities. He required all black officers on the base to sign a statement saying they had read and understood the new regulation, which called for continued segregation. Neither he nor the Air Corps command counted on the officers' determination. One hundred and one black officers refused to sign, and they were arrested on April 13. The standoff prompted the War Department to intervene. The officers were released without charges on grounds that they had not fully understood the implications of their actions in refusing to sign the regulation. Only the three officers who had been accused of pushing military police when they entered the officers club on April 1 were charged. Two were acquitted, and one was fined $150. The 477th was transferred back to Godman to a kind of de facto segregation. The officers club at Godman was open to all officers, but in practice most of the whites went to the club at nearby Fort Knox. The Army also decided to replace the 477th's white commanders with blacks.

I was assigned to the 477th during its last days at Freeman Field. I was sent to Selfridge for a few days and then joined the unit at Godman after the officers' revolt. I only found out the details later, when I began researching the 477th's history. In retrospect, it is clear that what happened in our group was not unusual. There were dozens of actions in all of the military branches to segregate and isolate black soldiers. The list is long and, in the light of history, so utterly stupid. It really was one of the great ironies of World War II that blacks had to fight for the right to defend their nation. More than one million African Americans served in the armed forces during the war. I suspect most of them ended up feeling the same way I did. It was a great experience, and I would not give anything for the people I met and the experiences and training I had in the military, but I was glad to get on with my civilian life.

At the time I joined the unit, however, I was still enthusiastic. As an enlisted man, I focused on being a good soldier and putting what I had learned in training school into practice. I was assigned as a radio operator to the 617th Squadron. We flew B-25s, the so-called Billy Mitchell bombers, which were medium range and required a crew of six. Each plane carried a 500-pound bomb, 50-caliber machine guns, waist guns, nose guns, and tail guns. B-25s were used extensively in the China-Burma-India Theater for low-level strafing duties. It was the type of airplane that flew off the deck of a carrier under the leadership of General Jimmy Doolittle and bombed Tokyo. I flew on a number of training missions in the waist or middle part of the B-25 until somebody noticed that I was oversized for an enlisted man on a combat crew. The maximum height was about six feet, and I was four inches over that. So, I was pulled out of the crew and assigned to become the air-ground liaison chief. Then a buddy, John D. Silvera, who worked as the public relations officer for the base, persuaded me to transfer from radio communications to public relations. He knew I had a writing background from high school and Nashville. So I wrote news releases, helped write the squadron's history, and became associate editor of the camp newspaper, the *Godman Field Beacon.*

Working in public relations, I became well acquainted with our base's new commanding officer, Colonel Benjamin O. Davis Jr., whom the Army had brought back from the 332nd in Europe to lead us. I had been a fan of Davis's ever since I was a boy delivering the *Pittsburgh Courier.* In 1936 he became the first black to graduate from West Point since the 1890s. It was all over the *Courier,* and we were so proud of him. During his time at the academy, Davis had no roommates. He was given the "silent treatment" by the other cadets during his first two years.

This did not dishearten him because his father, Benjamin O. Davis Sr., another remarkable man whom I also met, had prepared his son for the mistreatment he would receive at West Point. Davis Sr. was another military pioneer; he became the first black general in U.S. armed forces history during World War II. Anyway, Davis Jr. survived the isolation with a chilly reserve and remarkable self-discipline. When I knew him, Colonel Davis was what you expected a West Point officer to be: straight as an arrow, mentally and morally. We were proud of him and did our damnedest for him. He truly was a hero in the best sense of that word. He went on to become a lieutenant general. After his retirement he became head of public safety, briefly, for the city of Cleveland under Mayor Carl Stokes. Decades later, one of my brother's grandsons, Leon Rawlings, graduated from West Point. His good experiences there show how much times and attitudes have changed.

One of the more embarrassing moments in my Army career came when my mother wrote to then-Colonel Davis about me. While I was in the Army she worked for a young couple. She lived with the wife while the husband was off in the Navy. I had a savings bond program and used to have the bonds sent to my mother. They were in our joint names. As time went on, I wanted to use some of that money to have a little fun. So I would write my mother and she would send it to me. After a while, she became disturbed by the requests and wrote to Colonel Davis. He called me in and said, "Well, I got a letter from your mother, and she's afraid you're getting into some kind of trouble. Are you?" And I said, "No, I'm not. I just want to use a little bit of the money that I've saved." And he said, "Well, all right, take care." He looked kind of embarrassed. I know I was quite embarrassed. In retrospect I find it amusing—the extended care my mother was getting to me through my commanding officer.

Davis was not the only remarkable man on the base. Ours was quite a group. Most of the men had high morale and above average intelligence. Daniel "Chappie" James Jr., who had attended Tuskegee, was a first lieutenant and one of the best pilots. He later became a four-star general in the Air Force. Coleman Young became mayor of Detroit. William T. Coleman Jr. went on to graduate from Harvard Law School, clerk for U.S. Supreme Court Justice Felix Frankfurter, and become secretary of transportation under President Gerald Ford. Robert L. Ming, one of the nation's great civil rights lawyers, was our base legal officer. Before the war he taught at Howard University and spoke out against police brutality aimed at blacks. After the war, he became a professor of law at the University of Chicago.

Through my work with the base newspaper, I got to meet my childhood idol, Joe Louis. The Army put entertainers and big stars in Special Services to travel around and meet the troops. Joe came to our base for a two-day visit. I decided I was going to get the definitive interview, and I thought up all the good questions I was going to ask my hero. I dogged his footsteps, and at dinner asked if I could interview him. He said, "Not now, man." So, I stood at the table, hoping that sometime during the evening he could find time for me, but he kept waving me off. When dinner was over, he went to the gymnasium to put on a boxing exhibition with an amateur from our unit. I still could not catch up with him, so I decided to try and catch him the next morning. I went to the barracks where he was staying at about eight in the morning, walked over to his bunk, and said, "Hey Champ! Good morning." He raised up, looked at me, and said "Goddammit, man, leave me alone!" I said, "Okay," and backed away quickly, realizing that I still had one more shot because I had arranged to be one of his two hosts at breakfast. When Joe arrived in the mess hall and saw what was coming, this harassing young amateur reporter trying to interview him, he just took the morning paper out and put it up in front of his face as I sat across the table from him. I never got my interview, although, in a way, I did have breakfast with the Champ.

Godman Field had its own share of famous athletes. There was Malvin Whitfield, a tall, handsome guy who always seemed to be running. These were the days before an ordinary person would put on a sweatsuit and run, but Whitfield was running all of the time. No one at the time guessed that, once the war was over, Whitfield would become the world's premier middle-distance runner. He dominated the 800-meter between 1948 and 1954, setting indoor and outdoor records and winning Olympic gold medals in 1948 and 1952. After his great successes, he wound up in Africa trying to help produce runners for the 1956 Olympics. I also got to know Archie Harris. He had been the national discus champion for three years running and was also a star end on the football team while he was at the University of Indiana. When he arrived at Godman Field, the Army asked him to organize a football team. Harris left the service and became big in the International Longshoremen's Union in New York City. I used to read about him from time to time.

I covered the football team for the camp newspaper, and I will never forget one trip we took to MacDill, Florida, just outside Tampa. The black football team there included the great basketball player Goose Tatum, who for many years was the star of the Harlem Globetrotters. I went down to report the action and ended up having the most harrowing airplane trip of my life. The pilot was Chappie James, who was also a member of the Godman football team. I think there were about thirty of us on a C-47 cargo plane really made for twenty-two. We also had a huge air compressor that we were dropping off at Tuskegee Air Field in Alabama. We were scheduled to fly to Tuskegee, stay overnight, then go on to Tampa the next day. We took off in a cold November rain with poor visibility, but we all felt comfortable because Chappie was at the helm, and we considered him to be the best pilot on the base. Once we took off, we could hear the engines groaning from the weight. After we reached our assigned altitude, we realized that ice was forming on the propeller and wing surfaces. We came down to a lower altitude and descended into a violent storm that tossed the airplane all over the sky. We flapped around for half an hour or so, going up and down in powerful vertical drafts, probably five hundred feet at a time. You put a bunch of young guys together and they are usually macho and gung ho about everything, but instead of yelling and shouting "ride 'em cowboy," we all got damned quiet. On the final approach, we came so low over the little town of Tuskegee that we could almost touch the church steeple. The runway was full of water. We landed, skidded sideways, and finally straightened up. I do not know how many of us actually got down and kissed the ground. I think I did.

Perhaps the most important thing that happened to me while I was in the Army was that I met my future wife, Mavis Clare Livingston. In Detroit some people had started an organization to provide recreation and entertainment for servicemen. They would invite young women from the community to meet the soldiers and airmen at nearby Selfridge Field. When the 477th moved to Godman Field, Kentucky, the airmen wanted to have a social event that would reunite them with the women from Detroit. We planned a big weekend with a number of events, including track and field races, a dinner, and a dance. A couple of busloads of young women came down in the spring of 1945. At one of the events, I spied Mavis and was immediately drawn to her. There was some fellow who had met her previously who was horning in, and I tried to outmaneuver him. I got a chance to dance with her a couple of times. We had more time to talk at the nondenominational service in the chapel on Sunday, and we exchanged addresses. I started to write letters to her, and when I got leave, I went to Detroit to visit her and her family.

Things were heating up pretty rapidly. I became worried that we were going to rush to the altar, and so I did something very stupid. I told her that I was involved with somebody else. It was untrue. I was very much taken with her, but I thought I better try to go to school before I got married. I figured once I got married, the chances of my getting an education were much slimmer. Mavis had become very attached to me, and she was disconsolate. We stopped seeing one another. I always thought about her, and I hoped that we would get back together.

While I was in the Army, I tried to serve flawlessly, and I think I was a pretty good soldier. Eventually, I was promoted from private first class to corporal to buck sergeant. I was in that position when I left the service on February 18, 1946. By the time I left, I had soured on the Army. My disenchantment began when I learned from the classification sergeant that I had one of the three highest scores in the outfit on the Army classification test, including all of the officers. In order to be an officer, you needed to have scored at least 110. My score was 133. I guess I had expected to be promoted according to my contribution and my merit. Instead, I found that the system did not always work efficiently, and sometimes it took more than skill and ability to get ahead. During my last months in the Army, my consuming interest was in getting out of military service and returning to school.

Just before I left the Army I had an encounter that made me re-think some aspects of my life and ambitions. I was coming out of the chapel in a big hurry, as usual, just as our base's old, white-haired chaplain was coming in. He stopped me and asked, "Where are you going so fast, big boy?" We struck up a conversation, and he asked me what I intended to do when I mustered out of the service. I expressed my intention to hurry and finish college, then marry and settle down. In a highly symbolic way, he pushed his hand at my chest and said, "Slow down, you are going too fast." He then told me something I carried with me when I left the Army. "You are a young man, and you have plenty of time to prepare. Wouldn't it be wise to devote the first half of your life to preparing for the second half?" I thought about what he said, and after that I approached the rest of my schooling with an emphasis upon completing it well. I am sure that chaplain never realized how profound an impact his words had on me. Sometimes we never realize the effect we can have. In any case, I shall always be deeply grateful to this fine gentleman for the sound advice he rendered on the most casual of contact. It just goes to prove the old saying, "Our monuments and brickstone and mortar will some day be passed and forgotten, but the imprint we leave in the hearts and minds of people remain immortal."

All told, I was on active duty in the military from May 1943, when I was twenty-one years old, until February 1946, when I was twenty-four years old. I came out and was briefly a member of what was popularly called the "52/20" Club. The government provided an allowance of twenty dollars a week, for up to a year, for returning veterans who were unemployed. After leaving the Army, I went to Flint, Michigan, to stay with my Aunt Maggie and Uncle Sylvester and begin looking for work. The big General Motors strike, the longest in the history of GM and the United Auto Workers (UAW), was in progress. I could not find any work, but I kept busy while I was waiting for an opportunity. I wrote articles for free for the *Flint News Advertiser*. When the strike finally ended in March 1946, I was able to hire into the Chevrolet division of General Motors.

While at Chevrolet, I had another lousy job. This time I worked as a metal polisher, trying to get the nickel off of car metal to make it shine like a newly minted dime. I used a rag wheel, treated with lime, held together by grease, fanned by blowers that did not operate effectively. The rag wheel stock needed a lot of friction to get the nickel off of the metal. If you did not grip it properly, the rag would catch in the wheel, which was doing about three thousand revolutions per minute, then it would spin out toward your gut and hit you with enough force to take your breath away. We wore heavy, leather aprons for protection, but it was still easy to get hurt. The job was also dirty. I always got filthy, right through three layers of clothing, into the skin on my arms, face, and neck. I worked the third shift at night, so I could earn premium pay. I hated that job so much that I literally counted every day until I was scheduled to leave for Syracuse University in September.

2
Upward and Onward

✦ 5 ✦
College and Law School

I ENTERED CIVILIAN LIFE intent on becoming a journalist. I started this career in high school as editor of the paper and class annual. I continued working at it in Nashville and as an editor of the *Godman Field Beacon*. While I was still in the Army, my mother and I discussed the possibility of moving North so that I could study journalism at the University of Michigan and we could be closer to our relatives in Flint. I offered to use my savings for a down payment on a boarding house in Ann Arbor. She would run it, and I would stay in it, help out with the chores, and attend school while we both benefited from the income we would get from boarding students.

I abandoned the idea after I realized that the University of Michigan had a department rather than a school of journalism. I reasoned that relegating journalism to a department meant that the university did not take the subject seriously, so I applied instead to the William Allen White School of Journalism at the University of Kansas and the journalism school at Syracuse. I probably would have gone to Kansas because I had great admiration for White, the sage of Emporia, and the way he approached journalism. I wanted to go where he was. But when I heard that there had been racial trouble on the campus in Lawrence, I chose Syracuse instead.

When I arrived there in the fall of 1946, Syracuse was packed with students. It had accepted many more veterans than it could handle, so it had to house us in dormitories at the state fairgrounds, just outside of the city. We came to campus by local train every morning. Finally, the university was able to create housing for us closer to school. It obtained several Navy barracks from someplace and erected them about a mile from the campus. The university set up a Quonset hut, which we called a "Quonseteria," to serve meals. After dinner was over, a part of the Quonseteria remained open as a soda fountain and sandwich bar, which I managed. During the Christmas and Easter breaks, I also took work as a dormitory cleaner and porter, bringing in and taking out furniture and doing handyman jobs until school reconvened.

With credits from my year at Fisk, I began classes at Syracuse as a late freshman. I had intended to get a degree in journalism, but I also took business courses, including a year of accounting, because I hoped someday to buy my own newspaper. I was in a study group with a bunch of guys, most of whom were Jews from New York City. We shared a lot of information in studying economics and political science, and I found myself scoring well on tests and in classes. I was on the dean's list during the entire year, and I came even more to believe in myself and my abilities. It was probably during that year that I finally shed some of my last feelings of childhood inferiority.

At the same time, I began to worry that I was becoming an old man before finding a career. I still wanted to be a journalist, but I surveyed the journalism situation among the great colored race of the United States of America and decided that unless you owned a newspaper, the business was highly unrenumerative; you just could not make a decent living out of it. About that same time, my brother had the strange notion that I might make a pretty decent lawyer. We had been trading letters about careers, and he thought I might give law a try. His advice had always been sound, so I investigated further.

I went to the veterans' counseling center at Syracuse and took a battery of tests that were geared toward analyzing my skills and interests. The test results showed that I had an inclination for and probably an aptitude for three jobs—author, journalist, or lawyer. I began to think more seriously about a legal career. In the end, I decided that I could fulfill my desire to write by writing legal briefs. Besides, I reasoned, it would take me a much shorter time to earn a decent living as a lawyer than it would as a black journalist.

When I was considering my future, I recalled one of the most memorable scenes from my childhood in Memphis. I was about fourteen, and my brother and I skipped school and went downtown to the courthouse to get a look at the legendary Charles Hamilton Houston, the Washington, D.C. lawyer who was the Moses of the nation's early civil rights legal struggles. Charles Houston was the grandson of

slaves. His father, William L. Houston, worked his way through Howard Law School's evening division. He sent his son, Charles, to Amherst at age sixteen, where he was only one of three black students.
Charles graduated in 1915 as class valedictorian and a member of Phi
Beta Kappa. Later, he attended Harvard Law School and graduated in
1922 at the top of his class. He spent the following year in Spain,
studying civil law at the University of Madrid.

He returned to Washington, joined his father in practice, and
began teaching at Howard. One of his first full-time students was
Thurgood Marshall, who later became the first black to serve on the
U.S. Supreme Court. Marshall dubbed Houston "Old Iron Shoes" because of his high standards, which placed heavy demands upon his
students. Houston alienated some students but inspired others with
his intolerance of laziness and mediocrity. He believed that black lawyers had to be better than the average white lawyer to succeed, and he
drove his students and, later when he became dean, his faculty. Within
a few years of taking the helm, Houston transformed Howard from an
unaccredited night school into a fully accredited, nationally regarded
law school. He made it his mission to attract blacks into the legal
profession. Whereas white lawyers were perfectly adequate to handle
routine cases, Houston argued that only blacks could effectively wage
the legal battle for civil rights. He bemoaned the fact that, according
to the 1930 census, there were only about 1,230 blacks among the
nation's approximately 160,000 attorneys. Of those, only 487 were in
the South, where Houston claimed they were needed most desperately.

In 1935 Houston left the deanship of Howard Law School to direct
the NAACP's legal campaigns, where in collaboration with Marshall,
William H. Hastie, and others, he fought the Battle of Jericho against
segregation. Because of their efforts, the walls started to tumble down.
One of Houston's first priorities at the NAACP was to launch a campaign to equalize educational opportunities for blacks. He believed
that continued inequality in education would condemn the entire race
to an inferior social position in American society.

One struggle in that campaign took place in the Memphis courtroom where I saw him during the 1930s, when Houston challenged
the racially exclusionary practices of the University of Tennessee,
which had not opened any of its graduate schools to Negroes. Houston
was accompanied by one of Tennessee's most prominent black attorneys, Z. Alexander Looby, a native of the British West Indies who had
graduated from Columbia University Law School and settled in Nash-

ville in 1926. The courtroom was crowded; there was standing room only. I had been exposed to a lot of fine people in the community, but I had never seen black professionals in a professional setting. There were these two black men, in court on an awesome matter, presenting it with such poise, energy, verve, and confidence. What struck me most at the time—and I will never forget that scene—is that with all the hostility around him, Houston seemed to be so relaxed and utterly fearless, a quality that you did not see too often in those parts.

As I was growing up, Charles Houston became a living, breathing hero to me. I had a chance to pay homage to him later when I was in law school. Houston literally worked himself to death, dying of a heart attack in 1950 when he was only fifty-four years old. He fell, but he did not fail. And my brother and I—two Tennessee boys who had watched him with awe and admiration some fifteen years earlier— stood in Rankin Chapel at Howard University in April 1950 and, along with hundreds of other mourners, wept unashamedly at his funeral.

Houston's distant cousin, William H. Hastie, who participated in those NAACP battles, was another role model to me during World War II. Hastie, who was ten years younger than Houston, also had great courage and ability. He was a fellow Tennessean who was born in Knoxville, where he completed the first seven grades in school before his family moved to Washington, D.C. He was valedictorian of his high school class, then followed his exemplar, Charles Houston, north to Massachusetts, where he attended Amherst. He turned down fellow- ships to Oxford and the University of Paris in order to teach at a black high school in New Jersey. When he earned enough money, he went on to Harvard Law School, was elected to law review, graduated, and returned to Washington. He later returned to Harvard to earn a doc- torate in juridical science. In 1937 Hastie was appointed to be a federal judge in the Virgin Islands. After two years, he resigned that presti- gious post to take over as dean of Howard Law School. More impor- tant, he became part of the brain trust that mapped the NAACP legal strategies to end discrimination in education, politics, and other cru- cial areas. As had been true with Houston before him, Harvard trained Hastie's mind, but Howard University and what it stood for captured his heart.

In 1940 Hastie took a leave from Howard to become the civilian aide to Secretary of War Henry Stimson. He had always been known for his quiet dignity and cool, almost laid-back manner. Nevertheless, with his great courage and persistence, he became the burr in the saddle of the military establishment during World War II. With the zeal of a task force prosecutor and the poise and daring of a hang-glider pilot, Hastie pursued the military on every act of discrimination in its treatment of Negro soldiers both on and off the military reservations, culminating in his dramatic resignation in January 1943. For nearly three years, white military commanders tried their best to circumvent Hastie's efforts to expand the fight for democracy abroad to the fight for justice in the U.S. military. In some instances, War Department bureaucrats did not even provide him with the information about black troops that he needed in order to carry out his job. Finally, Hastie had enough. He came to believe that he could be more effective criticizing the War Department as an outsider.

His resignation may not seem like much now, but it was regarded at the time, with the war going on, as nothing short of an act of defiance and, in the eyes of some critics, as an act that could only give aid and comfort to the nation's enemies. I can remember thinking at the time, "It's a gutsy thing to do and the right thing to do, but I am afraid that public service will forever lose a person of truly outstanding ability." But Hastie did return. He became governor of the U.S. Virgin Islands, then a federal judge in the Virgin Islands, before he finally was appointed to the Third U.S. Circuit Court of Appeals in Philadelphia. Hastie said many times that he tried never to forget how little it meant for him to be the "first" black in so many important positions when blacks as a group were last among all Americans. I thought about that many times in later years when I became a so-called "first" in Michigan politics and corporate America.

Hastie left a great legacy on which all of us so-called successful African Americans have been able to build. I remember one speech he gave later in his life. He spoke with stridency against some black activists who for rhetorical effect or perhaps out of ignorance claimed that no progress in race relations had been made since the *Brown v. Board of Education* decision in 1954, that no real progress had come with passage of the Civil Rights Acts of 1964 and 1965. Judge Hastie, in his quiet way, said—and this is not a direct quote but is from my memory—something like: "We should be careful to avoid use of the language and symbols of defeat lest our enemies miscalculate our resolve. More important, if we say we are losing, we will adopt the mentality of losers and the strategy of losers. In the end, then, we will lose. We may still lose some battles, but although progress may be uneven, we are still moving ahead. We are winning." The last time I saw Judge

Hastie was at a meeting of the National Bar Association, the country's major organization of black lawyers that Charles Houston had helped found in the 1920s. In the curious way we sometimes treat our great people, he was left to stand around. I went up and asked him why he still came to meetings, and he said humbly, "Just in case they need me."

Houston and Hastie provided inspiring examples of what lawyers could do to eradicate social injustice. I decided if I could not accomplish much as a poor, struggling black journalist, then I might be able to make a difference as a lawyer. Meanwhile, my brother was beckoning from Washington, D.C., where he was living with his small family, and he said, "Come down, and let's get together again." We had always planned to do that because we were close buddies, so I inquired of various schools in Washington, D.C.

I cannot remember now why I did not seriously consider Howard University Law School, but it probably was because Catholic University Law School had an early admissions program for veterans. Under its policy, Catholic admitted veterans with only two years of college if they had a good academic background with a B average or better. If I had it to do over again, I would have gone ahead and gotten a bachelor's degree before going to law school. That way I would have had more time to study and appreciate a wider range of subjects. But from my perspective then, as a twenty-five-year-old, I was getting to be an old man. It was not an unusual view among the veterans returning from World War II.

The fact that I had converted to Catholicism by then also played a part in my decision. During my early days in Memphis, we attended the African Methodist Episcopal Church. In high school, when my mother resumed work as a maid, she had to be on the job and could no longer attend church on Sunday. My good friend Lytell Barrett was a Catholic, and I had some visceral feeling that because my father had been a Catholic, I should look into it. There was, too, the lure of my high school sweetheart, Odile Bartholomew, who was also a Catholic. Lytell never proselytized, but when he found out about my interest in Catholicism, he helped me delve into it more deeply, and I ended up joining when I was sixteen.

I applied to Catholic University and sent everything I could think of that was favorable in my application. Although I satisfied the formal requirements, the admissions committee was not very enthusiastic about me because they had pretty bright people applying—people with bachelor's and master's degrees and some fellows who had been in seminaries and had received excellent educations. So, at first, the admissions committee members were not too much persuaded by my comparatively meager accomplishments. But I kept writing to the committee, and finally its members admitted me. I was told later by a young law professor, Richard J. Blanchard, why they changed their minds. Blanchard, who had been an officer in the Navy and had just returned from active service, noticed that I had achieved a perfect score on my Army radio school test at Scott Field. Blanchard told me he had a tough job convincing the other two members of the admissions committee, but he finally was able to persuade them that anyone who could eager-beaver his way around four hundred other soldiers could probably study law successfully. That is how I got in.

During my final semester at Syracuse, I had my first major bout with illness. I had a perforated duodenal ulcer in the spring of 1947 and became quite ill. The doctor who performed the surgery was a nice old fellow who had been in the service as a surgeon. He came to me after the surgery and said, "No more drinking or smoking." I had done very little drinking anyway, although I did occasionally have a beer or two, but I smoked a fair amount, a pack or a pack and a half a day. I stopped smoking after that date, April 23, 1947. Later, there would be times when I was at meetings and people would pass around cigars or serve cocktails. I would chomp down on the cigar but never light up, and I would sip a little alcohol at ceremonial occasions and then just push the rest away. I always got something that looked like a drink, a glass of water or tea that could pass as vodka or whiskey, and just held it in my hand. I have never experienced any sense of loss by not being able to drink over the years. I used to say kiddingly that I could be in a room full of cocktailing revelers and be as stupid and silly as they could without having anything to drink. Still, it is a strange kind of experience to be among people at a cocktail party, whose tongues are loosened and are saying all kinds of things to you that they otherwise would not say. Interestingly, I could pick up things that I would not have learned otherwise because I was sober.

At the beginning of the summer, I left Syracuse and moved in with my brother and sister-in-law, who lived on Bass Place, in southeast Washington. I spent the summer recuperating and did not work. It was the only time I had rested and taken off from work since I had been a very young boy, and it felt strange. However, it did not take long for my life to return to its normal, hectic pace.

Once I began law school, I resumed my busy schedule of trying to attend school while supporting myself. I took the familiar round of part-time jobs. I worked Christmas holidays as a mail sorter at the main U.S. Post Office. The first summer I had a job as a mail, file, and information clerk with the Immigration and Naturalization Service because of my uncanny ability to find lost files among the six million or so they had there. I spent my entire summer going around figuring out where some dumb or inattentive clerk might stick a file in the wrong place. The next summer I worked as a teletype operator in the headquarters for U.S. Air Force communications in the Pentagon.

My law school class had about fifty students. There was only one other gentleman of color who started with us, but he left after one semester. Why I do not know. In any event, there were a lot of fine people in that class. Two became federal judges—Dick Conaboy and Bill Leland—both in Scranton, Pennsylvania. I never had any illusions that I was number one in the class, and in retrospect I am happy to believe that I was in the top third in terms of ability. That might even be stretching it a bit, but in any event, a law school class, particularly mine because it was so small and we took essentially all of our courses together with a few minor variations, is an interesting testing lab. We were together. We got to know each other pretty well. We had our great debates in the classroom and out. We had our study groups in which we argued the great issues of the day. My good friend Jim Pie and I met and had a magnificent argument the very first day about Franco and the Catholic Church. It went on for several hours. Jim probably had the best mind in our class, and because of him I ended up in some of the best study groups with some of the top students. We were a group of veterans, in large part, and we became a cohesive group during those three years.

I am proud to say that in none of my associations ever, dating back from 1947 to the present, have I ever had any indication that my classmates or teachers harbored any racist feelings toward me. In retrospect, that might have been in part owing to the fact that because no issue was made of it, a lot of people may not even have known that I was African American. To make sure that they did, I invited my brother, Hamilton, and my longtime friend, Bill Coleman, who was then a law clerk at the U.S. Supreme Court, as guests when I participated in the moot court. I suppose by the time my classmates found out I was African American, they had gotten to know me, and it did not mean anything to them. In any case, I was handled like everyone else.

I did fairly well in law school. With two other students I wrote a lead article that led to me being invited to join law review during my second year. Apparently word got out that I was a perfectionist—that I had insisted that we do the article properly. So the members of law review, who were among the top students in the class, voted me a special member of the staff.

Even more important, during my second year, my team won the final round of the yearlong moot court competition. The finalists had to win previous rounds in order to compete for the top honors. That meant being chosen the best presenter of the four people—two on one side and two on the other—in the arguments and briefs of the two preliminary rounds. Our team of finalists consisted of another second-year student, Joseph J. Urciolo, and a third-year student, Thomas Francis McKenna. Tom started law school, dropped out and worked in the FBI during the war, then came back to law school and finished. Our task was to present a highly technical argument on constitutional law before real judges—Robert H. Jackson of the U.S. Supreme Court, E. Barrett Prettyman of the U.S. Circuit Court of Appeals for Washington, D.C., and T. Alan Goldsborough of the U.S. District Court. I was fascinated with the research, so Joe and Tom let me do most of the work on the brief. Unfortunately, I did not do that well in the oral presentation. I found the questions from the judges too tough and had a rough time making my argument. Joe and I were lucky that Tom was on our team; he was an excellent debater, rescued the argument, and saved the day.

U.S. Supreme Court Justice William O. Douglas presented the three of us with gold keys and embossed law dictionaries for winning the competition, and Catholic University issued a press release that featured a picture of the ceremony in which I was shaking hands with him. It appeared in Flint, Michigan, which was listed as my hometown because I had lived there with my Aunt Maggie while I was working for Chevrolet before I entered college. That picture would play a major part in launching my legal career.

My last semester of law school was significant for another reason. I married Mavis Livingston. I had thought about her ever since I had broken off our relationship. But, as time wore on, it seemed increasingly unlikely that we would ever get back together. Then my Aunt Maggie intervened. I was visiting her in Flint during a law school break. I told her about my continuing feelings for Mavis. Aunt Mag was a great one for matchmaking and arranging things. When her nieces and nephews were involved, she was especially eager to help. Anyway, she wrote Mavis's family explaining everything; then I wrote Mavis and made elaborate apologies, and we reunited. I visited Mavis a couple of times, and the next thing you know, we were engaged to be married. I spent the end of my second summer in law school in Detroit, visiting Mavis and her family, and working as a metal finisher at Chrysler's Mack Avenue Plant on the east side of the city.

We were married on December 29, 1949, in Blessed Sacrament Cathedral in Detroit. We chose that date because we wanted to have a full-blown nuptial wedding, rather than an ordinary wedding mass, so we had to get past Christmas and past the Feast of St. Stephen and a couple of other important days on the church calendar. We chose the year because it was close to my graduation. We figured any children would come after I was already back in the workforce. We spent an abbreviated honeymoon—four or five days at a frozen lake, the Great Lakes Resort in Jackson, Michigan—and then we went back to Washington. Mavis worked for a brief time as a secretary on campus in the social work school, I was hard at work trying to finish law school, and we spent what little spare time we had getting to know each other better.

Even while I was a student, I appreciated the fact that Catholic University Law School was a special place. Now with years of hindsight, I can say that I really had three of the greatest years of my life there. Certainly the three greatest intellectual years of my life. I greatly expanded my knowledge base and sharpened my mind, and not just in the classroom. I had wonderful conversations with my classmates, many of whom were fairly sophisticated thinkers and scholars. Many had college degrees and had been in Catholic seminaries studying for the priesthood before the war came along. I learned much from those very talented people who were quick-witted, steeped in solid Catholic educations, and so thoroughly drilled in philosophy and logic. We did a lot of arguing in philosophy and history, and that was as helpful to me as the study of law, which, of course, also broadened my horizons.

By the time we graduated, my classmates and I left law school with a high sense of mission instilled in us by great teachers who insisted that lawyers should be something much more than skilled mechanics in the justice system. They believed and taught us to be-

Smith met his wife, Mavis Clare Livingston, while serving in the Army Air
Corps during World War II. They married on December 29, 1949, at Blessed
Sacrament Cathedral in Detroit, just before Smith's final semester at Catholic
University Law School.

lieve that every practitioner should be something closely akin to an assistant minister of justice, a skilled advocate to be sure, but one who also knows where good advocacy ends and chicanery begins. In addition to the usual courses on torts and contracts, we were required to take classes in jurisprudence—the science and philosophy of law. In those classes, Dean Brendon F. Brown taught us to analyze the moral content in cases on equity and to examine the historical bases of our juridical concepts. We read such legal and political theorists as Thomas Aquinas, Thomas Hobbes, Sir Bronislaw Malinowski, and Roscoe Pound. I left law school with an even stronger sense of what my mother had taught me as a child—what we seek and expect often in others, we must cultivate most carefully in ourselves: character. In all my varied years of law practice I tried never to forget that character covers the whole spectrum of conduct demanded from a lawyer, from honor to fair play, to good conscience, to hard work. I know that may ring of platitudes, but I have come to realize that platitudes are often, simply stated, the obvious virtues coupled with a disagreeable sense that we often fail to live up to them. It is easier to be forgetful of these virtues—and the difficulties in obtaining them—if we label them "platitudes," but somehow they remain hauntingly with us no matter what the age or the season.

I left law school with two heroes. My first was Father James Keller of the Christophers. Keller completed his theological studies at Catholic University in the 1920s, then spent more than two decades raising money for the Maryknoll Brothers and their overseas missions. During a trip to Italy in 1933, Keller reflected on the early Christian martyrs—the Christophers—who shed their blood as witnesses for Christ. Most were laypeople who did not need an ecclesiastical mandate to speak out. Their views and actions were the natural consequences of their faith. Keller melded his insights and experience into a simple belief best summed up by a Chinese motto that he cited frequently: "It is better to light one candle than to curse the darkness." I was deeply impressed with Keller's philosophy and his 1948 best-selling book, *You Can Change the World,* in which he argued that everyone was capable of improving the world. Keller believed in stressing the positive and motivated readers to choose careers in which they could do the most good, including law and politics. Many of his admonitions sounded as if they had come from the culture of my youth, including his advice: "You will never bring out the bit of greatness in you if you set your sights low."

My second hero during law school and after was Thomas More, the famous humanist thinker and Catholic martyr. More, as the famous play by Robert Bolt suggests, was truly "a man for all seasons." He had piety and humility, wit and wisdom. He was an extraordinary husband and father, a man of great talent as a lawyer and judge, a scholar and a man of letters. More towered above the other social, legal, and intellectual figures in sixteenth-century England. As one of the leading figures of humanism, More revered education and wrote widely. His most famous work, *Utopia,* describes an ideal community in which all children are educated in the classics and become adults whose time is divided between work and intellectual pursuit. He coined the term "Utopia" to describe an ideal society in which tyranny was banished, democratic ideals reigned, economic and social equality were the norm, and the human spirit was free to soar toward God unfettered by pride, greed, and the other human failings that take root in ordinary civil society. More, along with other humanists, was dedicated to understanding and improving the human condition. He was one of those rare human beings who managed to have it all. He was educated and contemplative yet still had a successful career. He was deeply religious and still had and enjoyed his family.

The outline of his life and martyrdom are well known. In 1529 Henry VIII appointed him lord chancellor, the top lawyer in the government of England. Henry VIII, upset at his wife Catherine of Aragon's failure to produce a male heir, sought papal approval to annul his marriage to her so he could marry Anne Boleyn. When the pope refused, Henry VIII removed the Church of England from Rome's authority. He consolidated his power by establishing the crown as the highest legal authority of ecclesiastical matters. He required that all church decrees needed royal approval, and he declared himself, as king, the symbolic head of the Church of England. More resigned in protest. He earlier had accused Martin Luther of encouraging heresy by abandoning church dogma, and he repeated the charge against Henry VIII. In *Utopia,* More criticized rulers who sought to increase their power at the expense of the welfare of their citizens. He also took up that charge against Henry VIII, arguing that no temporal ruler had the right to increase his extensive powers by taking over both the religious and political concerns of his citizens. He added insult to injury by refusing to take an oath recognizing Anne Boleyn's daughter, the future Elizabeth I, as a legitimate heir to England's throne. In short, More refused to distort the law so that the king would come out looking wholesome in an otherwise corrupt scheme. More was imprisoned in 1534, then beheaded on July 6, 1535. As he was facing his executioner, More uttered these immortal lines: "I remain the King's good servant but God's first." The Catholic Church beatified him in 1886 and canonized him in 1935.

More stands as one of the great heroes of history. He was a courageous man willing to sacrifice his own life rather than abandon his integrity and convictions. In all of my subsequent years of legal practice and public service, I kept a picture of Thomas More in my office to remind me that although I had loyalties to political party, loyalties to family, loyalties to employers, I also had duties to God, to the law, and to the truth. It is not exaggerating to say that More's example and ideals carried me through my early days as a lawyer and my later career as a public servant. For a number of years, I made speeches extolling his virtues and commending his life to various groups.

Perhaps, in part because More was my model, I did not begin my legal career thinking that I would achieve great fame and fortune. It never occurred to me that I would become a Michigan supreme court justice or end up as general counsel of the world's largest corporation. I began with only two goals when I started. First, I wanted to be regarded as an honest, able lawyer. Second, I wanted to be able to support my family. I succeeded at both.

✦ 6 ✦
Fascinations of the Law

D URING MY LAST semester of law school, Mavis and I were overjoyed to learn that she was pregnant. We decided to move back to Michigan to be near her family in Detroit and my relatives in Flint. When I finished law school in June 1950, Mavis's father, mother, and kid brother came to Washington in a Buick Roadmaster. They visited with her and vacationed while I studied for the bar exam, which I took about ten days after school ended. The next day we loaded up the car and drove back to Michigan. This was before interstate highways, so we took a ferry across Lake Erie. We drove from Washington to Pittsburgh, then on to Cleveland, where we boarded the Detroit and Cleveland Navigation Boat, which had staterooms. We left Cleveland at 11 P.M. and arrived in Detroit about 7 A.M. the next morning. Mavis and I moved in with her folks, who lived at 527 Woodland Avenue in Detroit, and I immediately began looking for work.

I looked everywhere. I even applied to become a deputy marshal in the United States Court House, hoping to get close to a courtroom. I made a 98 on the exam, but the marshal's office never called me for an interview. I assumed it was because the person doing the hiring realized that I would probably leave as soon as I passed the bar exam and could find a job as a lawyer. So I ended up working again as a laborer. My first job was in a car wash. After only a few hours, the owner came up to me and said, "You shouldn't be in a place like this." I disagreed, but he let me go anyway, and I began pounding the pavement again. My mother-in-law added to my anxiety because she was obviously afraid that I might remain unemployed. Of course, I had no such thing in mind, and I looked for work even more feverishly. Finally, the first week of July, I landed a job with the Ternstedt Division of General Motors at its plant on West Fort Street and Livernois in Detroit. My father-in-law was a foreman at the plant, but that had nothing to do with my being hired. Ternstedt needed metal polishers, and I had the necessary experience from my days working for Chevrolet in Flint. Anyway, I ended up polishing the metal trim that was placed on doors and around various parts of car interiors. It was not a pleasant job. There was a lot of dirt and grit and grime and metal dust, but I kept at it until I could begin work as a lawyer.

That summer I enrolled in the Abbott Bar Review course, which was given at the Rackham Building in midtown Detroit. I took the Michigan Bar exam in September 1950, just after I learned that I had passed the bar exam in Washington, D.C. Because we had no plans to move back east, I waited anxiously to learn the results of the Michigan exam. During the week after Christmas, I learned I had passed and decided to accept an offer with Dudley Mallory, a sole practitioner in Flint. I joined him as an associate on the second Monday in January 1951 and spent the next two weeks looking for a small, cheap apartment. After I found one, Mavis and our first son, Vincent, who had been born two months earlier, joined me. A new chapter in our lives began.

I was very lucky to have landed a job with Mallory. I first came to his attention during my second year of law school when I won the moot court competition. Catholic University sent out a press release that featured a picture of me shaking hands with Supreme Court Justice William O. Douglas. The *Flint Journal* ran the picture with a caption noting that I had lived on Carton Street in Flint with my Aunt Mag and Uncle Sylvester after I got out of the Army. Mallory saw the article and recognized the address as being in what was then the African-American ghetto of Flint. He contacted my Aunt Mag and invited me to interview with him.

I was only halfway through law school at the time, but I promised to keep in touch. I kept him abreast of my progress, including my activities on the law review. He was still interested when I graduated and, having nothing better to do, I thought I would try Flint. I did not want to return to Washington, D.C., where there were so many lawyers, and I did not particularly want to settle in Detroit for similar reasons. Flint proved to be a good place for me. As I explained to one of my nieces years later when she sought advice about how to launch a career, it is easier to make one's mark in a smaller city. The business atmosphere is less competitive, and there are fewer barriers to becoming active in politics and community affairs.

I had a wonderful time starting out with Dudley Mallory, who treated me as a son. He was a remarkable man. He was born in Madison County, Virginia, in the shadow of the Blue Ridge Mountains, on a farm that his grandmother had bought after she was freed from slavery. In 1911, when he was seventeen, Mallory left for Baltimore, where he worked as a stevedore on the docks. He held various other jobs in Washington, Newark, Pittsburgh, and Waterbury, Connecticut. He labored as a factory hand, a longshoreman, on construction crews, and in steel mills while attending night school to earn his high school and college diplomas. Both Yale and the University of Michigan accepted him to their law schools, but he chose Michigan because it was cheaper, and he believed it would be more racially tolerant. Apparently that was true because there were four other blacks enrolled in the law school when he attended it. Mallory supplemented his savings by firing furnaces in Ann Arbor. He graduated in 1926.

While he was in law school, Mallory became impressed with the success of a black doctor, J. L. Leach, who had established a medical practice in Flint. He wrote to Leach, who encouraged him and offered to rent him office space. Mallory liked to say that he arrived in town with forty dollars in his pocket, two suits of clothing, and an old fountain pen. He put fifteen dollars down on a large wooden desk and four wooden chairs, which he kept for the rest of his legal career—even after 1954 when he built a new office building.

Mallory moved into his office in what was then called the old "community building" on McClellan Street. He had just settled in when Leach gave him the bad news: a condition of his staying in Flint would be working as a bagman for the political machine run by William H. McKeighan. Mallory was always a straight arrow, and he would have no part of dirty politics. Leach visited him several times and threatened to run him out of town if he refused to cooperate. Mallory stood fast, and Leach or one of his cronies posted flunkies at the foot of the stairs leading to his office. Their job was to run off potential clients by telling them that Mallory was a penitentiary agent who was guaranteed to lose their case. Years later, Mallory took delight in relating those early battles against Leach.

Mallory persevered and prevailed. He moved out from under Leach's watchful eye and reopened his office on the corner of Industrial Avenue and Leith Street, in a second-floor office over a bank. He remained there for the next twenty-five years. Mallory was a good lawyer. He was not particularly gifted in public speaking, but he was adequate. His strengths lay in other areas, especially his thoroughness in legal research, or what lawyers used to call reading the law. He used to say that you could not practice law by ear. That is to say you could not hear from what other lawyers were saying what the law was; you had to read and research it yourself. Or, as he explained, very few matters are cut-and-dried, and it is up to lawyers to sort through endless legal decisions in order to find ways to tease out the law that applies to the unique set of facts in front of them.

In that era, before electronics and computer searches, this process could be very time-consuming. In law school I found that I loved research, and working with Mallory only enhanced my skills. With his guidance, it got so that I could always find some relevant case, no matter how obscure the facts that we faced seemed to be. Even in areas of the law that I thought I knew like the back of my hand, Mallory insisted that I go back to the books and reread pertinent statutes or rulings in light of the case in front of me. From my current vantage point, with years of experience under my belt, I see the wisdom of Mallory's dictum. Good lawyers never assume that they know the law. They always go back and check, time and time again, in order to see things in a fresh light.

These days there are electronic means of finding law. I am not sure how much that has helped. Now you can push a few buttons on a computer and bring up everything pertinent to your case on the screen. But that does nothing to foster the talent that Mallory and all good lawyers have of being able to analyze, then find analogies with which to persuade a court to help their client. Anyway, Mallory's thoroughness in reading law made him a very dependable lawyer, and I think it did the same thing for me. One day when I was arguing a case in Lapeer County, I spied a revolving book shelf next to the judge. I fell in love with it, and when I became a Michigan Supreme Court justice I had members of my staff locate one for me. I put all of the basic statute books and treatises fundamental to practicing law in Michigan in that bookcase, so I would never have an excuse for not looking up the law. One thing is certain. The search for applicable law is a lot like the search for truth; it is very often illusive, but it is certainly satisfying once you have found it.

Mallory's other great attribute as a lawyer was his character. There were several things that he believed in, and he believed in them strongly. He believed in truth. He believed passionately in justice, and for more than forty years he saw to it that his clients got it. In his personal affairs, he was just and fair with every man with whom he had business dealings. He also had true humility. Like the stoics of old, he did what was right, not because he might receive the praise of the crowd but because it was right. In other words, he had a code that he lived by, and he was one of the few men I have ever known who was absolutely faithful to his own code. For that reason, he was as predictable as the four seasons and as day and night. In a word, he was a man of integrity.

To many people, Mallory seemed like a loner. If he was a loner, it was probably for two reasons. First, he marched to a distant drummer whose cadences we could never hear, although we knew they were there. Second, he never wished to impose upon others even though he had strong views about things. He liked his privacy and he respected other peoples'. He filled up his nonworking hours as a civic leader, heading youth programs and establishing the St. John Street Center, a community meeting place in Flint's black neighborhood. He also helped several of his relatives through school. Even though he never married, Mallory ended up with many "sons." To each of us he meant opportunity, the chance through him to make our own way. Opportunity was what he wished for everyone. He had little tolerance for those he considered lazy or dependent. He once said, "If a young person will work and take advantage of the opportunities this community and this country offer him, he can succeed at anything he wants. But the man who sits down and waits for someone to give him a handout, regardless of the circumstances, will keep right on sitting there." He used to tell me, when I asked what he was going to do with all of his money and property, that he did not care. But while he was alive, he added, "I just want to cover the ground on which I stand." He succeeded at that far better than most men—a fact I pointed out when I spoke at his funeral in April 1969.

By working with Mr. Mallory I got a quick and immediate grounding in the law. It is no accident that so many film and television shows are based on the experience of lawyers. At base, law consists of the conflicts between individuals and between individuals and society. Frequently where there is conflict, one natural by-product is human drama. At least that is what I learned as soon as I began practicing law in Flint. My career got off to a running start. Mallory made a motion to have me sworn in on Monday. Tuesday I was appointed to defend a kid accused of stealing a car. Wednesday I was facing the jury. That was pretty much the pace that I maintained for the next six and a half years of private practice.

Mallory worked hard, and he expected everyone else to put in long hours. I would start work at 8 A.M., go home for supper at 6 P.M., then return to the office to see clients from 7 P.M. until 10 P.M. every evening. It was only after I had been in the office for three years that I began taking off Wednesday nights to be with my family. I continued to work every Saturday. Because we had a busy general practice, there was rarely a shortage of clients. I think my all-time record came one Monday morning when I managed to see twenty-six people—a number you would probably only find these days in a legal aid or public defender's office.

Every lawyer remembers his first case, and I am no exception. Mine was not exactly a disaster, but it would be safe to say that I was long on enthusiasm and energy but short on experience. Granted, I did not have much to work with. The judge who appointed me, the day after I was sworn in, told me in no uncertain terms that he was not going to grant any more delays because the accused had held up the court docket long enough by changing lawyers and asking for continuances.

My client was an Irish-American lad accused of taking a car. He was seventeen or eighteen years old, just old enough to be tried as an adult. He was out on bond, but his accomplice, who was only fourteen or fifteen, was in a juvenile home. My client claimed he had been at a bowling alley on Saginaw Street, Flint's main thoroughfare, when the younger boy came by and asked if he wanted to go for a ride. My client climbed in. A policeman spotted the pair, stopped them, and determined that the car had been stolen from the younger boy's foster parents. When I interviewed the younger boy, he told a different version. He claimed that my client had helped him jump the ignition, then they had gone to the bowling alley together.

The two conflicting tales did not bode well. So I tried another tack. I asked my client if he went to church. He named St. Agnes, a Catholic Church on the north end of Flint. I had met the priest there, so I called him and asked if he would testify as a character witness. After I gave him my client's name, there was a long silence for what seemed like a full minute. Then the priest said, "I wish I could help you, but that's the same kid we've caught out here robbing the poor box three times over a two-week period."

So, there I was. Facing a jury the next morning with my client, it boiled down to his word against that of the younger boy. He was convicted. His trial fit the well-worn joke about a quick verdict. According to that old saw, the defendant was so clearly guilty that the last juror was just leaving the jury box, walking to the jury room, when the first juror was coming out the door with the guilty verdict. Anyway, the judge ended up sentencing my client to probation because he had no prior record.

That case was my first lesson in what all lawyers find out after they have practiced a while: it is very difficult to rely on what your client tells you, and a good lawyer is always skeptical. People tend to see things their own way. As a result, wittingly or unwittingly, they often fabricate stories out of whole cloth. So lawyers must make damned sure they are getting the right account and check all the facts. Otherwise, they wind up finding out what really happened when they are in court, much to their embarrassment. No matter how many times a lawyer tells a client, "Fool me and you end up fooling yourself," it is the lawyer who ends up looking foolish. The challenging reality is that getting to the bottom of things is rarely easy.

This is especially true in criminal law. Invariably a client claims to be innocent, even when there is overwhelming proof of guilt. Sometimes, even under probing questioning, a client will persist in lying. Some clients can be good con artists. I remember one case in which a fellow was charged with breaking into a General Electric warehouse on the edge of town, then rifling the coins that were in the cigarette and gum machines. He was a giant, gentle fellow who asked me to come visit him in jail, where he was being held without bail because he was a parole violator. He claimed he was innocent and told an unlikely version of the events that led to his arrest. He said he had a fight with his wife and took a walk to cool off because he could not afford to get into any trouble. Somehow, without realizing it, he ended up at the warehouse. It was a very cold night, so he broke in to keep warm. He claimed the gum and cigarette machines had already been pilfered and all he did was pick up a few coins lying on the floor.

I pointed out that the door to the warehouse was four inches thick, breaking in was not easy, and it did not make sense that another thief had already been there. Still, he persisted with that story for several months until his case finally came up for trial. Then he admitted he had broken into the warehouse to steal, and he pleaded guilty. He was such a nice guy—except for his habit of stealing things—that even the probation officer wrote the judge a strong recommendation for leniency. He stayed out of prison—but not for long. A year later, after I left my law practice in Flint, he was caught red-handed in another theft and was sent to the state prison at Jackson.

Years later, when I worked for General Motors, we used to joke that we could not even take the word of the chairman at face value. Not because we distrusted him, but because the person at the top does not always have the most current information about what is really happening in the lower echelons. So we had a rule: before any of us spoke for the corporation, we had to find one and preferably two other sources to verify what the chairman said.

I remember one ludicrous case from my early legal career that amply showed why it is important to verify a client's story. A fellow came into my office and asked, "How much money could I get if I found a worm in a can of corn?" When I determined that he had not eaten the corn, had not gotten sick looking at the worm, had not, in fact, suffered any ill effects whatsoever, I said, "Well, about all it's worth is another can of corn." He seemed disappointed and insisted on going home, getting the can of corn, and bringing it back to my office to show me.

I refused to take the case, but I offered to write a letter to Robert Hamady, who was the president of Hamady Brothers, a local food chain, the largest in Genesee County, where the client said he had bought the corn. I looked at the can and saw that it said "Shurfine" and had been packed by a wholesale grocer in Detroit, but I did not think anything about it at the time. A few days later, I got a call from Walter Krapohl, a very fine old-time lawyer in Flint who represented Hamady Brothers. He assured me that the chain had never carried Shurfine.

I realized he was right. By that time Mavis and I had four small sons, and I did all of the family's grocery shopping—usually at Hamady Brothers—and I had never seen a can of Shurfine corn on the shelves. In any case, I had to believe Walt. In a small town, a lawyer's word is his bond, and I knew that he would not lie to me. When my would-be client came in the following week, I said, "Why did you tell me a damned lie? You know you did not even buy the can of corn at Hamady's." He said, "Forget about that; I have an even bigger case for you." I walked him to the door and told him never to come back.

I had another case in which my client was accused of taking a car. He worked for Summerfield Chevrolet on North Saginaw Street. The fellow was a car porter, an employee of the dealership who transfers cars around and washes them and does other menial jobs. One day he took one of the cars, and he and some buddies piled in and went for a joy ride. They ended up in Saginaw, which is thirty-five miles north of Flint. When they ran a red light, a police officer stopped them, learned they had no registration for the car, and arrested them.

My client denied that he knew anything about the car theft. He insisted that he had been in front of Eddie's Lounge, which was a local night spot on Industrial Avenue across from the Buick plant, when his cousin Joe drove by claiming that his uncle had given him the new car. He said Joe loaned him the car. I wrote down all the details, including what side of the street the car was on in front of Eddie's Lounge. He brought his cousin to see me, and I grilled him for details. I asked him which side of the street the car was on, and he made a bad guess. I said, "You were not even there, and even if you want to help him, I can't allow you to lie on the stand." We ended up settling the matter before trial.

Edward Littlejohn, a professor emeritus of the law school at Wayne State University, interviewed me about what it was like being a black lawyer in Flint during the early 1950s. I told him there was not really anything unique about it. Most of our clients were wage earners at General Motors plants, and we did all the kinds of work for them that is part of a general practice: real estate, estate work, criminal law, divorce, personal injury, and property damage. Occasionally we would get a business client, rarely any whites and never any large commercial accounts. Most of our business clients were small outfits or nonprofit corporations and social clubs.

Surprisingly, Mallory told me that when he began practice, most of his clients were white. In those days, there were fewer African Americans in Michigan, and many of those could not afford or did not think to hire lawyers. By the time I joined Mallory, most of his clients were black, which may not have been so surprising because our office was located on a commercial street in a predominantly black neighborhood. Apparently, all of Mallory's African-American contemporaries—Floyd H. Skinner in Grand Rapids, Leon H. Hubbard in Pontiac, and James R. Golden in Battle Creek—had witnessed a similar shift from a white to a black clientele.

Ironically, some blacks preferred white lawyers. Mallory told a story about a fellow who came to see him to borrow a hundred dollars so he could go to a white lawyer. Mallory refused the loan. My favorite story along these lines involved an acquaintance of mine who called me early one Sunday morning to come down to the jail and arrange bail. He and a buddy had been carousing the previous night and were arrested for disturbing the peace. It turned out they had been in a minor auto accident with a car driven by some whites. They got out of their cars and began arguing about who was at fault. A crowd of whites gathered, and the police—to defuse the situation—arrested the blacks. I understood why the police did it, but it was still unfair. So, I told the guy I would only charge him ten dollars—much less than my normal fee—as sort of a community service. I knew he could not afford to miss work the next day, so I told him I would handle the bail hearing and meet with the prosecutor. I ended up getting the charges dismissed.

The following year he got into more serious trouble and went to see a white lawyer instead of me. The attorney, who was not very good, charged him a thousand dollars, and he ended up going to jail. A few years later, the fellow came to see me about handling some minor matter for him, and I refused. As to the larger question of why many blacks went to white lawyers—a fact Professor Littlejohn verified in his research—I have one theory. I think it is because blacks, more than whites, perceive that politics plays a large role in the justice system. For that reason, some feel that it is better to have a white lawyer who is better connected to the power structure.

Mallory and I had a handful of white clients. I remember one very clearly. I had not been in Flint more than a month when I heard Mallory shuffling in his office next to mine. He came bursting in with a young white man in tow and introduced me, saying: "This is Mr. Smith, who is in my office and will handle your case. I'll be responsible, but he will take care of you." I shook hands with the fellow whose name—improbable as it may seem—was Daniel Boone. Earlier that morning, a trolley bus had rear-ended Boone's old Chevrolet and knocked the bumper loose. He went down to the Flint Trolley Coach Company headquarters, where a company representative offered him twenty-five dollars. Boone demanded fifty dollars, and the argument began.

I listened to his story and, having nothing better to do said, "Let's go." So, we took off for the trolley company's insurance company, the Maryland Casualty Company, which had offices in the south end of Flint. We just missed the adjuster, so I offered to write him a letter to get a better settlement. The next morning I got a call from Mrs.

Boone, who told me that Dan was in the hospital. He had tried to get up that morning. When he could not, she took him to the hospital with a sore back. I was suspicious and wondered how a guy who had been moving around quite well the previous day could now be on his back. I went to the hospital, and the doctors confirmed that Boone's back muscles were rigid, which could cause pain. How much they could not say. They kept talking about subjective signs and subjective pain. To make a long story a bit shorter, I had to work with a doctor who either did not like Daniel Boone or did not fully appreciate his injury. I finally squeezed an admission from him that Boone's injury, although slight, could be disabling for several weeks. I sent it to Maryland Casualty, which settled for something like three thousand dollars. It just goes to show the vagaries of the law. If we had caught the insurance adjuster in his office that first day, then we would have settled for seventy-five dollars and probably signed a general release. Then, when Boone developed his symptoms and missed several weeks of work, we would have had no recourse.

In any case, Boone told all of his friends about me, and my white client list began to grow. What made it strange was that Boone was from the South—Arkansas or Missouri. He and his friends came to see me from all the way across the county in Burton Township, a place that was known at that time as a haven for southern whites. Finally, I asked one of the men why he was coming to see me when there were so many good lawyers closer to his home. He told me, "Mr. Smith, I just don't trust these Yankee lawyers."

Another of my white clients was a teenager of about eighteen or nineteen who had come from Mississippi to work in the automobile plants. His father came to see me and said, "I have been told that you're the best lawyer in town and I'd like you to help my son." His son had been charged with armed robbery. The facts were pretty clear. He worked for several years and bought a big Buick that he could not really afford. When General Motors had layoffs, which were inevitable in those days, he was one of the first to go, and he lost his car. At about the same time he began hanging around with a girl who kept bad company. This rubbed off on the kid from Mississippi, and he got hold of a sawed-off shotgun. He saw a couple parked in a filling station lot that was closed and went up to the man, pointed the shotgun at his face, and said: "Give me your money." The victim tossed out his wallet, and the lad picked it up and ran back to his room. That is when he discovered there was no money. He panicked and decided he had better get rid of the gun. By that time the police were looking for him, and when they saw him running with something bulging from under his overcoat, they stopped him and found the gun. The victim identified him as the attacker.

I leveled with the father. The evidence was clear and there was very little that I could do. I advised him that the best thing would be to get the charge reduced from armed robbery, which under Michigan law at that time required a prison sentence, to unarmed robbery. If the son agreed to plead to that, I thought he could get probation as a first offender and return to Mississippi. It was clear to me that the boy was immature and unable to control his life. It was not just the robbery; there were other signs of instability. So I reasoned the best solution would be to get him back into the lap of his family where he could be supervised.

Even though he was a white from Mississippi, the father was respectful of Mallory and me. I particularly wanted him to meet Mallory so he would not be under the illusion that he was dealing with a white lawyer because of my complexion. He met him with complete aplomb and just said something like, "It's nice to meet you, Mr. Mallory," and we proceeded to do business. I told him I would need a fee and he said he would have trouble raising it but he would pay me.

I persuaded the prosecutor to reduce the charge, then I appealed to the judge before sentencing. I explained that we were trying to get the boy away from Flint. In small cities, like Flint was then, it was possible to do things informally. Judges invented means of doing justice and took advantage of their wide latitude under the law. In any case, the judge accepted the plea and sentenced the boy to probation, appointed me his probation officer, made it a condition of his probation that the boy return home as quickly as possible, and put me in charge of delivering the kid to his family. The boy, however, did not want to go home, and he stayed around Flint. I felt terrible about the situation and kept a vigilant watch. I finally caught up with him and gave it to him with both barrels. I swore at him and threatened to call the probation office and have him thrown in prison if he did not leave for Mississippi immediately. The threat of prison did the trick. He returned home, and his father called me several days later to verify his arrival. He also wrote me a very nice letter when it was all over.

I do not want to leave the impression that all of our white clients were southerners. In fact, Mallory and I had a fair number of white clients who were from Michigan. I remember one fellow whose parents died and left him an impoverished forty-acre farm in Saginaw County. His brothers and sisters just dumped the matter on him, even though he worked in Flint and lived in Genesee County and they lived in Saginaw County, where the estate was probated. The siblings were apparently afraid that they might end up paying their parents' bills, including a number of debts owed to the state. I got the state liens barred by statute, which left some private debts that could be paid with the proceeds from the farm's sale. No one thought the land was worth much until a family from Detroit fell in love with it and paid a price considerably above the appraisal. That meant that the bills could be paid and all of the heirs received a little bit of money. That apparently was not enough for them. Although they had not had any interest in the matter when they thought they could be financially liable, the brothers and sisters became very active when there was money to be had. They appeared in court and protested my fees. I told the judge what had happened, but in those days most lawyers would relent when there was a question about their fees. So the judge just held up his hand, and I accepted the minimal figure and walked out in disgust.

Those clients were unusual; most appreciated our help. In part, I think that is because of the way that Mallory and I conceived of our job. The role of a good lawyer is to be helpful to people who are in trouble. I spent a lot of my time just listening to people. Contrary to public opinion, good lawyers listen a lot more than they talk. I used to say that one of the wisest investments I made as a young lawyer was a comfortable chair because I ended up spending so much time sitting in it, listening to people's troubles. Lawyers not only listen and provide advice, they also try to help people. That is really the whole point of it. It is not just a matter of getting clients justice in court or getting them large settlements out of court. It is also a matter of trying to ease their burdens, whatever they are, real or imagined.

I remember one such case. A young man said that he wanted to get a divorce. He was a newlywed who did not get along with his in-laws. The couple was living with the woman's parents. The parents did not like him, and he did not like them. I told him he did not need a divorce. "What you really need," I said, "is a place of your own. No matter how small. A barn or a small room or anything. Just get out of there and get your own place and see if that doesn't work." He took my advice, and the last time I saw him he was still married.

There was another case of an up-and-coming young businessman who wanted a divorce. This was back in the days before no-fault divorces when couples had to have grounds to end their marriages. The grounds in Michigan were very limited; they were primarily adultery, mental or physical cruelty, and desertion. Most people brought their facts under mental cruelty, which could be stretched to include such things as nagging, talking too much, screaming, and not taking care of the home. I went through the whole litany of possibilities with the man, and he did not have any of them. It turned out that he had a nice wife, who was a practical nurse, and a young son. She had not done anything wrong. So I asked him why he wanted a divorce. He said, "Well, you know, I'm a college man, and she didn't go to college, and I think I could have done better." I was shocked and annoyed. I said something like, "I sit behind this desk and I hear all kinds of stories. And from where I sit, you are one of the luckiest men in town. I'm not going to frame any kind of false divorce charges against your wife. I'm not in the business of concocting evidence, and you don't have any grounds to divorce her." I charged him fifteen or twenty dollars for a consultation and sent him on his way. He was still married last time I checked, which was nearly thirty years after that conversation. He became fairly prominent in Flint, and the fact that he stayed married added to his civic success.

One last divorce story illustrates the counselor end of being a lawyer. A thirty-year-old fellow who worked for General Motors came to see me. He said he really did not want a divorce but that something had gone terribly wrong in his marriage that made one inevitable. After much questioning, he slowly and painfully told me that while attending a funeral down South, he had a passionate affair with an old girlfriend. When he returned home, he was impotent and ended up confessing to his wife. She forgave him, but he was still impotent.

I suggested a solution. I went through an elaborate warm-up to it because I could tell from talking with the man that he was not terribly sophisticated, and, besides, psychotherapy was not something that was talked about much in the early 1950s. I told him that if he had a cough or physical ailment, then he would go to a doctor. It was the same with emotions. If they became tangled, then it made sense to see a doctor who took care of the mind. I repeatedly assured him that I did not think he was crazy. In the end I referred him to a young psychiatrist whom I had met at a professional seminar a few weeks earlier. After several sessions, the young man was fine, and he went on with his married life as if nothing had happened.

I tell these stories because they illustrate an important part about being a lawyer. The consultation fees I charged these clients were negligible compared to what I could have earned handling their divorces. But I knew that my job was to help first; making money was secondary. Good lawyers offer advice and recommendations based upon what is best for the client rather than their own pockets. The legal profession comes in for a lot of criticism because some lawyers fail to recognize that, but I think most good lawyers keep their priorities straight.

Later in my career, I gave many speeches on this topic. I remember one at Michigan State University, where I was the principle speaker at the annual meeting of the Lansing Black Lawyers Association. My theme that night and on other occasions was: "We Stand on the Shoulders of Those Who Have Gone Before." The older I get, the more I realize how true this is for all lawyers in general and black lawyers in particular. I cited the obvious examples of the Howard University giants—Charles H. Houston and William H. Hastie. Then I named some of the early black pioneers who had preceded us in Michigan— Oscar Baker, Dudley Mallory, Leon Hubbard, Floyd Skinner, Jim Golden, and Cecil L. Rowlette, Joseph A. Brown, and Harold Bledsoe in Detroit. I realized in writing the speech that all of them had one trait in common: they understood the law as a profession and not as a business. Their primary motivation was to achieve justice. Making profits was second, if not third or fourth, on their agendas. I have urged young lawyers whose primary goal is to make a lot of money to get out of law and go into business because law should be a higher calling. I think this is particularly true of African-American lawyers. In my long legal career, beginning in private practice and continuing through public service jobs, I was acutely aware that if I stubbed my proverbial toe, it could embarrass not just me and my family but also the entire race. I believe that all young lawyers would do well to remember that they stand on the shoulders of my predecessors and my generation, and it is up to them to preserve and add to that fine tradition for those who follow.

Idealism aside, the reality is that one aspect of practicing law is recognizing that you will get into situations where there is no way you are going to make any money. Lawyers who think they are going to come out entirely whole in every case ought to get out of the profession because justice does not lend itself to those kinds of exact measurements. Maybe lawyers in commercial practices never lose any money, but in a general practice, dealing with people of all economic groups, you are going to lose money. Of course, you are also going to feel awfully good about yourself for having been able to right wrongs. That is the essence of being a lawyer, in my judgment.

I remember one case that demonstrates this principle. A man and his wife, who lived near the Buick plant in Flint, came into the office. They had two or three kids and were trying to buy a small house. He had been injured on the job and had not been able to work. In other words, they had to count every dollar. The Citizens Commercial Savings Bank, the largest bank in Flint at that time, threatened them with a judgment because they had supposedly not kept up with payments on one of their loans. The amount involved was something like fifty dollars, but to them it might just as well have been fifty thousand. They had three loans with the bank, and they paid them off in all kinds of ways. They did not have a checking account, so sometimes they paid in cash. Other times they paid with money orders from a neighborhood drugstore. Sometimes they sent their money in without a stub. I could not believe how much time I spent on that case. I talked to the bank four or five times. I talked to the couple more often than that. I sorted through all kinds of disorganized records without success. Luckily, I knew the druggist, and I persuaded him to go back through all of his records. There were a lot of them because it was a busy store. Finally, he found the receipt for the money order.

I called an internal auditor whom I knew at the bank. He came over to my office and took some notes. He indicated that there had been some suspicion of embezzlement, and my clients may have been victims. He promised to take care of the matter. Even by 1950s standards, I must have put at least four hundred dollars worth of time into that case. But what can you charge people who cannot pay anything? I may have billed them twenty-five dollars, which they could not afford to pay in a lump sum. They offered to pay two or three dollars a week, and I agreed. That was typical. Within a few years I was able to fill up my office with clients, but I never knew how to charge, so I never made a lot of money in private practice.

Every lawyer at some point talks about the jury system, and we all have one favorite story about how jurors did the opposite of what we expected. My favorite example came from when I was defending a small woman, the mother of a couple of kids, who had been charged with assaulting her husband with a deadly weapon. He was a big guy and had a history of wife battering. The couple would fight, then they would make up, then they would get into trouble again. After one of their umpteenth spats, she left him, took the kids, and moved in with her mother. After a few days, the husband became annoyed and tried to persuade her to move back home. When she refused, he grabbed her. She broke free and fled back into her mother's house.

She was a feisty woman, and a few days later, she decided she would no longer let her husband dictate her movements. So she left her mother's house to go to a movie. Her husband had been stalking her and attacked her while she waited at the bus stop. According to two eyewitnesses walking down the street, the husband slapped her, and her eyeglasses fell off and hit the ground. She reached into her purse and pulled out a pen knife and scratched his wrist. He started to back up, tripped over the curb, and fell into the gutter. She kept carving away at him with her knife. He complained loudly to the police, who agreed to press charges.

There is a gray area of the law—at least it was gray back in those days and I assume it still is and always will be—in which a person who is assaulted can use only necessary and reasonable force to repel an attacker. Once you fend off the aggressor you have to quit. You cannot just go right on beating another person because then you become the one who is guilty of assault. Because she kept attacking her husband after he was down, the prosecutor argued that the wife was guilty of felonious assault. She retained me to defend her, and we went to trial.

My client took the stand and described what had happened. Her story did not differ too much from what the eyewitnesses had seen. When the prosecutor was cross-examining her, he continued to question her about the details. If he had been smart, he would have sat down and asked the judge for a directed verdict of guilty. Because the facts were not in dispute and the law was clear, the judge would have to have found her guilty. Instead, the prosecutor droned on. The more he asked, the more apparent it became that the husband was a bully, the kind of guy who does not make out too well in the world, then comes home and takes out his aggressions on his wife, the proverbial "little woman."

That about summed up the argument I used to the jury. I knew it would be a difficult case if the jurors followed the law. Anyway, I focused my attention on the women jurors and pinpointed one in particular—a middle-aged woman who had a beaten-down look. I just guessed that the poor soul probably got the same kind of treatment from her husband as my client got from hers, so I talked to her a good bit. I did not pay much attention to two middle-aged men who were sitting on the second row of the jury box. My hope was to get a hung jury because the woman would ignore the technicality of the law and look for the equities in my client's situation as a battered wife.

The jury went out. It stayed out. And it stayed out. The judge wondered why the jurors were taking so long to decide what legally should have been an open-and-shut case. The judge even asked the prosecutor why he had not sought a directed verdict. Eventually the jurors came back and said they could not reach a verdict; they were a hung jury. It turned out upon questioning by the prosecutor that the two people who had hung the jury were the two men whom I had largely ignored. As soon as the jurors began their deliberations, these two said something like: "Don't ask us to convict this woman. The son of a bitch had it coming." No matter how much the other jurors cited the judge's instructions, the laws, and the facts, these two refused to budge. The prosecutor vowed to retry the case. I told him, "You're crazy if you do. You'll only get the same result." I told him I agreed with the two men. My husband's client was a son of a bitch who deserved the attack. The prosecutor relented, dismissed the case, and justice was done.

As an aside, the battered woman drama was one that occurred all too often in my practice, and I assume that was true in most general practices back then. I remember one woman who came to me and wanted a divorce and an injunction against her husband. I took her affidavit describing what had happened. Her husband had come home drunk and began beating her, and she ran for dear life wearing only her negligee. She had little or no money, but the situation was so abusive for her and for her three children that I took the case and filed the necessary papers. She never followed up, and I assumed that she returned to her husband. That was what happened in many of these cases. Anyway, a year later she came back with the same story of abuse. In the intervening time, she and her husband had another child. I cannot be sure, but I probably filed the papers again, hoping that she would leave him this time.

It is almost a given that once in a while young lawyers, carried away by a strong sense of justice, will be conned by their clients. I remember becoming outraged when a middle-aged man came to see me because he had been unable to obtain his driver's license. The fellow looked normal to me, so I could not understand why the state continued to suspend his driving privileges even though he had been released from the Pontiac State Hospital three years earlier. I advised him that the first step would be getting a psychiatrist to certify that he had returned to sanity. I was so naive that it did not seem the least bit strange to me that he appeared to know all of the legal advice that I was giving him.

In any case, I rattled off the names of several psychiatrists. He found fault with every one. Either, he claimed, they were no good or they did not like him. I finally remembered a new man in town whom I had met a few weeks earlier. My client agreed to see him. I immediately called up, made an appointment, and then went down to probate court to get my client's file. The clerks all looked around, and then one said, "You too?" I asked what he meant, and he said: "Well, everybody's had that file." It did look a little suspicious, but I was not deterred. I only realized the problem when my client failed to keep his appointment with the psychiatrist. Sometime later I saw him on the sidewalk in Saginaw and he looked at me strangely. I asked him how he was, and he said he was fine, apparently without recognizing who I was. I figured at that point that I could close the case.

One thing that many people do not understand about the law is that attorneys are advocates for their clients' causes; they do not have to identify with or even like their clients. As a matter of fact, anyone who has ever practiced law for any length of time, no matter what kind of practice, has come across people who are absolute scum. But even the scum are entitled to have their rights vindicated under the Constitution and laws. I had one client who was a rogue of a fellow. He was not stupid. He came from a pretty good family in St. Louis. His father and one of his brothers were doctors. The rest were teachers. My client was, by his own admission, the black sheep of the family. Somewhere along the line he had become a pimp.

One balmy summer evening he parked his Cadillac on a busy street and was talking with two or three ladies of the evening. Two vice squad policemen were watching, and when he sped off in his car, they were right behind him. They played traffic cop and stopped him for going fifty miles per hour in a twenty-five-mile-per-hour zone. They searched his car and found a rusty switchblade and a .25-caliber pistol under the floor mat. They charged him with loitering, speeding, carrying a switchblade, and possessing a concealed weapon. The first two charges were fairly bogus, and the knife could not have cut a banana. The gun charge, however, was punishable with a one-to-four-year prison sentence.

As I interviewed my client, it became clear that the vice squad officers were not pure either. The pair had visited my client at his home a few weeks earlier, presumably to solicit a bribe. When I suggested that their visit might have been related to some kind of investigation, my client just laughed and said, "You don't know these cops." Actually I did, and I also had my suspicions. After all, what were these policemen doing at his home? They did not have any clear business with him, and they certainly were not making a social call. Still, the officers had been cagey, and there was no way to prove that they had been trying to collect a payoff.

I figured the only way to help my client was to show that the police action had been questionable. During the preliminary examination, I asked the officers: "You visited this man, did you not?" They admitted they had. Then I asked, "And you did not go there to make an arrest?" They admitted they had not. I asked, "And you did not go there for a social visit?" They admitted they had not. I did not follow up by asking why they went to my client's home because I knew they would just start lying. Of course, the prosecutor did not seek to clarify the matter either. It was just left hanging.

The charges came to trial. The loitering charge was a loser, and the judge acquitted my client. He was convicted of speeding, and I appealed. Then came the two more serious charges. The judge, Stephen J. Roth, who later became state attorney general and a federal judge, had been a prosecutor in Genesee County, and I guess he knew how heavy-handedly some Flint police officers operated in the African-American side of town. In any case, he called me to see why I was not pleading out my client given the clear facts in the gun case. When the prosecutor and I were in Roth's chambers, I said, "Well, this guy is not a Sunday school character for sure, but I am not really happy about the way the police have handled him." I told the judge that I suspected a bribe attempt and showed him the transcript of my cross-examination of the policemen from the earlier hearing.

Roth did not say a lot, but he frowned noticeably as he read. Finally, he said: "If your client should plead guilty to the weapons charge, I'm not promising you anything, but I'm not likely to give him time. If he does plead, he should come back to court on sentencing day with a lot of money in his pocket." After my meeting with Roth, I felt fairly comfortable telling my client to plead guilty. He did, and the police seemed quite pleased. Of course, they did not know what the judge and prosecutor and I had discussed. On sentencing day the police came expecting to see this guy, who could cause trouble for them, sail away to the state prison. Instead the judge levied a heavy fine and urged my client to leave town. I had already warned him about this, saying the cops would be lying in wait if he did not leave. The upshot was that we got rid of this unsavory pimp and taught the police officers a lesson about abiding by the law.

By 1954 I had four sons and needed a steadier, surer income than I was earning from my private practice. So I accepted an appointment as an assistant county prosecutor working for Chester R. Schwesinger. The prosecutor's office was busiest on Monday mornings because so many bad things happened on weekends. People were robbed and shot or got drunk and got into fights. Those cases were waiting for us when we came in to start the week. Weekends were also a good time to discuss family problems, and so we got a lot of people coming in on Mondays to file charges in cases that were not so violent. One of the more common of these crimes was statutory rape. These cases almost always occurred when an underage girl had sexual relations with an adult man and became pregnant.

I remember one particular morning when a mother and daughter came in. I knew or at least I thought I knew what the trouble was. The mother spoke up first, saying her daughter was going to have a child. I nodded and asked the obvious question: "Who is the father?" There was a long silence, the girl started to tremble, and then she cried that it was her father. The mother nodded concurrence. I found such cases of incest disgusting, as I guess most people do. In that case the father was arrested and charged. I do not know if he served time in prison because another prosecutor took the case to trial.

One of the strangest cases that came in one Monday morning involved two teenage girls. What a story they told! They lived just outside the southwest corner of Flint in the county. They were leaving a football game when a big, blond, boozy fellow, his girlfriend, and his nephew asked directions to some place over in northeast Flint. The girls tried to explain, could not, then climbed into the car to show him. They drove and drove and finally wound up on Lover's Lane in Davison, which is on the northeast side of Flint. The girlfriend and the nephew climbed out of the car leaving the big fellow and the two girls. The girls fought when he tried to have sex with them. Finally, one of the girls gave in so he would leave the other alone. The man was arrested, and his lawyer came in and demanded that he either be charged or released.

The whole story sounded so convoluted that I told the lawyer:

"Oh, shut up. I'm trying to find out what happened." It required most of the day for me to piece the truth together. I talked with the girls separately, then I spoke with their mothers, then I spoke with the state trooper. It would have been very easy to accept the mothers', the girls', and the policeman's testimony on faith, but no self-respecting prosecutor would ever take a tale like that at face value. I finally ended up charging the man with gross indecency, attempted rape of one of the girls, and rape of the second girl. I had doubts about it. I could not understand why his girlfriend and nephew stood around while the man attacked the girls. The case ended with a plea bargain, in which the man admitted attempted rape.

That year in the prosecutor's office was tough. I took between fifty and sixty cases to preliminary examinations in the lower courts and twenty cases to jury trials. Of those, I only lost one—a difficult, two-week abortion case. At the same time, I was trying to hold my private practice together at night and on weekends. Then Mavis and I learned that our youngest son, Steven, needed surgery for a hernia. Several times, I just prayed for the strength to keep going with my jobs and with helping to guide my family through the year while Steve was recuperating. When it was over, I guessed I could live through anything. I suppose it just goes to show that if we had any idea what was coming down the road, we probably would head in early rather than stay around and suffer the things that come later.

I finally decided that I had had enough. I knew Mallory wanted me back full-time in private practice and was depending on me to help him. I was also generating an awful lot of work myself. So I returned to full-time private practice in 1955. I stayed in the prosecutor's office long enough to help break in my good friend Jerome F. O'Rourke, who succeeded Schwesinger as Genesee County prosecutor. O'Rourke would have kept me on, but I had no desire to stay. In addition to the huge volume of work I was doing, I was growing weary of criminal law. It was often exciting, but there was also a downside, seeing the worst side of human nature on a daily basis. Between my private and public work, I had more felony cases pending than all of the other lawyers in Flint combined, according to the *Flint-Genesee County Legal News*. In my last few years of practice, I stopped taking criminal cases.

After I left the prosecutor's office, I accepted an appointment from the state attorney general's office to become one of Genesee County's two public administrators—a position in which I did various jobs for the probate court. I handled quite a few estates of people who died without wills and with no apparent heirs. The probate judges also appointed me as guardian for a number of children and mentally handicapped people. At any given time, I probably had about three dozen of these matters pending.

Often the estate cases involved quite a bit of detective work. I remember one in particular involving a Polish fellow who worked as a toolmaker for GM. He owned a small farm in Fenton, south of Flint, and had accumulated a bit of cash. His estate was worth seventy-five thousand dollars. Judging by his house and the number of whiskey bottles lying around, he drank heavily. Piecing together clues from his belongings, I figured out that he had hunted gold in the West somewhere along the line before he became a toolmaker. He had been married but was living by himself when he died. I found a picture of a young man—whom I guessed to be his son—dressed in an Army uniform.

I arranged for the man's funeral, then talked to everyone who showed up, trying to learn where the son was. Neither his neighbors nor his banker had any information. I combed the house in vain looking for letters with relevant addresses. I checked with the Army for the son's name and variations of it without much success. Finally, I got some information that the son might be living in Chicago. I got a Chicago telephone book and just began making calls. I guessed that the first few people I contacted knew the dead man but did not want to say so for fear that they would end up paying for his funeral costs and debts. I realized I was on the right track. At one point, I located a man who said he was the nephew. He must have sensed that there was money involved because he gave me some cock-and-bull story about how his uncle had no other heirs except him. I replied that he was probably thinking of someone else. I gave up and turned the money over to the state. I do not know if any of those folks ever got curious and ended up making a claim.

In another case, the court ordered me to represent the adult child of an elderly man who needed care and financial support. The court was trying to determine whether any of the man's sons or daughters, who were in their thirties and forties, had the means to take care of him. The case turned my stomach when I saw how bitterly the children were fighting each other to avoid taking any responsibility for their father. I determined, based largely on that case, that I would never fight with my brother about supporting our mother. I guess that probably had something to do with how willingly I stepped forward to help her financially even when my brother could not. I reasoned that she was 100 percent my mother, and if my brother could not help, it did not matter because I could and would. In fairness, he had more children than I did and a lower income. And although he did not help financially, he did what I could not when he persuaded her to leave her home for a retirement community and, when she could no longer live alone, to enter a nursing home. Even if I had had any inclination to be resentful, my memory of the ugliness of that probate case would have eliminated it. All of which points up one last truth about being a lawyer: one of the legal profession's greatest fringe benefits is that seeing the worst in human behavior can help you take a better path.

✦ 7 ✦
Monuments in Passing

THERE ARE MANY kinds of public service. Like many lawyers—especially in small towns—I ended up doing a lot of free community work. Little did I know that my volunteer service would pave the way for a career in political life that would have been impossible by the standards of my youth growing up in Memphis. It was almost unimaginable for the times in Michigan, and the United States as a whole. Within a very short span, I became the first African American to head a major state agency not connected to welfare and prisons and the first of my race to be elected to statewide political office since Reconstruction.

While I lived in Flint, I was asked to serve many charities. The only organization I sought to join was the NAACP, largely because of my positive experience years earlier as a member in Nashville. After a year, I was elected vice president and legal redress officer—a position I held for four or five years. On one occasion, I sued the city of Flint and also a couple of policemen for shooting a man in the back as he was leaving a private home that was being used for illegal gambling. Back in those days we called them "Harlem rent house" parties because they moved from one place to another. Flint police officers frequently raided these houses, when they could find them. During one of those raids, my client, who did not want to get caught because he was a church member, ran out the front door, jumped over the porch railing and headed off. Police spotted him and shot him. He lost a kidney. The policemen claimed they were justified because they were investigating a complaint about a possible felony. I checked the telephone and police records and found no record of such a call. Even so, city officials dragged their feet, and I had to pursue the case vigorously before they agreed to settle for a reasonable amount. I provoked even more controversy when I sued to integrate Flint's bowling alley. A few whites who did not want to socialize with African Americans called my home making threats. Someone even took a pot shot at my window. It got to the point where my wife had to leave all of the outside lights on when I came home late.

My work for the NAACP drew the attention of Arthur J. Edmonds, executive secretary of the local branch of the Urban League. He asked me to join the board, and I accepted. It was quite different from the NAACP. The NAACP's board consisted of a lot of good church people. Most were not college educated, but they had a deep commitment to civil rights and were not above raising hell on occasion. They were far more militant in their opposition to racial prejudice than the Urban League people, who spoke out in careful, measured tones. The Urban League drew on more college-educated members and invited white business leaders to serve on its board. It attacked discrimination from the inside, while the NAACP worked from the outside.

I also joined my neighbors to fight construction of a gas station at the corner of Twelfth Street and Lapeer Road, which formerly had been the site of an old mansion that had been the Women's Hospital of Flint. Residents within a three-hundred-foot radius of the lot hired me to sue and promised to raise money for my fees and court costs. Ironically, I lived one hundred feet outside the radius of those who could sue. In any case, I persuaded both the Planning Commission and the City Commission that there was no reason to allow a commercial venture in a residential neighborhood.

That prompted the lot's owners—two Flint lawyers, Arthur Weiss and John Damm—to sue. They claimed that the Lapeer Road was quickly becoming commercial, and, therefore, it was unfair to deny a building permit based on the fact that the neighborhood was primarily residential. I was proud of my lawyering on that case. I rebutted Weiss and Damm's argument by showing that the two or three businesses on the road had been there for twenty or thirty years. I also called in a mortgage correspondent from Metropolitan Life Insurance Company to testify that the most appropriate use of the land would be for housing and that he would recommend that his company provide lending for that type of construction.

When the case came to trial, Art Weiss was the principal witness for the partnership. John Damn acted as the lawyer. Art was a big, expansive guy who made a fair amount of money on the side in real estate. During cross-examination, I tried to show that he could finance any use for the land, including housing. My goal was to make him admit that on the stand. I began by flattering him because I knew he was susceptible to it. He was a nice guy, but he was a mite pompous and really proud of himself and his real estate acumen. I began by asking him if he had any banking connections in Flint. When he said he had ties to all of the local banks, I asked him about Detroit. When we determined that he had banking friends in Detroit, I asked him about his other connections, and he conceded that he could obtain financing from banks in Chicago and New York. By this time, Damm could see where I was going and began trying to signal Art to stop. But I made sure I stood between them, so they could not make eye contact.

After the hearing, I scrounged around looking for court cases dealing with this kind of problem and wrote my brief. Then, as every lawyer does, I watched the advance sheets carefully. The advance sheets are the temporary paperback publications that print the latest court decisions. The brief was due on Monday, and during the weekend I learned from the advance sheets that the Michigan Supreme Court had recently decided a case involving the City of Holland, Michigan, in which the facts were just like mine. The decision upheld the city's failure to rezone. I scrapped my original brief and hurriedly wrote another one. Our side won, and I became a momentary hero in the neighborhood. I received about seventy dollars for my services, which worked out to about twenty-five cents an hour.

I did not have the nerve or really the strong desire to charge a full fee for that kind of community service. My decision paid off later when I ran for school board in 1953 and municipal judge in 1955. Although I was defeated in both elections, I never lost more than ten votes in my home precinct. I found that very satisfying. When you get right down to it, to have that kind of endorsement from your own neighbors—the people who know you best—is one of the highest honors that can be given to a person.

I also served as a board member for a number of groups in Flint. They included the Michigan Children's Aid Society, the Red Cross, Big Brothers, the Boy Scouts, and the YMCA. When people ask me why I always devoted so much time to civic activities, I have an easy answer: it was part of my family heritage beginning with my great-grandmother, the one my brother and I visited back in Rodney, Mississippi, as children. After she was freed from slavery, she helped clear the ground for Alcorn College, now Alcorn A&M College, in Alcorn, Mississippi. From my earliest childhood, I also remember how my mother went to help those she heard were in need. So it is not surprising that my brother and I always believed we had an obligation to help others.

Those examples in public service took on added light given my fascination with Thomas More and Father Keller. Because of them, I came to believe that I should get involved with government as a form of public service. To do this, I knew I had to become politically active. I considered which political party to join. The Republicans in Flint kept somewhat of a closed shop in those days, so I looked to the Democrats. I did not really become a confirmed Democrat until I heard Governor G. Mennen Williams speak. He was a liberal and a progressive with a vision. I was taken with him because he was the first politician I had ever met who did not insult voters' intelligence. Williams always talked issues, and that really impressed me. I worked hard for his campaigns for governor in 1952 and 1954.

I eventually became secretary of the Genesee County Democratic Committee. I also served on the mayor's charter revision study commission and the city election commission. The party asked me to run for school board in 1953, and I lost. Two years later I decided I would make a pretty good judge, so I ran for municipal judge in 1955 and lost. If you had told me in those days that I was destined for greater things in politics, I might have laughed at the notion. I temporarily gave up my ambition to run for elective office. Besides, Mallory kept telling me that I could not be effective by keeping one foot in government and the other one in our law practice.

My civic activities prompted the Junior Chamber of Commerce to name me Flint Man of the Year in 1956. I told the audience, "If you really think I have made some slight contribution, consider it a down payment on what I intend to do. I promise in the future to do something more genuine to merit the award." That honor brought me to the attention of officials in Lansing in a way that they had not thought of me before. Of course, they knew me as an ardent campaigner. In addition to working on Williams's campaigns, I had traveled all over Flint with Thomas M. Cavanagh, who was elected Michigan Attorney General in 1954. I had worked with and had great affection for Philiip A. Hart, who was lieutenant governor. Phil later told me that when the governor's legal advisor, Alfred B. Fitt, threw my name into the discussion about filling the position of chair of the Michigan Public

Service Commission (MPSC), he kicked himself for not having advanced it himself.

Long before I ever knew I was being considered for the job, someone leaked my name to industry. I suppose it was someone in the governor's office, hoping that if anyone knew or found any dirt on me, my name would never go forward, and there would be no political embarrassment. One reporter, Tommy McIntyre of the *Detroit Times*, apparently went all over Flint trying to uncover some skeletons, but he could not find anyone to say anything against me. I passed muster, and the county chair George Stevens called to tell me that Governor Williams wanted to appoint me to the MPSC.

I had not asked for it, and I did not know anything about it. So in a half-humorous way, I asked: "What kind of a welfare agency is that?" Back in those days, most African Americans appointed to political offices ended up in welfare work. Still, I was flattered by the governor's interest and faith in me. I decided the least I could do was to visit Williams in Lansing. He asked me: "What is your regulatory philosophy?" I answered truthfully that I did not have one. He seemed disappointed and pressed for a better answer. I finally said, "I think I know a fact when I see it, and I think I can follow the law pretty well, and I am fair-minded." He still did not seem pleased. He said, "Well you can't just go over there and be a housekeeper." I said, "I know what you're asking for, Governor, but I have not thought about the matter much, and I just don't have a regulatory philosophy."

I was not too disappointed at the way the meeting went because I decided I was not particularly interested in the job. I had checked into the pay, which was $11,500 a year—about $2,000 less than I was earning in private practice. I was surprised, then, when the governor's office called and told me that Williams wanted to go ahead with my appointment. I asked for time to think about it. I talked to Mallory, who told me to make up my own mind. All I wanted him to say was that it was foolish and I would have stayed. I found out later that he was not in favor of my going, but he did not want to tell me that. I thought about it and thought about it and finally decided that I could not take the job because of the financial sacrifice. After all, I had a wife and four young sons to support.

I saw Phil Hart at the Democratic Party's annual fund-raiser, the Jefferson-Jackson Day dinner. I told him, "Tell the governor that I appreciate his thinking of me, but I want to be taken out of consideration. I cannot afford to come." Phil must have relayed that to the governor because I got a call asking me to meet with Williams again. When I got there, he asked, "When can you start?" Like a babbling idiot, I could not say "no." I really did not go there to say "yes," but I held Williams in too much awe to turn him down in person.

That is how I became the first African American to serve as chair of a state commission having nothing to do with the penal system or welfare. I felt enormous pressure—as if I were carrying the great burden of race on my shoulder. I had an awful fear that if I did not succeed—and succeed very well—then the black cause could be set back tremendously. We African Americans who were modern-day pioneers in government knew that our every action was scrutinized by a doubting public. Wade McCree, a Michigan judge who later became U.S. solicitor general, and I discussed the fact that Charles Jones, the first black appointed to the recorder's court in 1949, was chased out of office by a barrage of bad publicity in the 1950 elections because of a small technical violation. We were determined that this would not happen to us and, through us, to our people. Too much was at stake, and we knew it.

I think it is hard for people now to realize the kind of pressure that "pioneers" were under. One example comes to mind. In *Balm in Gilead,* Sarah Lawrence Lightfoot describes how her mother, Margaret Morgan Lawrence, left Mississippi to attend Cornell in the mid-1930s. After she graduated from college, Margaret Lawrence applied to Cornell's medical school. She was shocked when the dean of admissions told her that despite her fine academic record and her promise as a physician she could not be admitted. He explained, "Twenty-five years ago there was a Negro man admitted to our medical school, and it didn't work out. He got tuberculosis."[1]

Such stories seem incomprehensible now, but they were fairly common to people of my mother's and my generation. We carried with us a fear that if we failed, then somehow we could prevent those who came after us from having the same opportunities. The fact that this has changed has been one of the most gratifying signs of progress that I have seen in my lifetime. In the early 1990s I had lunch with Leroy Richie, a black man who was vice president and general counsel of Chrysler Motors Corporation. He said, "I want to thank you for one

1. Sara Lawrence Lightfoot, *Balm in Gilead: Journey of a Healer* (Reading, Mass.: Addison-Wesley Publishing Co., 1988), 175.

thing in particular. . . . By succeeding as general counsel of General Motors, you have made it possible for me to succeed or fail at Chrysler as Leroy Richie without having to carry the burden of race on my shoulders." I appreciated the compliment and his insight. In working with younger people, I find that they are much more concerned about failing as individuals, not as members of the race. I think that is a wonderful step forward.

In 1957 I was conscious of the possibility of failure when I took over the MPSC because there were a lot of eyes on me. However, I tried not to let that dog my tracks. I just set out to do the job as well as I could. Even though I was still comparatively young at thirty-five, I knew I had been well trained as a lawyer, and I had good enough moral and political instincts to do reasonably well. I said to any and all that I had not asked for the job but I would bust a gut trying to do it well, and if the governor did not like my performance, all he had to do was nod to me that it was not working out. I did not need the job; I earned more from my law practice than I did at the MPSC. In terms of being the first African American, I said to myself at the outset: "I'm not tiptoeing around here like some nice humble colored guy, just glad to get the job." I determined to be a strong chairman, not an arrogant one, just a strong chief executive officer for the one hundred people who worked for me. In other words, I reasoned that I would do the job right and the rest would take care of itself, and it did.

When I arrived at the MPSC there were no other people of color there. I did not let that bother me. While I was living in Flint, I had finally thrown off the last vestiges of my feelings of racial inferiority. It was during this time—through the practice of law and my many community activities—that I began to think of myself first as a person and only secondarily as a black man. I would offer this advice to anyone: you really have to define yourself; do not let other people do it for you. It did not bother me to be regarded as African American, but to myself I was a person first. The point is, when you look at yourself as a human being first, it frees you to look with more compassion at everyone else and to try and see the good and evil in everybody. If you do not do that, then your first instinct is to react racially to everything. Before you know it, you apply a racial tag to every possible kind of human conduct.

It is important to remember that most aspects of day-to-day life have nothing to do with race. This is true in state government, the private sector, or any other work setting where organizational practices and general rules of conduct between people are more important than the personal attributes of employees. There are all kinds of things that go on that have no particular bearing on race. There is assertion of authority. There is acceptance of authority. More often than not, organizational dynamics settle considerations of race. I learned this soon after I arrived at the MPSC on July 1, 1957. I discovered that the woman who was my secretary had announced that she would not work for a black and was leaving. After we began working together, she never said anything about it to me. Two years later, when I left the job, I found out she was upset that I had not taken her with me.

As the independent regulatory agency overseeing railroads, trucks, buses, electric, gas, and telephone companies that do business in Michigan, the MPSC had a large order to fill. It determined where utilities could operate, the rates they could charge, and the standards of service they were required to meet. As if that were not complicated enough, the commission had a poor reputation for favoritism and inefficiency. The other two commissioners—Democrat James H. Lee of Detroit and Republican Maurice E. Hunt of Sault Ste. Marie—were feuding with each other. Hunt's term had expired and he planned to move to California, but he refused to step down until he had decided some of the pending cases. That created a quandary for Governor Williams, who could not appoint Hunt's replacement until he formally resigned. I liked Hunt; we hit it off immediately. He finally handed in his resignation and after five weeks was replaced by Thomas M. Burns of Saginaw, who became my close friend and ally.

Jim Lee was an interesting guy and an impassioned advocate of the peoples' interest. Early in his political career, around 1911 or 1912, he had been the only Democrat in the Michigan Senate. Later, he served on the attorney's staff for the City of Detroit. Those experiences left him with an inherent distrust of utilities. While working for the city, he had battled against rate increases and fought for improved service. Robert A. Derengoski, who was chief counsel of the MPSC at the time, said: "If there was ever a man who was dishonest because he played favorites, it was Jim Lee because he always favored the public." Jim just did not believe that the utilities, including the railroads, ever had much of an argument when they came before us.

Perhaps because of his strong emotions on the subject, Jim never learned how to put a rate case together. Determining a reasonable rate of return for a utility is complicated. It involves looking at historic, current, and projected studies of costs and expenses, engineering studies of construction projections, wages, and so on. The records in some cases constituted a mountain of material. For example, when I took over there were two large cases pending. One involved a $12.5 million rate increase request from Michigan Bell Telephone Company and the other was an application from Michigan Consolidated Gas Company to add eighty thousand space-heating customers. The records of testimony constituted eleven hundred pages in the Bell case and two hundred pages for the gas company.

When confronted with that amount of complex material, Jim was just not able to sort through it all in a step-by-step fashion to reach a reasonable conclusion. If a consumers' or citizens' group lobbied against any increase or conceded the need for a very small one, Jim would usually embrace it. That made it difficult for Tom and me to get something reasonable through. This was especially challenging because I worked hard to ensure that most of our decisions would be unanimous so they would carry more weight with the courts. On the small cases unanimity was usually not a problem. But on big cases, Lee almost always decided against the utilities even when Tom and I decided for them.

Given Jim's attitudes, it sometimes became difficult to conduct fair hearings. At times, he would literally point his finger at witnesses for utility companies and accuse them of being mistaken or of lying. He would sometimes get very upset if he could not get a witness to agree with him. To maintain some level of decorum, I usually intervened and announced that we would take a break. Sometimes Jim would cool off, and sometimes he would not.

Other times, he would lead a weak witness around, confusing the record by getting the witness to say unintended or confusing things by the way he asked his questions. After he was finished, I would step in and ask some questions to clarify, such as: "When you said this, did you mean that?" Jim would tap his desk impatiently. He never really got angry with me, although he would sometimes become angry with the situation. On one such occasion when I had finished reconstructing the record of a hearing, he jumped in at the end and said, "That was just the question I was going to ask. I don't know why you persisted and would not let me ask it." His comment was so incongruous that the hearing room erupted in laughter. I had to smile a little, but I tried to keep a straight face because I did not take any delight in embarrassing a friend and a colleague.

We had very different regulatory philosophies. I tried to operate with what I considered to be complete honesty, and that did not mean always kicking the business guys in the teeth. Sometimes they were terribly wrong and sometimes they were right, and it was up to us to follow the facts. To Jim they were always wrong, and regulation meant trying to beat them at their own game. That does not mean Tom and I normally sided with utilities. It would have been easy for a regulatory body such as ours to listen to the utilities and then fail to get the rate payers' side of the case. The approach we took was to get a comprehensive set of facts from both sides before making a decision.

Philosophical differences aside, Jim, Tom, and I agreed on the basics: we worked hard to ensure that our decisions were made in a timely matter without any appearance of political favoritism. We worked hard to restore faith in the commission. It took two years and long hours, but together the three of us were able to clean up a docket that was terribly in arrears. Some of the transportation cases had been pending for five years. Nowadays, most public utility commissions rely on administrative law judges to hear cases. We heard them all ourselves and wrote all of our own decisions. It could be time-consuming. It was not just a matter of quantity. We also worked to achieve quality in our opinions. We aspired to be accurate and to achieve results without political favoritism. As a result, there was a huge decrease in the number of appeals from the commission's rulings.

Another of my goals was to eliminate all appearance of impropriety. This was how I became known as the "Chairman who Shot Santa Claus." Perhaps the most unpopular decision I made with some of my staffers was my decision to reform the commission's traditional Christmas party. It was really more of an orgy, the biggest, most lavish party in Lansing. The MPSC sent out invitations to utility, railroad, and trucking companies and sold tickets for a dinner dance with entertainment for the evening. The MPSC charged the companies more for tickets than its employees and made enough money from the event to fund another big in-house party in the spring. About a quarter of MPSC staff members were inspectors who drove Michigan highways checking for trucking and transportation violations. At the Yuletide, these same state employees would stop truckers to sell them tickets.

Soon after I took office, Jim asked me to cancel the party, saying it was a disgrace. I did not like the idea of MPSC staffers soliciting the industries we regulated, charging higher prices for tickets, and then using the huge profits for other social events. I decided, however, that it would be unwise to cancel the festivities until I could actually see for myself what was happening. Jim was right. That first year it became clear that things had to change. The partying began in the morning at hospitality suites the utilities rented near the capitol. The most popular location was the Olds Hotel right across the street. MPSC staffers took off work and partied all that day, that evening, and into the next morning. What bothered me most was that so many of the industry attendees felt compelled to come. I drew this conclusion after talking to one fellow from the Soo Line Railroad who was clearly exhausted from traveling. He said the only reason he came was because he feared what would happen if he did not make an appearance.

I clamped down. I told members of the MPSC social committee that they could continue the party, but they could not openly solicit sales, they would have to charge everyone the same price for tickets, and they would have to adopt a budget that would be just large enough to cover the party without making any profits. They complained and reminded me that Governor Williams had attended several of the parties. When I refused to relent, they decided to embarrass me by canceling the following year's party. They warned me that the industry folks would complain bitterly about not having this wonderful social event. I stood my ground. It became clear that many industry executives were relieved. They told me that they were glad to spare the expense and the pressure of trying to outdo their competitors by having more lavish suites and more employees attend. Thereafter, we had nice tame Christmas parties for the staff. People brought cakes and cookies, and we had a good time.

In that same vein, I thought it was important not to accept meals or any kinds of gifts that came my way. I told my secretary to advise people who wanted to send me something for Christmas that I would be happy with a card, but that I never wanted anyone to think they had to be on my good side, ever. As I explained to anyone who asked, the taxpayers paid me to be on everyone's good side. Officials of several companies did not believe what they were told. I received a ham, a turkey, a fruit basket, and some wine. I sent the well-wishers nice notes, saying that I appreciated their thoughtfulness but it was not required and I had sent their gifts on to the St. Vincent's orphanage. I did not get any more gifts, and neither did my staffers. Some were used to getting substantial presents and were displeased. But Tom Burns and Jim Lee approved of my decision, and that was good enough for me.

I made similar decisions about meals. Many utility executives

129

wanted to talk with me not about pending cases but about their general problems, and I felt it was my obligation to meet with anyone who asked to see me. The Bell Telephone people were the most persistent, but several natural gas companies, including Michigan Consolidated Gas Company, also sought regular conferences. I always tried to schedule meetings with these folks between meals so there would be no question about the check and no appearance of impropriety. When that proved impossible, I always insisted on paying my own way. The president of Michigan Bell found this especially amusing considering that he earned about twelve or fifteen times more than I did. Another advantage to my "no lunch" policy was that it gave some MPSC staffers, the other commissioners, and me a chance to get away together and relax in the middle of the day.

My vow to remain free of influence did not deter lobbyists from trying. Michigan Bell made the most concerted effort, probably because it had a huge rate increase case and a rehearing during my two years at the MPSC. Anyway, Bell's vice president of revenue tried to get on my calendar every week, whether the company had a pending issue or not. I think he just had to show his superiors that he had met with me or another member of the commission weekly. I finally told him that I could not afford that kind of time and would not meet with him unless he had something substantive to discuss.

In reality, it did not matter how many times I met with the fellow; it had no impact on my decision. I remember one tempest in a teapot involving Michigan Bell. The company was filing for either the rate increase or a rehearing to get additional money. By law, we had to notify its customers of the request, but Bell argued that we did not have to include the amount it was seeking. Company officials feared that if consumers found out the figures involved, more would show up to complain. I believed that the company was obligated to inform the public of the sums involved. After all, I reasoned, when the governor and the state legislature asked for tax increases, they had to tell the people of Michigan how much money they wanted. Officials at Michigan Bell were not satisfied with my decision and asked for a meeting with all of the commissioners.

The phone company's lawyers made their pitch, and I countered that the commission made its decisions on facts and figures, not on how many people showed up screaming at public hearings. After all, I pointed out, if it were left to the popular will, there would never be any increases at all. I had done most of the talking, and one of the lawyers asked: "Does the chair speak for the commission?" It was a touchy question because it implied that I was just some damned fool talking off the cuff. There was a moment of silence, and then Tom said, "Well, he speaks for me." Jim Lee did not have to say anything because he was known to be hostile to utility companies. The company backed down, and we published the notice including the figures.

Jim, Tom, and I agreed that in order to restore confidence in the commission it was necessary to remove any appearance of political favoritism. In the early days of our administration, just after I took over, companies would try to make a political identification with one of us. It took a while for us to get the message across that politics would play no part in our decisions.

I remember one man who was one of those fairly rare creatures in Michigan—a wealthy Democrat. He was part owner of a natural gas pipeline, and he came to see me soon after I took office. He explained that he had access to Governor Williams and wanted "to help me understand how to operate the Public Service Commission." It was clear that he had an ax to grind about our regulation of gas pipelines. I listened and tried to be polite. I assured him that if I ever needed his insights or advice, I would call him. I saw him a couple of times after that at Democratic Party functions and around the capitol. He was apparently miffed that I never took him up on his offer, and he came by to see me. I allowed him the privilege of explaining the work of the MPSC. Then I got my dander up and told him he did not need to importune me again.

He was offended, but he backed off. It all boiled down to a judgment about how I wanted to run the office, which really was not very complicated. I wanted to serve the best interest of the public and keep out of the clutches of special interests. Officials who cross the line usually do it because they become personally close to the lobbyists or people seeking favors. They forget that their mandate is to serve everyone equally. I call it the erosion principle, which I read about someplace, then adopted as my own philosophy. That is, nobody ever gets corrupted by one free lunch or dinner, but if you are forever accepting favors, just like a drop of water on a stone, little by little, it erodes your independence. Somewhere along the way, you lose your virtue and become the captive of the person who has an ax to grind or a favor to ask. At that point, you are no longer a public servant.

In any case, once I had set the tone and the companies and special interests got the feel for how I would operate, they left me pretty much alone. That was not always true of some staffers. There was one case involving about twenty small telephone companies that were upgrading their equipment from old hand-rung bell telephones to dial phones. This cost a lot of money, depending on the size of the company and whether it could buy in bulk. To secure their purchases, these small companies issued securities, giving their suppliers a financial stake in their operations until the equipment was paid for. Most of these companies were too small to have in-house lawyers who could have told them that under Michigan law it was a felony to enter into such agreements without the permission of the MPSC. The rationale behind the law was to prevent utility company employees from making sweetheart deals with their creditors that required high amounts of interest that could then be passed on to consumers. Of course, that was not the situation in any of these cases.

It turned out that Lawrence B. Lindermere, head of the state Republican Central Committee, was also chair of one of the companies that had improperly issued securities, the Stockbridge Telephone Company. One of the lawyers for the MPSC who was a Democrat came to me and pointed out that as an officer of the company Lindermere was liable for Stockbridge's violation. He suggested we use that information in an upcoming election. I refused. The violations had occurred out of oversight, not intent, and the amount of interest that would be passed on to customers was negligible. I told representatives of all the companies involved, including Stockbridge, to file retroactively and get on record as having complied with the law. The Democratic counsel was disappointed, but I was not going to be part of any plan to politicize the commission.

While the Michigan Bell rate increase case was pending, a representative of the Communication Workers of America, the principal union that organized the employees of Bell, showed up to lobby on the company's behalf. He told me, "Our pay increases depend on the rate increase." The implication, of course, was that I was a Democrat and would be sympathetic to the union's request. I explained that it was not the MPSC's job to determine what Bell paid its workers, and I repeated the line I always used in such cases: "Whatever you can negotiate, fairly and legitimately, the company will put in as an expense, and we will consider it along with all of the other costs in weighing a rate hike." Tom Burns and I used to laugh at the lengths to which groups would go in trying to persuade us. That was just part of the job, and we were determined to operate purely and completely within the facts of the law and not be guided by anything else.

I remember only one case in which we broke that rule. There was a fellow up near Bay City—on Michigan's thumb—who had a one-truck operation, hauling agricultural fertilizer. He had been doing it for a number of years without the required operating license from the MPSC. His competitors turned him in to our enforcement officers on the highway. The officers felt sorry for him because he was a poor guy with a big family to feed and was working as hard as he knew how. They persuaded some members of our Lansing staff to show him how to file for a permit because he could not afford a lawyer.

At the hearing, the big truckers protested that there was no reason to extend operating authority to this guy. On legal grounds, they were probably right. He had been operating illegally, and there were enough fertilizer haulers in the area already. But Tom Burns stuck his head in my door after the hearing and said, "I just want to tell you that the guy has a wife and six kids." He had a smirk on his face and was soliciting my vote. I said, "Well, we'll do something we don't normally do. We'll grant him his operating certificate, and if the fat cats want to appeal, they can take it to court." That is the only case we did not decide solely on the facts of the law, and I am not ashamed of it. Our decision made sense, and it was just. We did not hurt the existing carriers, and it would have been inequitable to have put this fellow out of business.

Most people who had doubts about my ability to do the job were apparently won over when it became clear that the MPSC, under my leadership, would decide cases purely on the facts and the law. Most of our press was good, although I remember one situation where it was negative. I learned a valuable lesson in media relations in that instance. Otto Pressprich, who was editor of the *Saginaw News,* wrote a negative editorial about me and a decision that the MPSC had made. He was completely wrong in his understanding of the case. I wrote him a note setting out the facts and explaining his misunderstanding. I told him my letter was not for publication; I just wanted to ensure that next time he covered the subject, he would not make the same errors. He was so touched that he tried to persuade me to release the letter for publication. I refused and reassured him again that I was not seeking a retraction. Although I had no such ulterior motive, after that, I could do no wrong according to Mr. Pressprich and the *Saginaw News.*

I found my time at the MPSC satisfying because I was able to accomplish so many reforms. I think I did a better job there than in any of my other major positions. Tom, who had more experience in government than I did, once told me: "I never thought I would be a part of any agency that worked like this one—it works like a textbook case." Years later, Mennen Williams told an interviewer that I had accomplished "an impossible job on the MPSC." He said, "The mark of this man is that both producers and consumers had praise for him all the time I was governor."

By contrast, my work as Michigan's auditor general was less challenging. When I first learned I was being considered for the job, I was not even sure I wanted it. In October 1959 Frank S. Szymanski of Detroit, who was auditor general of Michigan, persuaded Governor Williams to name him to a local job as a probate judge in Wayne County. Based on our time together at the MPSC, Tom thought I would make a good replacement for Szymanski. He talked with his good friend, Larry Farrell, who was the governor's executive secretary, and I was offered the job. My nomination had to clear the state Senate Public Business Committee, which was chaired by a Republican, Frank J. Beadle of St. Clair. He told reporters that I enjoyed unusual bipartisan support because of my accomplishments and fairness and said: "The only thing that would stand against him is that he has done such a wonderful job on the Public Service Commission that we would like to keep him there." I was confirmed by the senate with no problem, and I began work on September 23, 1959.

A few cynics said the only reason I was appointed was because of race. That seemed a bit ironic given the fact that I was the first black appointed to such an important statewide elective office. But publicly I took a more diplomatic approach. I told one reporter: "When it comes to race, I can't ignore it. It is important for Michigan, for the City of Flint, and important to my group that I am recognized and honored. I certainly will not rest on that account." I told another, "I just hope I can bring something worthwhile to the job. I don't want to be just an officeholder, and I don't want the rarity of my appointment to be my only contribution. In years to come I'd be terribly disappointed to hear a conversation like this: 'What about that Smith fellow?' 'Well, he was the first Negro to be appointed to that job.' 'What else?' 'Well, . . . let me see.' "

Auditor general was at that time the sixth highest job in the executive branch of Michigan's state government. The auditor general was responsible for auditing the books and records of all the state agencies and county governments in Michigan. I had responsibility for supervising a staff of approximately one hundred people. There were three divisions. The largest was the State Agency Audit Division; the second was the County Audit Division; and the third was Real Estate, which kept track of all the plats filed by developers and filed defaults, when that became necessary. Much of the work on my watch was routine. We implemented a new system for standardizing accounting procedures at the state universities, for example.

We also had a few small scandals. Auditors uncovered some problems in Washtenaw County's social welfare department, which led to prosecutions and indictments. The biggest scandal while I was auditor general involved a probate judge in Flint who was caught with his hand in the till. He borrowed money from Genesee County on a regular basis. He always left IOUs, but his actions were still illegal. The auditor called me, knowing I was from Flint, and asked me what to do. He assumed I knew the judge and would want to give him a break. I did know the judge—I had practiced before him in Flint—but I told the auditor to handle the case like he would any other.

Our practice was to give public officials who were criticized in our reports a chance to comment. When the Genesee County judge received a copy of the report, he asked me for a meeting. I told him I would be coming home to Flint and would stop by his chambers on the way from Lansing. When we met, it became clear to me that he was not attacking the accuracy of the report, he was simply asking for some softer statement of his misdeeds. I let him talk and finally said: "Is there anything inaccurate about the report?" He admitted there was not. I said I could not change it. When the report was made public, the bar association called for his resignation. He quit and moved to Florida, and that was the last I ever heard of him. I did not think what I did was unusual. Being honest should be nothing unusual, so I do not take any credit for that.

I remember an incident involving racism. There was an opening for an auditor in Alpena, in the northeastern part of the state. At the time we had a few black auditors in Wayne County, and I suggested that we promote one to the job in Alpena. The deputy head of the State Agency Audit Division protested. He argued that the population of northeastern Michigan was nearly all white, and officials in those five or six counties would never cooperate with an African American. I listened to him but finally said: "Well, ultimately, we won't know

unless we try, will we?" I met with the fellow who was being transferred and asked how he felt about it. He was eager for a promotion
and was willing to move. I concluded there was no legitimate reason
for not reassigning him. A year or so later, a supervisor told me that
this fellow was one of the most effective and popular auditors in the
area. That is what I had hoped would happen, and I was glad I had
taken a small stand and it had worked out.

Another personnel matter was fraught with a different kind of
politics. The longtime head of the State Agency Audit Division took an
early retirement, and Governor John Swainson wanted to handpick
his replacement. He had a fellow in mind who used to work for the
state auditor general but had moved on to the highway department.
Swainson mentioned the man to me several times, and I put him off
by saying, "I'm studying it." I was not inclined to appoint the man
because we had a very good career person in the agency who wanted
the job. He actually had been running the division for the previous
two years while his boss had been ill. I worked with him and was
impressed with him and the job he was doing. By contrast, Swainson's
man had not been well liked by his colleagues.

My third reason for not wanting to appoint the fellow was more
personal. As I lived and breathed in the capitol environment I kept
hearing from one and all that this gentleman from the highway department was going to return to the auditor general's as head of the
State Agency Audit Division. Apparently, he had assured everyone that
was going to happen. Well, that made me more determined than ever
to resist. So I did not take any action. The governor would ask me
every now and then, "What are you going to do about that vacancy?"
I would assure him that I was considering the matter carefully.
Frankly, my tactic was to wait him out. He was my friend, the leader
of the party, and the head of government. Still, it was one of those
times when you have to stand fast for what you believe in, and I
thought I would do just that.

Finally, the governor, apparently a bit peeved, turned the matter
over to his executive secretary, Zolton D. Ferency, a brilliant guy with
great stamina and integrity who was very outspoken and did not mind
rattling a few chains. He asked for an explanation, and I told him I
wanted to promote the better qualified internal candidate. Ferency
said he would check into the matter. He learned that the highway
department employee had supported Swainson in the hard-fought primary battle against James Hare. Ferency also found out that the guy

expected the job because he had contributed fifty dollars to Swainson's campaign. Then Ferency told me, "You know we don't sell jobs around here. But if we ever started selling them, we're going to charge a whole lot more than fifty bucks." He told me to do what I wanted, and he would clear it with Swainson. I appointed the internal candidate and never heard anything more about the matter.

I do not pretend that any of these things that I have done are very unusual, but I give examples because they reflect my attitude toward government. I consider it to be a great public trust to serve the people. One of the highest honors you can give, next to serving God directly, is serving other people through effective, honest work in government. My views were formed long before I got to Michigan. I had seen bad things growing up in Memphis during Boss Ed Crump's reign, and that style of politics became a negative model for me. Thomas More provided a positive model, and I kept his example before me. I was also fortunate to serve in an era that had such fine public servants as Mennen Williams and his other appointees. I think we all shared a belief that we would do what was right, no matter whether we were loved for it or not. We all had the sense that if we were not up to a job, we would leave it. The main point was service, not keeping ourselves on the public payroll for selfish reasons.

In other words, we shared a political philosophy and certain fortitude. In public life, there are always opportunities to make the popular decision at the expense of what is right. It is then when you need to be steadfast in adherence to principle, and that takes guts. Particularly, when that decision could ride you out of office. Looking around from my current vantage point, I think one of the things that the city, state, and country need to cure our political malaise and the government's inability to take needed action, particularly at the federal level, is a lot more people who are willing to be one-termers, public servants who dare to be objective and make tough and unpopular decisions. I think if people are not prepared to do that, then they should not be in government. It is just too important.

I ended up taking a position that would have ended my job when I was auditor general. In those days, the job was elective. In 1960 I was duly nominated by the Democratic Party to succeed myself, and I ran statewide along with John Swainson for governor. I won handily. My plurality was something like 135,000 over my Republican rival, John B. Clements from the Upper Peninsula. As a matter of fact, I had more votes in the plurality than John F. Kennedy had in his victory over Richard Nixon in the presidential race that year. My victory was significant for another reason. It was nationally noted that I was the first African American elected to a full-time statewide post since the Reconstruction days of the 1870s.

I was proud. But I also was a little dismayed that my election seemed to be such a big deal. The problem with being the "first and only"—which I was at the MPSC, then in the auditor's general election, and later when I became the first black state supreme court justice in modern history—is that it is too easy to get the wrong impression that I was the first qualified. That, of course, was absolutely false. There were plenty of African Americans who came before me who were as worthy and certainly as qualified, if not more so. I tried to keep in mind that I was lucky to have lived at a point in history

Although he would later be dismissed for not being "black" enough, in 1960 Smith was considered an African-American icon in Michigan politics. This November 1960 picture shows him with, *left to right,* Dr. D. T. Burton, Rep. Adam Clayton Powell (NY), Rep. Charles C. Diggs (MI), and John D. Dingell.

when things came together, and I was allowed to make a little history myself. I realized, however, that my successes were just little sign pointers along the way to measure racial progress, and they indicated how far we had come and how much further we still had to go. I finally coined a phrase for my "firsts," describing them as "monuments in passing."

Running for election as an African American in 1960 was quite different from what it would become in the 1970s. In later years, African-American candidates made much of their origins, and the media and voters went along. When I ran in the years before politics had opened up, black politicians had a different philosophy. At least, I knew I did, and I do not think I was unique in this regard. I essentially argued: "Just give me a chance and judge me by my abilities and not by anything else; race is irrelevant, or at least it should be." The newspapers, of course, picked up on the fact that I was black, but I never tried to make it an issue, and I do not think it ever became one in any major way. I ran on the basis of my record and my programs. That, combined with my strong support within the Democratic Party, seemed to be enough to satisfy black and white voters alike.

Anyway, I was serving as auditor general when Michigan held a constitutional convention. One large item on the agenda was the future of the auditor general's office. At that time, the post was part of the executive branch. That was different from the federal system in which auditing functions rest with Congress. Reformers argued that the federal model made more sense, and I agreed with them. The legislative branch appropriates the money, the executive branch spends it, and it seemed logical that it should be up to the legislative branch to figure out whether the money was spent honestly and fairly. The other big question was whether the auditor general should remain an elective post or whether it should be appointive.

With the help of my staff, I conducted an elaborate survey of all the states to find out what they were doing. How were their auditors' staffs formed? Were they elected or appointed? Which branch of government were they in? What were their functions? We ended up with a huge spreadsheet of information. It was probably three feet tall and five feet wide. I thought this would be useful for the Constitutional Convention, but it was never used.

That Constitutional Convention was a study in the weakness of the political process. It was dominated by Republicans, who appointed staff members who were party loyalists or who were thought to be loyal to the Republican point of view, whatever that might be. One of these staffers, a Michigan State University professor, called me and asked what my office did. I offered to meet with him and told him I had gathered the survey material in anticipation of our conversation. He did not want to look at and never asked for my conclusions about whether the auditor's office should remain elective or stay in the executive branch. He assumed because I was a Democrat that I would oppose any changes. Although I objected to the politicking in what should have been a more open discussion about good government, I did not object to any of the changes that the new constitution mandated about my office. It was moved to the legislative branch, it was made appointive, and it was mandated that a certified public accountant hold the post.

I could not quibble about any of it, especially the last point. My year of accounting at Syracuse helped me as chair of the MPSC, where I was the only commissioner who understood the accounting aspects of rate cases. But my limited knowledge became glaringly obvious when I became auditor general. My weakness in this regard became apparent one evening during my campaign for reelection. The joke was on me. I attended a dinner in Ann Arbor hosted by Neil Staebler, who was chair of the Democratic Central Committee and a wonderful man of great integrity, learning, and political skill. It was a meeting of the Economic Club, whose members included such folks as the president of the University of Michigan, the president of the Ann Arbor Trust Company, and Robert McNamara, the head of the Ford Motor Company who went on to become secretary of defense.

After dinner, I gave a little talk about the work of the auditor general's office and invited questions. The first were relatively simple. I had brought our annual report. It had been in preparation when I took office, and I had reviewed it and signed it. It was printed over my imprimatur, and my picture was on the cover. I had familiarized myself with it as much as I could, and then someone at Neil's house asked me about the state aeronautics fund. That was one of the state's smaller budget items, and I did not know much about it. I struggled over the charts and accompanying written material, and I finally told the group: "I am not going to try to bluff you. I don't know the answer." At that point, McNamara, in a gentle way, started to help me. He looked at the chart, pointed to one part of it, and said, "I wonder if this is part of the answer." I said "yes." He continued to ask similar questions until he led me to the answer. It was a very nice thing on his part, and it pointed out how very bright he was. A very sharp guy.

That incident pointed up the need to have someone serve as auditor general who was an accountant by training. I was never as effective in the auditor general's job as I had been at the MPSC. I did not do the job any harm, but I did not do it any exceptional good, either. I ran an efficient shop, thanks to a very good staff, and I maintained the integrity of the department. That was about all.

It may seem strange in retrospect, but I rarely experienced any kind of discrimination while I was chair of the MPSC or auditor general. I thought about that an awful lot, and I think there are several possible reasons I did not. Some would say my light skin color made it easier for me to merge into white society, at least professional society. Another is the fact that I am Catholic. Some whites who might have been bigoted otherwise seemed to feel a special bond with me because of our shared faith. On a more pragmatic level, my success also stemmed from the fact that I went in as the boss. Life is a lot easier if you are in charge. But those things aside, I attribute my success to my attitude about myself and about everybody else. I just took people as they came. I did not look for trouble, and it rarely came my way.

One of the nice things about being in public life is that you get a chance to meet so many wonderful people. I had the great good fortune in the late 1950s to be invited to a daylong meeting of thirty or thirty-five prominent Democrats from across the nation that was held at the Pierre Hotel in New York. The event was chaired by Eleanor Roosevelt, who at that time was in her mid-seventies. She was still very sharp—incisive and thoughtful about current issues. Along with everyone else, what I noticed most about her was her grace and poise. That came through even though she was quite businesslike and ran a very orderly meeting.

In 1960 I met John F. Kennedy. Mennen Williams arranged for a small group of political activists in Michigan, including me, to spend a day with Kennedy at his Georgetown home. He sent the family jet to fly us to Washington. Quite frankly, I was not too excited about Kennedy's presidential ambitions. I preferred Stuart Symington, the senator from Missouri. But Williams was hooked on JFK. He called me into his office one day to discuss the presidential race, and I said: "What the hell has Kennedy got except a lot of good looks and a lot of money?" Then I realized I was looking at Williams—a guy with good looks and a lot of money. I was so embarrassed that I wanted to go right down to the floor.

Williams persuaded me to go to Washington with him. We spent four hours discussing issues with Kennedy, who had just returned from the campaign trail and was very tired. Williams chaired the meeting and kept pushing Kennedy to be more explicit about some of his views, particularly on civil rights. After the meeting, I became a convert to the cause. Kennedy was a very bright fellow. I liked his incisiveness on the issues, his great clarity and vision, and his ability to lead. The country, in general, and Flint, in particular, were trapped in the

Smith was skeptical about John F. Kennedy's run for the presidency in 1960. Then, during the campaign, Smith and several other prominent Michigan Democrats met with Kennedy for a day at the candidate's home in Washington. After that, Smith became an enthusiastic supporter, publicly endorsing Kennedy at this rally in Flint.

malaise of the 1950s—a period of letdown after the war years. JFK expressed concern with the direction we were going and openly warned against the slow drift. He tried to get people fired up. He was thinking about moving forward into space and moving forward into human rights areas we had not been into before. That appealed to me.

After he was elected president, Kennedy offered to appoint me to the Federal Power Commission, which later became the Energy Regulatory Commission. I did not even think about accepting the appointment because I felt I had an obligation to the people of Michigan who had just elected me auditor general.

♦ 8 ♦
The Michigan Supreme Court

I N 1961 Governor John Swainson asked if I could join him on a short trip to Grand Rapids, which is about sixty miles from Lansing. As we got on the highway, he asked me who I thought should be appointed to the state supreme court vacancy left when Talbot Smith resigned to accept a federal district judgeship in Detroit. I advised Swainson to replace Smith with one of the very fine Wayne County judges whom Mennen Williams had appointed. I mentioned a few, including Horace Gilmore, Victor Baum, Joseph A. Sullivan, and one or two others. Swainson found fault with each one. Finally, he asked, "Well, how about you?" I guess my mouth must have dropped to my chest because I really did not expect the offer. I said I had to consider it, and he asked: "What's to consider?" I pointed out that it was a big move, and I needed time. So I took a couple of weeks.

Most of the attorney general's staff and many of the lawyers in Michigan were ambitious to be on the state supreme court. I, by contrast, had never thought much about it. My focus was on getting my public service over and returning to my law practice. I originally planned to stay in Lansing only a couple of years. I still had not moved to the capital and was commuting home to Flint. The longer I stayed in state government, of course, the harder it got to return to my law practice. In any case, the supreme court appointment was too important not to consider.

I decided to go to Flint and ask my friends what they thought. I figured that in Lansing everyone knew me as a politician. I wanted to return to my legal roots, as it were, to find out if people thought I was really up to the job. My first ringing endorsement came from Mallory.

In his usual blunt manner, he said, "Well, you can't do any worse than some of the bozos who are already down there." I asked another friend, John M. Wright, with whom I had worked in the prosecutor's office, and one or two others. They seemed puzzled by the offer and not overly enthusiastic. After all, I was fairly young, thirty-nine years old, and had only practiced law about ten years, the last four of those working more as an administrator than as a lawyer at the MPSC and as auditor general. Still, none of my friends seemed to think the idea of my being on the supreme court was absurd, even though I worried that I had neither the experience nor the ability to perform adequately.

Governor Swainson thought I was taking too long and called me, demanding my decision. We met and I expressed my concerns but agreed to take the post on one condition: "If I don't work out, I will quit and let you appoint somebody in time for the next election." By law an appointee has to run in the next scheduled general election, which in my case meant 1962. Swainson's response was, "Don't worry about it, you'll do fine." So I put on my black nightgown and took my seat on the Michigan Supreme Court in October 1961.

I was not very productive during my first year. When I hit the court and saw the kinds and volume of material there to be decided, I quaked in my boots. I was afraid of making a fool of myself by committing mistakes. I took too much time to write and rewrite opinions, trying to make them perfect. My colleagues were very kind to me as we came up time after time to opinion day and I was still working on the cases assigned to me. Eventually, I realized that I had seven teachers on the court—my fellow justices—who could help save me from error. Reassured by that insight, I hit my stride sometime in the second year, and I was able to get my work out on time as I gained confidence.

I was definitely the junior member of the court in experience and, with one exception, in age. The court had eight justices—a strange number given the fact that most appellate courts have an odd, not an even, number of members. In 1903 Michigan's legislators set the number at eight because they believed that any majority decision of the court would carry more weight if it were decided by more than a single vote.

My Republican colleagues included Chief Justice John R. Dethmers, a former attorney general of Michigan who was in his sixties. He was originally from Holland, Michigan, but had moved to Lansing some years earlier. Leland W. Carr Sr. had been a circuit court judge

One of Smith's best friends and supporters was Wade H. McCree, the nation's second African-American U.S. solicitor general. When Oakland University honored McCree with an honorary doctorate, Smith and McCree's son-in-law, David Baker Lewis, were serving on the board of trustees. Lewis founded the nation's first African-American commercial law firm, now known as Lewis & Munday, which Smith joined in 1984 when he retired as general counsel of General Motors on April 1, 1984. Pictured also is Dr. Donald O'Dowd, president of Oakland University from 1972–78. *Left to right:* Smith, McCree, O'Dowd, and Lewis.

in Lansing for thirty-some years before he was appointed to the supreme court. He had sat on the high court for more than twenty years and was in his seventies. Carr had been appointed by Harry F. Kelly, who had served as governor and secretary of state. He lived in Gaylord, upstate, and commuted to Lansing.

The Democrats included Eugene F. Black from Port Huron. He had been a Republican attorney general in the late 1940s, but he switched to the Democratic Party and won election to the court in 1953. Black was in his late fifties. Thomas M. Kavanagh from Carson

City had also been Michigan's attorney general. George Edwards had come up through the ranks of labor as a firebrand, then served as city council president and a probate and circuit judge in Detroit. Kavanagh was in his early to mid-fifties, and George was in his late forties. Ted Souris, who was also from Detroit, was the youngest and one of the most persuasive members. He was three years younger than I was but had served since early 1960 when he replaced John D. Voelker, who was better known by his pen name Robert Traver, author of the famous book *Anatomy of a Murder.*

The court for several years before and after I joined it had a reputation for divisiveness. There was a split between the "liberals" (mostly Democrats) and the "conservatives" (mostly Republicans). Soon after I arrived, the liberals asked me to join them in pre-meeting caucuses on crucial cases. In other words, we would meet together before we met as a whole court to map out our strategies and decisions. I think this was suggested out of the belief that the conservatives, translated into Republicans, were getting together and voting consistently on certain kinds of cases.

It smacked too much of partisan politics for me, and I declined to join, which left me out there by myself. It probably would have been easier during my first year if I had joined, but it just did not seem like the right thing to do. I did not mind discussing cases with anybody, including both my liberal and conservative colleagues. But in the end, I thought my job on the court was to make judgments and to dispose of cases with my own individual views about who should win based on the law and the facts. I understand that such caucuses exist and have existed on many courts, including the U.S. Supreme Court at certain points in its history. To those who participate in them, they have some justification, but I could not go along with the system.

Michigan's Supreme Court was not unusual in terms of the contentiousness of its members. A collegial court—that is, a court where all the judges sit and decide cases together—is prone to such factiousness. During my more than five years on the court, I became acquainted with justices across the nation, and I never heard of one collegial court on which there were not strong enmities. It is not that appellate judges are kooks, but they have to live in isolated circumstances away from the bar and the public. In addition to their isolation, they sit together and work together constantly and get to know each other and each other's outlooks and foibles well.

I never believed that my colleagues were captive of anything but their own philosophies and individual views of life. But sometimes those differing philosophies could create controversy and, as a result, every justice had some reservation about one or more of the other justices. Judges just do not see procedural and substantive differences and distinctions the same way. They do not analyze cases the same way. After considerable discussion, they may narrow the areas of disagreement, but they still come to different conclusions. Each judge's position becomes well-known to the others, which raises another possible problem with consistency. If a judge casts a vote contrary to one he or she made six months earlier, it raises a question mark. Colleagues begin to ask themselves, "What's wrong with this man? Why is he voting this way? What is his secret agenda? What's on his mind? Is he being stupid or political?"

These factors occasionally led some judges to think that others were less than intellectually honest, but I never held such views of my colleagues. I did think there were some curious temperaments on the court while I was there. Sometimes, this made for what I will call "interesting" discussions. I never thought, however, that any of them were less than honest in what they did. I believed we all made a very, very strong effort to do the right thing, and I thought we shared a distinct sense of honor. We never took anything lightly. We had good discussions about cases, considering them from every angle.

It is important to remember that in most instances court decisions are pretty standard and have little to do with partisan politics or philosophies. We wrote decisions in approximately three hundred cases each year. We were united on most things but sharply divided on others. In a survey I conducted during my last years on the court, I found that in the great majority of cases, something more than 80 percent, our decisions were unanimous. Most of these were proverbial "bread-and-butter" cases involving property rights, domestic relations, child support and child care, and criminal cases. In another 10 or 12 percent of cases, the court split all kinds of ways, irrespective of ideological or philosophical differences among the members. Then there was a small percentage of cases, somewhere between 6 and 10 percent, in which the splits appeared to be partisan. These involved such touchy issues of law as personal injury, workmen's compensation, governmental immunity, and political questions such as reapportionment of the legislature. The splits were usually, but not always, along what the press liked to call "party lines." We thought of ourselves more as liberals and conservatives, although philosophy often did follow political affiliation.

One of my own personal claims to fame is that I had the highest "convincing rate" of the justices. In other words, 83 percent of the opinions I wrote were for the majority—which was several points higher than the next justice. I do not think this was because I was smarter. I think it was due in large part to the fact that I did not have any agenda and I was a plain vanilla type writer. I did not write a lot of colorful philosophy into cases. I just wanted to be clear, and I wrote simply without a lot of adornment and without too many footnotes. I was aware that judges who write in a highly stylized fashion, unless they happen to be great craftsmen like Supreme Court Justice Benjamin Cordozo, who wrote eloquently in a grand style, just do not have the talent to pull it off. I certainly did not. Instead, I strove to decide cases simply and clearly so that lawyers and judges could apply my rulings with a minimum of effort. I was not trying to impress anyone with my scholarship, in part, because I thought that was something that I did not have very much of, actually. I always tried to keep in mind the mandate of the late U.S. Supreme Court Justice Louis Brandeis, who is supposed to have said "When we get cute, somebody gets hurt."

Certainly another factor in my "convincing rate" was that I was in the center of the court philosophically. I had thought I was quite liberal coming in, and I guess I was more liberal than I was conservative, but essentially I wound up in the middle ideologically. I did not worry much about labels, reasoning that such concerns create bad judges. I called cases as I saw them and let the proverbial chips fall where they did. I never set out to become a moderate liberal. That is just where I wound up.

As I approached each case, decision by decision, I found that I could not always go along with my more liberal colleagues. This was true in some workmen's compensation cases I thought had no merit. It was even more true in criminal cases. I had far more experience in that kind of trial work than any of the other justices. As a result, I came down a little harder in some instances. I was familiar with the rights of the accused, and I thought they should be protected. I also thought we should apply some common sense, and, in my judgment, we went a little overboard for defendants in some cases.

I remember one. There was a petition from a fellow whom I shall call Gorski. Gorski was serving a life sentence for murder and was a

150

very shrewd and active jailhouse lawyer. He, along with dozens of other prisoners, usually long-termers, would petition the court for habeas corpus, claiming their rights at trial had not been accorded justice. They were forever seeking the new wrinkle, the new point, the new discovery, the new fact that might change the situation and allow them to get out of prison. Gorski was by all odds the most prolific writer of all the prisoners who were incarcerated at that time. Before I arrived, he petitioned the court many times, and after I joined the court he filed four or five more pleadings. The court took all of his many petitions seriously, but by the fourth one I had seen enough. I spent a lot of time on the first three, each time intrigued by Gorski's ability to raise new issues. But enough was enough. I told my colleagues something to this effect: "I have given Mr. Gorski all of the due process I am going to give him. Next time he files a petition, I am going to tell you in advance that my vote will be 'no.' I think we have to put an end to this kind of thing. I appreciate the sincerity of all the members in trying to divine an issue, but after he has been up here eight or ten or twelve times, it is clear that there is no issue, and the court should spend its time serving the rest of the people who have legitimate matters to be adjudicated." The court concurred.

In addition to clamping down on habeas corpus petitions, we implemented quite a few other reforms during my time on the court. We followed the Federal Rules of Civil Procedure by abolishing the procedural distinction between law and equity and adopting something called the General Court Rules. This was an enormous step forward in the procedural realm. When we got to the point where we decided that we ought to adopt new court rules, we turned to one of our members, Justice Dethmers. Because of his special skills, we suggested that he take a crack at the first draft, and he did. Once he completed it, we invited response from the cochairs of what was then known as the Michigan Joint Procedural Commission—Jason Honigman of Detroit and Charles W. Joiner, who at that time was assistant dean of the Law School of the University of Michigan and went on to become dean of Wayne State University Law School and a federal judge. They were quite candid. They carefully reviewed the first draft and said rather bluntly: "You're so far off, we think you should abandon the project and let us take a crack at it." They then explained so many things that we had done wrong that we were persuaded to back off and let them draft the rules. When they were finished, we made the final decision as to what would go into the rules and adopted them.

In 1962 I ran for reelection to keep my seat and was opposed by an old friend and former colleague at the bar in Flint—Louis D. McGregor. The Republican Party nominated him to oppose me, even though judicial elections were officially nonpartisan. In nonpartisan elections you do not have the ballot appearance of being part of a ticket. In other words, voters cannot pull the lever, vote for the straight ticket, and sweep you into office. They have to find your name and vote for you individually. That made the fact that I beat McGregor by more than 100,000 votes more satisfying. I won with strong help from liberal and ethnic voters in southeastern Michigan—especially Wayne and southern Macomb Counties. I also had strong endorsements from public officials and newspapers.

The historic significance of my appointment and subsequent election was that I became the first African American to serve on a state supreme court since Reconstruction. Some people said I was the first in the nation's history. To my great pleasure, however, that was actually not the case. Jonathan J. Wright had served on the South Carolina Supreme Court *during* Reconstruction. So I was number two.

The same year I was reelected, Edward W. Brooke was elected attorney general of Massachusetts. *Time* and a few other magazines reported that he was the highest elected African-American official in the United States. A number of my friends, including whites in the Lansing press corps, urged me to fire off a correction to *Time,* pointing out that I actually held that distinction. I refused. They countered that it was not personal; it was a matter of state honor that Michigan was ahead of Massachusetts in this regard. I told them that it would be unseemly to argue about who was the first or the highest ranking, especially when there were only two of us in a black population of twenty million. Besides, I added jokingly, "When I ran for the court, I did not run to become head nigger." They got the point. I never advertised myself as the first and only because it always occurred to me that anybody who reveled in being the first and only was taking too much pride in an artificial distinction. Being first did not matter as much as doing a good job once I got there. Besides, while appointing or electing a "first" showed how far the nation had come, it also showed how much further we had to go before we really had something about which to boast.

The 1962 election was personally significant for another reason. The man who became my best friend on the court, Michael D. O'Hara, a red-haired Irishman from Menominee on the Upper Peninsula, was elected that year. Mike was the Republican nominated to oppose Paul Adams, who had been appointed to replace George Edwards, who had left the court to become Detroit's police commissioner. Adams and I ran on the same ticket. Strangely enough, I won and he lost. Mike defeated him, in large measure because his Irish name carried the day with Catholic voters in Detroit and southern Macomb County. Adams ran again after Judge Carr retired in 1963, and he was handily elected to regain a seat in 1964. In any case, O'Hara defeated Adams in 1962. Mike was part of a great family of O'Haras and Doyles, many of whom were lawyers or in public service. We lived only a few blocks from each other in Lansing. Mike was a spirited fellow who loved to do things on the spur of the moment. Even though we were very different temperamentally, we became good friends. We would go home together and discuss our cases. We did not agree on everything, but we certainly discussed an awful lot.

The Constitution of 1963 significantly changed the role and workings of the Michigan Supreme Court. It created the court of appeals, an intermediate appellate court that heard cases before they came to us. We had the job of writing the new court's operating rules, and after its members were elected in 1964, our workload decreased significantly. Before the intermediate court, we had a very large docket, and I can truthfully say that there was hardly an hour of my waking life when I was not preoccupied with one of these cases.

The constitution also reduced the number of justices from eight to seven, which eliminated the need to seek consensus on most opinions by allowing for a one-vote majority. There has been another significant change on the court since I left it—a huge increase in its support staff. When I was there, we probably had ten people around in addition to our law clerks. There are more than ninety now, and each justice has three clerks. Back then, we could hire one law clerk, although not all the justices wanted one. John Dethmers, for example, said law clerks got in his way. He did his own research and his own writing. When I was on the court, about half of us, including me, did our own writing. My clerks checked facts, and I let them write analyses and then read and challenge my opinions. I did not think, however, that I would have enough intimate familiarity with the facts and the law to make a decision unless I actually wrote it myself. My clerks were probably smarter than I was, but the people of Michigan paid me and not my clerks to exercise my judgment and to write my own opinions. The common practice in most courts now is to have clerks draft an opinion, which the judges review and edit to reflect their own thinking.

I enjoyed being a supreme court justice for all kinds of reasons. One was sharing my insights about the job with members of the public. One such encounter took place on a Saturday around noon or one o'clock. I had been in my office working and was leaving to go home. I ran into a black lady with eight or nine Cub Scouts from Detroit. She recognized me and identified herself as the wife of a lawyer whom I had met. I did not remember him, but that did not matter. I told her that it was a poor time for sight-seeing because all of the buildings were closed, but I would show them what I could.

We started on the ground floor of the capitol where there were public exhibits and worked our way up to the third floor where the supreme court was then located. (It has since moved to the G. Mennen Williams Building, behind the capitol.) A middle-aged white couple asked to join our group and tagged along. I opened the courtroom where the justices sat to hear oral arguments. I had several speeches that I used to give to the hundreds of schoolchildren who would come to the capitol in the spring. I picked one, mounted the bench, identified the chairs where people sat, and gave my spiel.

In the talk I used for kids this age, nine or ten, I compared the court's work to a softball or baseball game. I said something along these lines: "On the field of play, you have an umpire who calls the balls and strikes and when people are safe or out. . . . Well down in your home county there is a judge who sits in the trial court and his job is somewhat similar to that of the umpire. . . . Now often the parties have a dispute about whether the umpire is correct, and appeal to the commissioner or whomever runs the league. That's the kind of function we serve. We're kind of the commissioners of appeal who review and determine whether the trial judge made the right call."

I provided a few more details, and the kids filed out, but the middle-aged couple lingered. The man said my description of the legal system was one of the best explanations of the judicial process in lay language that he had ever heard. I thanked him and asked if he was a lawyer. I repeated that I was Otis Smith, and he said, "My name is Harry Phillips." At that time, Phillips was the chief judge of the Sixth U.S. Circuit Court of Appeals. In other words, he was the highest ranking judge in Michigan, Ohio, Kentucky, and Tennessee. We ran into each other several times later at conferences, and he would tell the story of our first meeting. Harry was a fellow Tennessean, and we became friends. Later when the Fisk alumni club held Otis M. Smith day in Memphis, Harry drove all the way from his office in Nashville to help honor me.

Every judge is accustomed to the elaborate courtesies paid him by the public and by lawyers in particular. This was especially true in Lansing, where everyone seemed to have titles and basked in the trappings of status. When I was auditor general, for example, a few people would call me "General," which was a little elaborate given what I did. When I joined the supreme court and people would ask what to call me, I would say, "Well, the very formal way is Mr. Justice, the more informal is Justice, the quite informal is Judge, and if you call me by first name, Otis, I won't be offended at all." There was one guy who took me at my word. He worked for Western Union, delivering messages around the capitol. He was in his mid-to-late twenties and was mentally handicapped. He would always say, "Hi, Otis," and I would say, "Hello, Joe" or whatever his name was. People would stare, especially if I was standing around with a group of lawyers and justices. I was not about to try and educate him about protocol. Besides, it was the kind of situation that relieved some of the stiffness around there.

The court handled several highly charged cases while I was on it. Perhaps the worst were child custody cases. Although they had less legal significance than other matters, I found them more trying. After all, nothing is more explosive than a child custody case because everybody is sympathetic to the child and no matter what you do, you are going to have people who are going to feel that it is the wrong thing. Perhaps the most notorious of these cases while I was there was the Mathers case, which became a cause célèbre.

The case of *Pearl Jean Mathers Hatmaker v. the Michigan Children's Aid Society and Mr. and Mrs. Edward Furlong* had an eight-year, tortured history in the courts. I found it extremely difficult to decide. Paula Marie Mathers was born in 1953. She was placed in foster care after a court found that her mother, Pearl Jean Mathers, had neglected her. The Michigan Children's Aid Society placed Paula in foster care with the Furlongs. The agency never told the foster parents that the placement would be temporary. After a month, the Furlongs received bad legal advice and began fighting to adopt the child. They tried to use charges of neglect to circumvent the adoption code. In the meantime, Pearl Jean Mathers rehabilitated herself and sued to regain custody. At a trial in 1958, a jury decided that Paula should remain with the Furlongs.

I wrote a decision granting custody to the natural mother. The law was fairly clear. Michigan state policy was to keep children with their natural parents. Pearl Jean Mathers may have been young, divorced, and guilty of certain misconduct, but that did not justify severing her parental rights permanently. In 1954 she reestablished a home with a man who would make a good husband and father. She did not make extraordinary efforts to see her child, but the Michigan Aid Society did not make it easy for her either.

As I asked in my opinion, "How can it be said that a mother who rehabilitates herself and then wages an eight-year battle for her own flesh and blood has committed some unpardonable sin that now makes the state master of her destiny and that of her child?" I rejected the argument used by the Furlongs that it would be wrong to take Paula away because she had lived with them for so many years and hardly knew her mother. Just because it took eight years to litigate the matter did not seem reason to keep Paula away from her mother permanently. I concluded, "It has often been observed that nothing surcharges a case with emotion as much as a fight over a child. Perhaps because each participant instinctively identifies with one of the emotional symbols ever present in such proceedings. Unfortunately, in this case, emotions have triggered advocacies bordering on the unethical. The hostilities fairly leap from the pages. It is a good example of how not to handle a custody case."

One of the most complex decisions I wrote was in a huge business case involving alleged pirating of six million dollars in assets. The case took thirteen weeks to try in the Wayne Circuit Court. Nowadays such lengthy cases are not unusual, but they were rarer back then. The record was the largest ever accumulated in any case that had been before the Michigan Supreme Court, according to the clerk's office. I spent the better part of three months reading the record, digesting the facts, and writing my April 1965 opinion in *Fenestra, Inc. v. Gulf American Land Corporation, et al.*

Fenestra manufactured automotive springs and was listed on the New York Stock Exchange. Gulf American, one of Florida's two largest land investment companies, had bought a large chunk of Fenestra stock. Fenestra argued that Gulf bought the stock not as an investment but as a way of gaining control so it could exploit Fenestra's assets. The judge in Wayne County held that Gulf's stock purchase was unlawful and contrary to public policy. He ordered divestiture and removal of the Gulf directors from Fenestra's board. There was very little disagreement about the facts—who did what when. The question was merely one of law. I ended up overturning the Wayne Court decision. It was clear that Gulf, along with all of the other parties involved, had acted out of self-interest. But, as I wrote, "one of the risks of a publicly held corporation is that a total stranger may purchase a controlling interest. As long as that purchase is not illegal, as it was not in this case, then the courts have no right to superimpose their suspicions, predilections, and judgments upon the actions of the entrepreneur." Justice Black concurred in result but wrote a separate opinion. My other colleagues joined in my opinion to reverse the trial court.

The most significant cases the court decided while I was there involved the apportionment of the state legislature. This was a national issue that has long since been forgotten because it was adjudicated largely in the 1960s, although it does come up for application again after every decennial census. There is always a dispute somewhere in the country. Political folk, including some Democrats and Republicans, historically have been alike in seeking more power for their party by using their control, if it exists, to diminish the impact of the political opposition by gerrymandering political districts, usually of state legislatures.

The issue, as it came to a head in the 1960s, was somewhat different. As a long-standing practice, the courts stayed out of disputes about how state legislatures set voting districts. The reasoning was that republican government worked best if the federal government stayed out of state business, and if the courts stayed out of questions best decided in the political realm. In many states, including Michigan, legislatures established voting districts by geography rather than population. With the growing size of urban areas, this led to huge variations in the number of voters in each district, with rural areas enjoying a disproportionate amount of voting strength. For example, the state senate district of Oakland County, outside of Detroit, was twelve times the size in population of the district at the western end of the Upper Peninsula. Most states followed the U.S. Senate model, guaranteeing geographic representation despite population disparities. Critics claimed that the system was unfair because it diluted the say of voters in more populous areas. They proposed a new system called "one man, one vote" that gained growing acceptance in the 1950s and 1960s.

The apportionment fight in Michigan began in the late 1950s

when August Scholle, president of the state American Federation of Labor and Congress of Industrial Organizations (AFL-CIO), filed suit on behalf of the Democratic Party against the state about the disparity in voting districts. Essentially, with the growing power of Democrats under Mennen Williams, the fight about redistricting became very partisan. In an attempt to block such suits, the legislature passed an amendment to the state constitution that was beguilingly called the "Balanced Legislature Provision." The provision kept apportionment of the Michigan Senate based largely upon geographic size rather than population. However, it also tried to strike a better balance between rural and urban interests. The problem with the provision, among other things, was that it froze forever, in law, districts that were still vastly different in population.

After the 1960 census, Scholle renewed his fight. The Michigan Supreme Court refused to rule in his favor. He appealed to the U.S. Supreme Court where his case was pending along with eight or ten others. His lawsuit, which became known as *Scholle v. Hare* was either on file or filed shortly after the U.S. Supreme Court handed down its famous 1962 ruling in *Baker v. Carr.* The Court ruled that the apportionment of state legislatures was a constitutional question open to judicial consideration, but it failed to take the next step of setting out the standards by which legislatures should redraw districts. The Supreme Court sent *Baker v. Carr* back to Tennessee to let local judges draft a plan. All of the other pending cases, including *Scholle,* were sent back to their respective states.

There was intense speculation about what our court would decide in Scholle's case. Six of the justices had already given their opinions in the first case, and they were divided three-three. Two of us, who were relatively new members of the court, had not. Justice Paul Adams could not participate because he had been Michigan attorney general when his office argued the first *Scholle v. Hare* case. That left me to break the tie. I was doubtful about not following the U.S. Senate model, which ensured geographic representation. So I polled members of both sides—the conservative Republicans and the liberal Democrats. I did not get much help. All of the justices told me to make up my own mind. For them, the issue was easy. They had already gone through the agony of making up their minds.

After two or three weeks, I decided according to what should be an obvious principle for anybody in government: when in doubt, vote with the people. So I decided to vote in favor of reapportioning the

Michigan Senate, and the stuff hit the fan. A couple of state senators promptly appealed. Their lawyers had to trek all the way to Littleton, New Hampshire, where U.S. Supreme Court Justice Potter Stewart was vacationing. Stewart granted the stay that temporarily stopped our reapportionment from going forward.

Nineteen sixty-two was an election year, and George Romney was running for governor. He went around the state criticizing the Michigan Supreme Court, calling our decision for reapportionment "the most amazing power grab" in the state's history. I winced every time I heard him say that. I believed his criticism was completely unfair because the U.S. Supreme Court had opened the gates in *Baker v. Carr*. To me, it was just a matter of trying to decide a very difficult issue in the best interests of the people.

I have often thought since then that Justice Stewart's stay of my opinion probably saved my political hide. I was running for reelection, and if the order had gone forward reapportioning the Michigan Senate, the Republicans, with the strong backing of the press, would have chased me out of office. Who knows, they might have hounded me out of the state as well. Stewart's order had the effect of temporarily averting the question, which returned two years later. In the meantime, I won reelection.

The case came back after the reapportionment committee—made up of four Democrats and four Republicans—filed their predictably gerrymandered plans. Having reviewed these proposals in open court with the lawyers and the other justices, it was clear that a very strong partisan job had been done on both sides. I told one of the Democrats on the apportionment commission whom I knew, "You submitted a god-awful gerrymandered plan. Why in hell don't you submit a simple, pure 'one man, one vote' plan so that if the supreme court does decide in the way you hope it does, there will be something up here that we can vote for without having to hold our noses?" I know that my comments were extrajudicial, but I did not care.

I later heard that the Democratic Party bigwigs debated my suggestion long and hard before deciding to take my advice. Two Democrats—Richard H. Austin, who later became Michigan's secretary of state, and Robert Kleiner—had submitted a plan, which, like the Republican version, was badly gerrymandered. After the party leaders met, Austin and Kleiner went back to the drawing board and came up with a pure plan that was adopted by a clear majority of the court. But a lot of dramatic things happened before we finally adopted their plan.

During the early part of 1964 we had been waiting for the U.S. Supreme Court to decide *Reynolds v. Sims, et al.,* which would set the standards that should be applied to redistricting. It appeared that we were going to run out of time before the state legislative elections. When the U.S. Supreme Court did not decide the case by April, it looked as if Michigan would not be able to have orderly primaries. I worried that if we did not draw districts, then the candidates would have to run in at-large elections. That did end up happening in Illinois. All of the candidates ran with the entire state as their election district. It took until spring of the following year for the people of Illinois to know who their representatives were. It was government at its worst. I may not be the smartest guy in the world about how government works, but I knew enough to know that the one thing I did not want to do was to vote to essentially dissolve the most important branch of government, which in my judgment is the legislative because it is closest to the people.

I decided to vote for timely and orderly elections. That meant crossing the line and voting with the Republicans on their plan. I reasoned that in the absence of instruction from the U.S. Supreme Court, we were merely looking at the question of which plan submitted by the apportionment commission most accurately complied with the state constitution. Clearly, the Republican Hannah-Brucker plan did just that. I reserved judgment on the federal question and decided that in the interest of a sound and workable election, I would vote for the law as it was then. My vote on May 23 gave the Republican plan a five-to-three majority.

My action was not very popular with a lot of Democrats, but I voted my conscience and tried not to worry about whether I would fare well in popularity. I wanted to be reelected, and I wanted to be liked by the people who nominated and elected me, but I figured I could not pervert the rules because of my friends and political supporters. I was not sanctimonious; I just felt that in the operation of government, the question of honor was supremely important and public servants owe it to the people to be brave enough to vote on the basis of principle. If that resulted in my being chased out of office, so be it.

On June 16, before the apportionment committee could implement the plan, the U.S. Supreme Court came down with its decision in *Reynolds v. Sims et. al.* We took another look at the proposals and voted to adopt the Democratic Austin-Kleiner alternative. Mike

O'Hara, a Republican, voted with me and the other Democrats. Referring to my earlier defection, he joked: "You're not going to be more gutsy than I am." I think what he wanted to do by joining the people on the other side of the aisle was to ensure that nobody could look at us and accuse us of being engaged in partisan politics. When he joined us, our decision gained the appearance of nonpartisanship, which helped get the plan approved in Washington. So we became the first court in the nation to adopt a "one man, one vote" apportionment plan. It was because we were sitting there waiting for it, so we were able to implement it in a matter of weeks.

Chief Justice Earl Warren, who visited us about a year later, said: "Everybody was watching who was going to be first and you were the first and all the others fell over like ten pins." I found it interesting that Warren said a number of times that the most important decision the Supreme Court made during his tenure was not *Brown v. the Board of Education,* which desegregated schools, but the apportionment cases, which had a profound impact on the makeup of legislatures in all fifty states by ensuring that one person's vote was equal to another's.

After I had been on the court five years, I did a survey and found that since I had joined, we had issued approximately 950 formal opinions and about two and a half times that many motions. I wrote 108 of those formal opinions, and after reviewing them, I came away with a very high respect for my own objectivity. None of the other justices were more objective than I was, and a few gave into their biases of one kind or another. This objectivity—perhaps *independence* is a better word—would get me into trouble, especially with labor unions.

In particular, I found myself voting with the Republicans in many workers' compensation cases. I just could not find it within myself to say that some of these plaintiffs had a substantial claim, and I ruled against them. This caused problems with organized labor, as I quickly learned. I attended Democratic Party conventions whenever they were held, even when I was not seeking renomination. I believed that the people who supported me had a right to ask me legitimate questions about my performance in office.

On one occasion, in the Olds Hotel in Lansing, I was approached by some "pork choppers"—low-level union officials off from their normal workbench duties with the shops as paid officials. They had been drinking. I was standing in the lobby, thanking people for their support and answering their questions. These fellows approached me, and one of them wagged his finger and said something like, "We've been hearing about you going South on us. You voted with the other side." That made me angry, and I responded with something like, "You damned guys support me because you know that I understand the legitimate needs of labor unions. I was a shop steward in the automobile workers as well as the steel workers. I know as much about it as you guys, but if you think that every time your name appears on some file that you're going to get my vote, you're crazy. You vote for me, you vote for integrity. I am going to vote for cases as I see them, and you can tell anybody that." I was so loud and threatening in appearance that two other judges stepped in to restrain me. I had no intention of hitting anybody; I just wanted to make it clear that while I appreciated political support at election time, I was not somebody who could be bought.

I am sure that this incident had something to do with my defeat in 1966. If it did, I am glad of it. By the time that election came around, I had become a pretty good judge. Every daily newspaper in Michigan endorsed me for a full eight-year term. The *Detroit Free Press,* for example, even endorsed me above Thomas M. Kavanagh, who was the chief justice. The newspaper called me "the class" in the field and noted that my only "serious weakness was over-working." Many of the newspapers that endorsed me were Republican, but that did not seem to make any difference.

Thomas Kavanagh and I ran as Democrats for the two seats on the court. We were opposed by Republicans Thomas E. Brennan, a handsome circuit judge in Wayne County, and Meyer Warshawsky, a Republican from South Haven. Kavanagh won handily. Brennan came in second. I came in third, and Warshawsky was fourth. There were several factors in my loss. More Republicans turned out to vote than Democrats in the election. Many of the ethnic and Catholic voters in Wayne County chose Brennan because of his Irish name. There were other things, like the huge ballot with some eighty-odd names just having to do with judges in Wayne County. So I also got lost in the shuffle. There may have been other facts which I probably would not want to know.

I took the loss hard. I felt I had really hit my stride as a judge. All of the major newspapers in the state endorsed me, and I believed their view that I was one of the better justices on the court. I certainly thought I was as good as any of the other candidates. Still, I was not entirely shocked. In the middle of the campaign, I realized that I might lose. I remembered that Paul Adams had lost his seat four years earlier to Mike O'Hara, and I worried that the same fate could befall me since I was running against two men with Irish names. I expressed my concern to my dear friend Phil Hart, who by then was a U.S. senator, and asked him to reserve a federal court appointment for me. Phil, who was really a straight arrow and not one inclined to make loose statements, told me: "Otis, I've been all over the state, and I think everybody's for you." He waved me off, as if my losing the election were impossible.

Unbeknownst to me, Damon J. Keith, an African-American lawyer in Detroit who was serving as finance chair for my reelection campaign, was also lobbying for one of the open seats on the U.S. District Court in Detroit. I heard later from several people that a mix-up occurred. Hart told me later that he was not holding the nomination for anyone, but Damon interpreted a conversation they had just before the election as a commitment. After I lost the election, I called Phil in Washington, and he told me he was very upset but had to proceed with Damon's nomination. Or at least he became upset when several people tried to convince him that he had made a mistake by choosing Damon over me.

The *Detroit Free Press* got wind of the story and ran two editorials endorsing me over Damon. In its editorial on December 3, the newspaper praised Damon's civic contributions, especially his work as a member of Detroit's Housing Commission and cochair of the Michigan Civil Rights Commission. But it gave the edge to me for my judicial experience and temperament, saying: "Anyone appearing before Justice Smith would feel he'd had his day in court. He has a willingness to listen, to follow an argument and to weigh opposing views." I am not sure how the *Free Press* got onto the story. I suspect that it had something to do with my good friend Wade McCree, who was by then a federal judge. It could also have come from the chief U.S. district judge, Ralph M. Freeman, who was from Flint, had been a classmate of Mallory's, and knew me and my record. I never did find out.

Phil Hart searched for a way out. He sent Jerome Cohen, who was chief of staff on his Senate Subcommittee on Antitrust and Monopoly, to convince Damon to withdraw. I heard later that Damon was about to withdraw, but the young lawyers in his law firm of Keith, Conyers, and Anderson convinced him that he should stay in the hunt. John Conyers, who was a fairly new congressman at that time, and other people from Detroit's black political establishment were in favor of Damon, and they were pulling for him.

The black establishment's support for Damon over me signified the shift that had occurred in racial politics. Although I had been and had received publicity as a "first" in my various political jobs, I never went around with a sign on my back saying, "I am colored or Afro-American or black" or whatever. I did not approach any of my positions that way because I thought my race should be irrelevant. And, as far as I could tell, it usually was with voters and my colleagues.

I was especially careful not to make racial speeches as a member of the supreme court. The speeches I made were very measured in judicial tone and substance. As a matter of fact, because of my desire to appear to be a judge for all of the people, I did not attend the historic march on Washington in 1963. I would love to have gone, but I thought about it and decided that if I went down to Washington and was seen on television, then people in Michigan who had racial issues before the court might conclude that I was biased. In retrospect, maybe I was a little too careful about my perception of my judicial duties, especially when it came to missing Martin Luther King Jr.'s "I Have a Dream" speech in Washington.

That does not mean I was oblivious to racial questions. There were two cases decided by the court while I was there in which I believed racism played a part. I thought in confirming the boundaries of that curiously shaped municipality called Dearborn Heights, there was a subtle unspoken understanding among my white brethren that the city's white residents wanted to protect themselves from having a substantial black influence in their community. There was also an incident involving a little girl whose white mother divorced her white husband and married a black doctor. They moved to California, and the father kidnapped the girl and brought her back to Michigan. It was clear to me that the girl belonged with her mother and stepfather, but the court ruled that she could remain in Michigan with her grandparents. I thought the other judges were motivated, in part, by the feeling that the child should not grow up in a home with a black father. They never said anything to me along those lines, but they were clearly voting against the law and the best interest of the child, as I pointed out in my dissenting opinion.

I suppose the point is that I had always stood by my principles for racial equality, but to me that did not mean trumpeting the fact that I was African American. That stand became less politically acceptable in the black-power politics of the 1960s. In any case, between the time I lost the election in November and January 1, when I left the court, I tried to persuade Phil to do the right thing and appoint me. He was having all kinds of difficulties that I only found out about later. Damon's supporters were pressuring him. Phil was still trying, through Jerry Cohen, to get Damon to withdraw. I was putting a lot of pressure on Phil because I felt very deeply about the job. I knew I was a good judge and wanted to stay one. The federal appointment appealed to me because it was lifetime. I would never have to campaign again. I also wanted to be a federal judge in the Sixth Circuit, which included Michigan and my native state of Tennessee. I had not asked for the MPSC, the auditor generalship, or the supreme court nomination, but I had a strong desire to be a federal judge.

Phil and I were good friends. I had worked with him on his first elections, even before he was a senator. We had become close when he was lieutenant governor. We discussed some of the great Catholic lawyers, including Thomas More. We had similar views of what a judge should be. Temperamentally we were soul mates in that we had very low anxiety levels and tried very hard to please everybody. When we found that impossible, we commiserated with one another.

I will never know what happened or what Phil really thought about my nomination. He is long since dead. He may really have thought that I would win reelection. Or he may have thought that I was not a particularly strong candidate for the federal appointment. In either case, I have always felt bad that he did not take my aspirations seriously. I felt let down because I had asked him well in advance. Besides, I thought the appointment was my due because I had done everything one is supposed to do. I had run in elections, had been a fairly decent operator in public office, and had won the confidence of voters in two out of three elections. I had also worked hard in the party, and I had judicial experience.

I was the one who put an end to the controversy by withdrawing. The nomination was turning into a mess. The newspapers were for me and against Damon. I did not worry about that, but I feared that the whole thing would degenerate into a kind of black/white spectacle. If I had wanted to, I could have gone around the state and gotten endorsements from county chairs and bar association leaders, most of whom were white, while Damon cultivated African-American support in Detroit. I talked to most of the people who supported Damon and asked them to reconsider. Instead, they asked me to drop out. I finally acquiesced after a meeting at black leader Horace Sheffield's house in December. And that is how I came to lose two judgeships inside a couple of months.

✦ 9 ✦
My Years at General Motors

AS IS OFTEN the case with situations that at first appear discouraging, my failure to get a federal judgeship turned out to be a blessing in disguise. My life and career took a dramatic and exciting turn when I joined the legal staff of General Motors on my forty-fifth birthday in February 1967. I was skeptical about whether I would fit in at the world's largest corporation, and it took me a while to discover that I loved it there. I stayed seventeen years, eventually becoming a vice president and general counsel. It would have been hard to predict that degree of success when I began.

A few days after the election, I received a call from my old friend Waldo E. McNaught, who was one of the top public relations men at GM. He asked what I planned to do. I told him I was hoping for a federal court appointment, and he asked me not to make any decisions until I had talked with a representative of GM's legal staff. Louis Bridenstine, the corporation's associate counsel, then came to see me. I said I still hoped to serve on the federal bench. He assured me that I would have a job waiting for me at GM if I needed it. When it became clear that I would, I contacted him.

When we met, I pointed out that I had never been too favorable to GM in the cases that had come before me as a Michigan Supreme Court justice. Bridenstine and his boss, Aloysius F. Power, who was then general counsel, reassured me that what mattered was my overall record, not my decisions against the corporation. We discussed my salary. I was only making $25,500 when I left the court. Considering what I believed to be the larger salaries in industry, I thought I was worth $35,000 to GM. Apparently Al Power was not very impressed with politicians or ex-supreme court justices and offered me $30,000. That put me fifteenth down from the top in terms of salary. Bridenstine assured me that when Power retired in a few months, my salary would be raised to what it should be, and it was.

Neither Bridenstine nor Power made any promise about my duties. In acknowledgment of my experience as a supreme court justice and head of the MPSC, they created a new title for me, "attorney in charge of appellate and regulatory matters." A number of people asked me why I did not have a fancier title, such as associate or even general counsel. I had no such illusions; I had no experience in a corporate counsel's office and was not even sure that I would like it at GM. I was more than willing to bide my time.

My first three years with the company were really a "feeling-out" period. The corporation and I had to find out of if I really fit in, and at times I had my doubts. There were hardly any people of color when I began working there; I could count all of the black folks in the headquarters building on two hands. I was also the lone Democrat in the top ranks. After I had been at GM for a number of years, one of the officers asked me if I was still a Democrat. I said that I was. He asked me how I could remain a member of an "antibusiness party." I said it was simple, "If it were not for the Democrats who were promoting and still promote the notion of an open society, I would not be at GM because if they had not given me the opportunity to serve in a high capacity of government, GM would never have known about me." There was supposed to have been one other Democrat in the executive suite, but nobody had ever been able to find him.

Not surprisingly, perhaps, I was also more liberal on many political and social questions than my colleagues. I will cite one example. When I joined GM in 1967, the war in Vietnam was raging, and I was the only person there who opposed it. I always had some reservations about that war, growing out of my differing perception of communism. I feel safe in assuming that I was the only member of GM's top management who had been a communist sympathizer in my youth. In large measure because of my experiences in Nashville, I believed that communism was most likely to take root in places where the political and business leaders were not sensible enough to accommodate the needs of the average person.

I never put much stock in the domino theory by which U.S. policymakers justified our involvement in Vietnam. I could not share the view of cold warriors who believed that if one country became communist, then its neighbors would also succumb, like dominos. Instead, I believed that in all of the countries where communism had taken root, including Vietnam, the inspiration came from within because of the country's unfair leadership. If the Soviet Union wanted to waste its resources trying to turn local fights into an international movement, I figured the United States should let it. There was no reason why we had to waste millions of our own dollars in the fray. Everyone else in GM management with whom I spoke was gung ho about the war. Interestingly enough, the following year, when there was a lot of talk about the United States having really lost any chance of winning, these same people all believed we should pull out of Vietnam.

Although I may have felt like an outsider with some GM executives, at the same time I also was surprised at the breadth of knowledge and vision a lot of them had. The more I became familiar with some of the top management people, the more I became impressed with their grasp of situations—not just in the auto industry but in the world at large.

For example, I worried when I first arrived at GM that many of its leaders would be antiunion. I was surprised to learn this was not the case. One day after I joined the company, I went to lunch with GM's chief labor lawyer. He had been with the company since the famous sit-down strikes of the 1930s. I asked his opinion of the United Auto Workers. He said, "First of all, unions are here to stay. No question about that. Nobody's going to refight that battle." He then described the UAW as one of the better unions in the nation. Walter Reuther, its president, was still alive, and the lawyer singled him out for praise. "Walter yells and screams sometimes about things he doesn't like about what we're doing, but when we're negotiating a contract he can read our financial statements as well as we can. He will push and push to get all that he can for his members, but when we resist, he reads our figures and knows how and when to close a deal."

There was an interesting footnote to this. Some years later, in 1970 after Walter Reuther and his wife died in a plane crash and Leonard Woodcock became president of the UAW, the union was in a long strike against GM. I saw James M. Roche, who was then chair of the corporation, in the lobby and asked him how it was going. He said, "If Walter were alive we wouldn't be in this fix," indicating that Reuther knew more than Woodcock about settling a strike. Roche seemed to be making the observation more in sadness than in anger. I suppose the main point is that although GM and the UAW had a number of opposing interests, I never, during all my years there, heard any top management people make disparaging remarks about UAW leadership.

Despite my initial misgivings, people were very courteous to me when I began working at GM. Everybody wanted to call me "Judge," but I would not let them because I thought it got in the way of good communication. It would have preserved for me an artificial status that I no longer had. Instead, I insisted that everyone call me by my first name. Only a couple of people on the staff seemed to resent me, including a black lawyer. I think he wanted to be the one and only. GM aggravated that situation somewhat by issuing press releases announcing that I was the highest-ranking black in corporate America. I took the same position about that distinction as I had in public life; my hiring showed how far the country had come and how much farther we had to go. It was not a matter of personal pride.

Needless to say, my experience at GM was quite different from anything I had ever had or ever even imagined. Coming into the legal department of the world's largest industrial corporation was a little scary, but it was also exciting because so many things were happening.

Three qualities of my new employer impressed me immediately. The first was that the people I worked with were uniformly bright, which was not always the case in government. The second was that most of the top executives were very keen and active listeners. I used to say that GM was the one place I had ever been where the client hears you the first time. The GM crowd knew the value of time and therefore wasted precious little of it. You could be in a room with thirty or forty people with one person laying out a problem for half an hour. You could hear a pin drop as everyone listened, took notes, and thought. They did not miss a point.

The third thing that impressed me was the speed with which GM took action. In government, leaders often discussed things without making a decision. When there was a lack of consensus, doing nothing was usually the right course of action. In the private sector, by contrast, based upon my exposure not just at GM but at other corporations on whose boards I served, there was no time to consider everybody's likes or dislikes. At GM there was discussion, and a decision was made within a matter of weeks. The appropriations were made and teams were formed, and before you knew it the building was built, the article was on sale. It did not happen overnight, but results were quick. In a competitive world that is the requirement. One objective of a business is to seek out the opportunities quickly and make the profit. Businesses do not, of course, have the problem of serving so many different constituencies. I suspect other reasons why businesses act more decisively are the considerations involved: the need to do things efficiently, to make profits for shareholders, and to earn higher salaries for executives.

During my first six months, I focused on familiarizing myself with GM's history, its largest legal cases, and the breadth of legal matters that its counsel's office handled. Occasionally, I gave advice on questions involving government regulations or policy. Then, in July 1967, the worst race riot in the nation's history rocked Detroit. Because African Americans were such a rarity at GM, I was assigned to help Roche, who was then president, to interpret the needs and desires of the black community.

I participated in a number of "race" decisions. I attended many of the early meetings of New Detroit, Incorporated—an organization formed to prevent future riots by bringing together business, labor, the black community, and civic groups to address the problems that had prompted the unrest. I listened to the huge agenda and advised Roche that GM should focus on a narrow list of fundamentals—jobs, education, and housing. I reasoned that some of the other issues that African-American leaders advocated—such as reforming the judicial system—were far removed from the corporation's expertise and wherewithal.

I also gave speeches to civic groups. But the more people asked my advice, the more I realized how little I knew. I had lived in Detroit only briefly, and my career had not focused on racial politics. Admittedly, I had held public office, and I knew African-American leaders. Still, there were urban affairs specialists far more conversant with the contemporary needs of the black community than I was. After several months, I suggested that GM hire some of these folks in its marketing department and other staffs. The company took my suggestion, but, more important, recognized the ebb of social change and hired some very bright young African Americans. By the time I left, there were several hundred blacks working at GM headquarters. In any case, being a black affairs expert was not a role for which I was prepared or a role to which I aspired. I was trained as a lawyer and wanted to stay one. I told that to Bridenstine, and he understood.

I switched my attention back to the law and handled a variety of questions. I reviewed and helped prepare testimony for congressional hearings and other federal, state, and local government agencies. Bridenstine assigned me to that job because of my general knowledge of government and the fact that I knew some of the committee and regulatory people. I was assigned to several large lawsuits involving the method by which GM was compensated for warranty work. My cases took me across the country. At one point, I had major litigation pending simultaneously in Hawaii and Puerto Rico. Some younger members of the staff kidded me that I had arranged the cases just so I could be in warm spots during the winter.

It took three years for me to decide that I fit in at GM. I still remember the day when I reached that conclusion. Several staffs were preparing testimony to present to a congressional subcommittee, and I was concerned that some of the "facts" were, at worst, not true and, at best, misleading. I insisted that we stick to the truth. There were a number of vice presidents who disagreed, but that did not bother me because I did not know and did not really care about corporate hierarchy.

Finally, someone decided that the best way to get the question resolved was at a meeting with Chairman Roche. About ten people attended the session at our New York offices. I presented the views of the legal staff after those on the other side had presented their argument. Roche agreed with some of the things I said and disagreed with others. What left the deepest impression on me was one point in the conversation when someone advocated taking an action that was not supported by the facts. Roche said something like, "At General Motors we don't make the facts. We just live with them the best way we know how." I could have jumped up and shouted with joy. At that moment, I realized that I was working at the right place.

My career began moving ahead. In 1970, Rosser L. Malone, who was then the general counsel, walked into my office and said he wanted to put me in charge of general litigation to replace Edward J. McGratty, Jr., who was retiring. My appointment was a surprise to me and to others. There were several other good candidates—one in particular—and McGratty was a Harvard-trained lawyer who had come to the corporation from the prominent Wall Street law firm Davis Polk & Wardwell. My background seemed too different to put me in the running. Nevertheless, I got the job. Two years later, GM put me in charge of three more sections in addition to general litigation.

In September 1974 GM promoted Frazer F. Hilder from associate to general counsel. I was named to his old job and became number two on the legal staff. I also received the title of vice president of the corporation. This was unusual. Normally, each staff had only one vice president, the person in charge. I took my new title as a sign that if I did not stub my proverbial toe I would succeed Hilder when he retired.

In 1974 or 1975 Hilder asked me to personally handle a twenty-million-dollar contract dispute between British Leyland and General Motors. I designated two men to help me—one was an engineer and the other was one of our lawyers in New York. They gathered all of the relevant facts, and I went over them. The final product consisted of about nineteen volumes of documents, briefs, and research of all kinds. We reviewed it with our solicitors in London, and I decided to use what is a fairly common tactic in these kinds of cases in the United States. To show that we had no intention of paying the twenty million dollars, we prepared as if we were going to file a lawsuit.

Our English solicitors suggested, at that point, that we hire a well-known barrister. In England there is a sharp divide between solicitors, who handle matters outside of court, and barristers, who appear in court. We met with the barrister in his office, which, according to the cornerstone, had been built in 1545. It was a shabby place, not in the grand style of major litigation lawyers in the United States. The barrister was a short, stocky man with a lovely Oxford accent. His assistant had a cockney accent and swallowed his words as he spoke; I could not understand most of what he said. There was also a young clerk who looked like a character out of Dickens. When he took a seat on one of the side chairs, he cupped his chin in his palm and rested his elbow on his knee. He did not appear to move or even blink his eyes for the next two hours.

I began listening to the barrister's summation of our case. I was utterly charmed until I realized that he was simply regurgitating the information that we had sent him in our nineteen volumes. It sounded far grander and more eloquent coming from him, but it was clearly the same material. There were no new revelations about English law or insights into our case. When he was through, I complimented him on his fine summation and asked him to assess our chances. He said they were less than fifty-fifty. I lost my enthusiasm for him at that point, especially when I remembered that we were paying him about four hundred dollars an hour, which was quite a lot in those days. We stood fast and eventually settled for about seven million dollars, which surprised and pleased then-chair Thomas A. Murphy.

One of the most interesting things I learned at GM was how the law works differently around the world. We dealt with legal issues arising from our international contracts in such varied places as Nigeria, France, Spain, Belgium, Germany, Brazil, Argentina, and Venezuela, to name just a few.

Sometimes conflicts arose not because of legal matters, per se, but because of differing expectations. I remember one situation in Argentina that came to my attention sometime in 1979 or 1980. GM was having a difficult time making any money there and was reorganizing its operations. A member of my staff told me that the very prestigious law firm we had hired there was overcharging us. Apparently the local GM management staff had negotiated a contract with the firm, under which it charged us four or five hundred dollars an hour even for such simple cases as workmen's compensation disputes, which are fairly routine around the world. Among other things, the contract included an escalator clause, tied in large part to the inflation rate, which was quite high in Argentina. On top of everything else, the law firm was paid in U.S. dollars rather than Argentine pesos, which made the contract even more lucrative.

After doing some calculations, we estimated that the firm had overcharged us several million dollars. I determined that merely firing it was not enough, so I assigned one of the best problem solvers on my staff, Julius L. Russu, to visit Argentina and ask members of the law firm what kind of plan they could come up with to take care of the situation. The firm's two senior members rushed to Detroit to see me. The lead lawyer, who spoke English and was quite cosmopolitan, pointed out that GM's own people had negotiated the contract. I told him that it was a lawyer's duty to represent clients fairly, and when he learned how onerous the contract was to GM and how lucrative it was to his law firm, he had an obligation to advise our management that it was disadvantageous. We parted company civilly. Within a short time, he indicated that his firm was willing to take steps to reimburse us. However, he did not want to pay us back in cash. Instead, he offered to give us credit for future work. It all came to about $1.5 million, and I agreed. At the same time, we began looking for different counsel in that area. When our credits ended, we switched law firms.

After my dealings in other nations, I concluded that the United States has the best lawyers in the world because we are essentially oriented toward the facts. In many other places, particularly in Europe and South America, lawyers tend to act like judges. If you are an outside lawyer and you bring them a carefully formulated question of law, they will give you an opinion as to whether or not your client is correct. By contrast, in the United States, lawyers represent their client's position and just start digging for the facts. After they decide what really happened, they are more than halfway home in deciding what is the best position for their client to take. Because of that trait, I believe that our lawyers have an edge in representing clients in many situations all over the world.

While I was associate general counsel I received several feelers from headhunters who were searching for general counsels for other corporations. I turned down most of these without much discussion. I reasoned that by making me associate general counsel and vice president, GM had signaled its interest in promoting me to the top legal job. I did end up meeting with one especially dogged recruiter. He was on an executive search committee looking for a general counsel for a mini-conglomerate based in Connecticut. He insisted on coming to see me. He discussed the advantages of being the top boss and he threw out various salary figures. When I told him I was already making more than he was offering to pay, he tried to sell me on how much nicer Connecticut was to live in than Detroit.

Finally, to get him off of my back, I told him he ought to contact my friend Wade McCree, who was a judge and might be ready for a career change. I did not know if Wade would be interested, but I thought he should have the opportunity to get off the bench and triple his pay if he wanted. The recruiter was very enthusiastic and went to see Wade, who was then on the Sixth U.S. Circuit Court of Appeals in Cincinnati. Wade, however, was far too much the consummate public servant to leave the bench, and the money did not faze him. I think his ambition was to go the U.S. Supreme Court, and it would have been wonderful if he had. He did end up as the second African American to serve as U.S. solicitor general after Thurgood Marshall.

In 1977, when Hilder retired, Chairman Murphy called me in to talk about the general counsel's job. He said, "Now it's one thing to promote you, but if it doesn't work out for some reason, it would be very difficult to fire you." It was clear he meant that given my race a dismissal or demotion would be hard to explain. I assured him that if things did not work out, I would leave without his having to ask me.

The question turned to who would replace me as associate counsel. My most likely successor was Paul H. Zalecki, who had worked with Hilder on a well-publicized Securities and Exchange Commission (SEC) investigation in 1976 and 1977. He was a brilliant lawyer, although some people thought he had a prickly personality. In any event

Smith joined General Motors' legal staff in 1967 and spent the next three years deciding if he could fit in. He was one of the few African Americans at headquarters, and he was unsure how his public service experience would mesh with the company's needs. He was impressed with his colleagues' intelligence, grasp of world issues, ability to listen, and willingness to make tough decisions. In 1977 Smith replaced Frazer F. Hilder as general counsel, shown here with him.

he was Hilder's choice, and I did not object to him. We always worked well together, and I expected our good relationship to continue. Murphy, however, had another candidate in mind. He suggested Robert A. Nitschke, an assistant general counsel who had a long tenure with GM and was our chief antitrust lawyer. In our past evaluations of him, Hilder and I had always thought that he should stay in antitrust litigation because he was so valuable to us there. But after Murphy mentioned him, Hilder and I agreed that the promotion would be a fitting capstone to Nitschke's career. Murphy then asked if I thought he should be made a vice president. I believed his question was some sort of test. In any case, I said, "Well, I would be awfully embarrassed if you did not name him to be vice president. After all, I've had the title for the past three years." That was the appropriate answer, and it was also clearly the one that Murphy hoped to hear.

Nitschke and I worked very well together for the two or three years until he retired. Roger B. Smith, the new chair, and I decided that we would replace him by promoting both Paul Zalecki and Eugene Hartwick to associate general counsel. This was my idea because I did not know how much longer I would stay. I wanted them both to get the experience of working with the staff as a whole rather than running units of it. They had opposite personalities, but they adjusted to the arrangement quite well and worked cooperatively.

In terms of my work as general counsel, Murphy once told me that the most singular contribution I made at GM was to change the way in which the legal staff interacted with the corporation's business managers. I believe the role of a corporate lawyer is to advise, not to decide what the businesspeople should do. For years before I came, members of the legal staff would take a position, then try to sell it to management. If management rejected their idea, then they felt compromised. I took a different approach. I believed that our job was to advise the managers and committees about the legal risks inherent in different courses of action. We were not exactly dispassionate; we always indicated what we believed was the best alternative. But, under my leadership, we never tried to force management to adopt our way.

As a matter of fact, there were many times when lower-level managers would love to have had the legal staff's backing in a purely business decision masquerading as a legal problem. Their hope was to use the legal staff to bolster their idea with their bosses. No matter how heady the suggestion, I tried to keep the two separate. We were trained as lawyers, not businesspeople. The one exception was when the proposed action might violate criminal law; then my staff's advice was always a firm "no."

Top managers liked this approach, but there were times when it also backfired. I remember a situation in which we strongly urged one course of action but then GM president Elliott M. P. Estes decided on another. The corporation ended up getting sued from one end of the country to the other, and the legal staff worked doggedly to protect it. Estes told me afterwards, "I don't understand you guys. You fought me like hell over this and now you're defending my decision like hell." I explained we were just doing our job. It really was one of the more amusing examples of an interaction I had with a top executive that I can relate without violating a confidence.

GM's legal staff, during the whole time I worked there, prided itself on its independence. Our lawyers felt they had the authority and the obligation to take independent stances. That continued to be true when I became general counsel. I always believed that top managers encouraged me to give advice even when they disagreed with it. I met very few people during my seventeen years at GM who did not want to do what was legally proper. There was a handful of folks who wanted to skate on thin ice and liked to run close to the edge, but they were few and far between. We would often get chided for being conservative. There was a joke that the legal staff should be placed on the top floor of the GM building for safety against bomb attacks because nothing could get through us. I took the humor as a sign of respect.

There were always big decisions to make in the general counsel's office, and, at first, I worried about them. In addition to heading a large staff with a big budget, I was also in charge of legal affairs for my client, the world's largest manufacturing corporation, that had a huge impact on employees, consumers, and folks all over the world. I had a long-time friend and counselor, a psychiatrist who was familiar with my background. I would go to see him when I felt that I was losing objectivity and getting too tense. He would help me refocus. On one occasion, I told him about my fear of "blowing" a large decision as general counsel. He thought about it for a minute and asked, "You were on the supreme court and you have been at GM for some years, how many decisions have you blown?" I thought about it and realized that I could not think of any—at least not major decisions. The realization was very reassuring. Usually, my hardest decisions at GM consisted of choosing whose advice to follow, especially in such highly specialized areas as tax and antitrust law. I never made decisions easily. However, I think I decided most matters soundly because I listened well and I had enough in the way of general legal knowledge and experience in working with people to be able to assess what was being offered.

One of the most important matters during my tenure was a federal grand jury investigation of GM for alleged tax violations. The probe centered on whether GM accountants had mistakenly written off $500 million worth of parts and equipment between 1972 and 1975 and then lied about their misdeeds to the Internal Revenue Service (IRS). GM claimed the write-offs, which lowered its taxable income for those years, were proper, and its employees had never misled federal agents. To lose would have meant not just great public embarrassment but also criminal indictments and fines and penalties that could have run to $1 billion. We were very careful to select an outside law firm that had strong tax counsel and good experience defending white-collar crime cases. We chose a Cleveland firm that had both those traits.

For the first six or eight months, we had a crew of about a dozen people working virtually around the clock, seven days a week. In a large company, that is the kind of furious activity that can be spawned from the issuance of even the simplest-looking subpoena or demand for information. I held many meetings with members of our in-house staff and attorneys from the Cleveland law firm. I had to make many decisions while the case was pending, which I would do after considering arguments pro and con. Most of my decisions turned out pretty well, not because I was so smart but because we had such excellent lawyers working on the matter. In June 1980 the U.S. Justice Department dropped the case, in essence proving our contention that the government was wrongly pursuing a civil audit with a criminal investigation. The following year, U.S. District Judge James P. Churchill agreed with our logic, when he ruled that the IRS could not use the 300,000 pages of records and 30,000 pages of transcripts obtained by the grand jury to prepare a civil case. Not surprisingly, GM's legal bills in the case were enormous.

Not all of my efforts as general counsel involved courtroom work or even GM directly. As general counsel of an influential corporation, I believed I had the wherewithal to help make meaningful changes in the law. I remember one case involving attorney-client privilege that could have had devastating consequences for corporate counsels nationwide. In the late 1970s, Paul Zalecki told me that the U.S. Justice Department was trying to compel the general counsel of the Upjohn Company to disgorge privileged information. Gilbert Merritt, a judge on the Sixth U.S. Circuit Court of Appeals, wrote an opinion in the case that narrowed privilege to communications between a corporate counsel's office and only a handful of very top officials. If the ruling had gone into effect at GM, members of our legal staff could have been called to testify about advice given to anyone outside the executive committee, from vice presidents on down. In practice, it would have been equivalent to setting up a grand jury inside most large U.S. corporations.

I looked into the matter and concluded that Judge Merritt's opinion was about the most restrictive I could find, and I thought it was terrifying. I contacted the general counsel at Upjohn and promised to rally support. I called general counsels at other corporations, and when the response was lukewarm, I took the matter to the national association of general counsels. The association rebuffed my overtures, insisting it could not become involved in litigation. Finally, I turned to Jones, Day, Cockley and Reavis in Cleveland, one of the best law firms in the Sixth Circuit. Its senior partners shared my concerns and suggested we join together in filing a brief with the court in support of Upjohn.

I thought that would be a bad strategy. Anytime major corporations—especially GM—seemed to be launching an effort to keep their operations more secret and confidential, the reaction of the courts was negative. I suggested that Jones, Day lawyers try, instead, to rally trial lawyers to petition the Sixth Circuit for a rehearing. I also contacted attorneys in New York City, who persuaded bar groups there to enter the fray. The Sixth Circuit refused to rehear the case. We wanted to make sure that the Supreme Court took the appeal, and several folks suggested that I speak about it with Wade McCree, who was then serving as solicitor general. The feeling was that if he flagged the case as important, the high court would be more likely to hear it. I knew McCree would be offended if I tried to trade on our friendship by approaching him about the matter, so I asked Erwin N. Griswold, who was at Jones, Day to do it. Griswold, a former dean of Harvard Law School, had served as U.S. solicitor general.

McCree followed regular procedures and assigned the question to his staff, and the Supreme Court did agree to hear the case. In its 1981 opinion *Upjohn v. the United States,* the high court substantially modified the Sixth Circuit decision. Its ruling, which was wider than Merritt's, was thoughtful and reflected a much better understanding of the problems of trying to render legal advice at a large corporation. My name never appeared in any records of the case, but I did play a crucial role. I was well aware that my influence stemmed not from me personally but from my position at GM. As its general counsel, I was in touch with a lot of lawyers, and together we had an impact.

Perhaps my most visible role at GM was as counsel to the board of directors. I attended their regular meetings, which were usually held the first Monday of every month. The August meeting was held in Detroit to coincide with the auto show; the rest were in New York. These meetings were impressive. Everyone I have ever discussed it with admits that he or she has been intimidated going into a corporate boardroom for the first time.

I first appeared before the GM board as associate general counsel. I had been invited to speak about the legal staff, its work, and its problems. This is a typical way of acquainting board members with someone who is being considered for higher office and whom they will have to approve. Anyway, I prepared carefully with the help of my staff. We compiled a write-up about our office, including the kinds of cases we handled, our budget, our staffing, and comparisons of various kinds. We turned over the information to the treasurer's office in New York, which made visuals to accompany my presentation. I rehearsed on Sunday and was ready to go on Monday. I had focused on what I would say, not on how it would be reflected in the visuals. When I was ushered into the board room, I became keenly aware of the huge screen to my right. Blues were succeeded by reds and greens. It got to be so exciting that I damned near lost my place because I looked up to see what was going on. I survived that first appearance.

Nevertheless, I was still a bit awed when I first took my seat as general counsel at the end of the table and saw the board members lining up on either side. When I was general counsel, GM's board consisted of twenty-three members, most of whom were from outside companies. A large number were either CEOs or just-retired CEOs.

During my years there, GM's board of directors was an impressive group. It included Catherine B. Cleary, president of First Wisconsin Trust Company, who was quiet, thoughtful, and very smart; Anne L. Armstrong, the former ambassador to Great Britain, who was very aggressive; John D. deButts, chair of American Telephone and Telegraph Company, who was stately and a great conversationalist; Walter A. Fallon, president of Eastman Kodak, who was obviously very bright but also dour and conservative; Dr. Marvin L. Goldberger, president of Cal Tech, who had an astounding intellect; Robert Hatfield, head of the Continental Group in New York City, who was one of the friendliest people I had ever met; and W. Earle McLaughlin, chair and president of the Royal Bank of Canada, who was a man of great wit and charm.

Others included John T. Connor, who had served as secretary of commerce under President Lyndon B. Johnson; Charles T. Fisher III, chair of the National Bank of Detroit and the grandson of one of the five Fisher brothers who founded the Fisher Body Works; James H. Evans, chair of Union Pacific, who was a lawyer by training; J. Stanford Smith, chair of International Paper Company; Raymond Herzog, chair of 3-M, Minnesota Mining and Manufacturing Company; and Howard J. Morgens, chair of Proctor and Gamble.

It took me a while, but I finally recovered from my awe. After reflecting on it for a few months, I concluded that although I was in no way as accomplished as most of them, I had earned my own way to the table. I realized that most of them had not been born with silver spoons in their mouths and like me had to work hard to get where they were. I have been lucky in one regard. I was never one to brag about the folks I had met, per se, but I have always been fascinated by their lives. As a youth, I was struck by that famous quote of Lord Chesterfield's in Carnegie's *How to Win Friends and Influence People*: "Every man I meet is my superior in some way, and in that I learn of him." This became part of my philosophy and carried on into my dealings with board members at GM. I would ask them about their philosophies and how they achieved what they had. Some businesspeople, of course, just had the desire to be big shots. But for most, it just boiled down to a desire to do well, along with energy, imagination, good communication skills, and the main ingredient—a lot of luck. With a few notable exceptions, most had a strong sense of right and wrong. They may have differed in what they believed was "right," but they were well intentioned and dependable. In other words, most of them shared my outlook on life.

I prepared carefully for board meetings. GM's financial staff put the chair's materials and the other matters on the agenda in a huge red book, copies of which were sent to all of the board members a week before the meeting. Using that as our guide, my staff and I prepared a blue book—a loose-leaf binder I filled with relevant legal opinions on matters pending before the board. I also carefully read newspapers for articles, usually involving legal matters pending with other corporations, about which the CEOs and presidents at the board meeting might ask my opinion. They were often seeking information for their own purposes because they had or might have similar problems.

Those first Mondays were crammed with activities. Mornings were devoted to board committee meetings. The most important of these was the finance committee, which was composed of GM's chair, vice chair, president, executive vice president for finance, the most recently retired chair, and three or four of the CEOs from other corporations who sat on our board. The finance committee meetings began at 10 A.M. and usually provided a preview of the board meeting because the committee members considered all of the tough strategic questions and big-ticket items. The agenda would begin with smaller items— matters involving fifteen to twenty-five million dollars—and then work its way up. I cannot remember one instance when the committee did not meet into the lunch hour, which left us scrambling for a bite before the board meeting began at 2 P.M.

Our lunch conversations were usually interesting. Most often they were about business matters; sometimes they concerned politics. Staff members, including me, had freedom to join in the talks up to a point. Good manners always dictated that I would defer to others in the room, especially the board members, who were in essence my employers. I never had any problems. But I did hear of one young executive whose career was sidetracked when he began freely offering unsolicited, hip-pocket advice to board members during lunches.

As general counsel I was required to submit a monthly report to the board on significant happenings in my office. It did not take me long to realize that almost nobody read these reports. So I decided not to elaborate on them. When the chair would ask me to comment toward the end of the meeting, I would pass over routine matters and focus on only a few pressing matters, such as huge lawsuits or where we stood in regard to federal governmental investigations. If there was no large item, I would just say, "I do not have any special topic, Mr. Chairman." When Murphy was chair, he would call on me by jokingly asking: "Is there anything from the generous counsel." This was an inside joke because some executives called us "Generous Motors"— especially when they thought the company was being too liberal in expenditures. Murphy referred to me that way when I recommended large settlements to avoid the possibility that we would lose verdicts. He would say, "There he goes again. The generous counsel." He always had a twinkle in his eye.

Because I had my blue book with me at board meetings, I was usually able to respond to any questions. I kept my answers brief because I knew that time was precious, and there was no reason to go into lengthy explanations about how my staff reached its conclusions. On rare occasions, when someone asked a question for which I was unprepared, I would give a guarded answer. I was never uneasy about the things I knew. Of course, there always were some legal questions I could not answer, and I was reluctant to give advice about those without checking them thoroughly. Surprisingly, most of these never came up at board meetings. Occasionally, I had problems with decisions that had been accepted by management without my knowledge. I would tell the directors that I wanted to check into these matters before the board members voted on them. Usually, they could wait until the next board meeting. On those rare occasions when a decision had to be made immediately, I would go outside and make a few phone calls, especially to people whose recommendations ran against my first instincts. Sometimes, I would change my mind; sometimes I would not. At least, I had a clearer grasp of what was happening.

Perhaps it is obvious, but I could never have succeeded in any of my jobs—especially as general counsel at GM—without a good staff. I was educated as a lawyer, but what I have been best at over the years is managing. "Participatory management" became a big trend in the 1980s, but I had practiced it instinctively from my first management job at the MPSC. I always believed that no one person could know everything, and the best results were obtained by melding everyone's views and talents.

I believe that what people call good administration usually boils down to being fair to everyone. I always tried to give employees what they deserved whether I liked them or not. Of course, I liked some people better than others, but I had no close friends on the staff and I did not play favorites. Years after I left GM, Bob Nitzschke and I were reminiscing, and he reminded me that nobody ever had any inside tracks with me, and my staff members came to realize that playing politics or mind games had no impact on me. I always believed that how workers perform for the organization should be the only standard for judging their performance. I put this maxim to work in two situations at GM.

The first involved Tom Watkins, a lawyer who seemed to resent me from the outset. I do not think it was racial. It was a matter of pride and insecurity. Before I arrived, other GM legal staff members looked to him as the reigning authority on appellate matters because he had worked as a clerk for the Michigan Supreme Court. He was a good lawyer, but clearly my experience outweighed his in this area. When I took over as general counsel, I called Watkins into the privacy of my office and said, "You know, when I came here you were the only person who I thought resented my coming." At first he demurred, then he tried to explain it. I stopped him and told him that I always believed he was a good lawyer and had a lot to contribute. Because he had a clear talent for personnel and budget matters, I asked Tom Murphy to create a new position on the legal staff, another assistant general counsel, and I placed Watkins in it. I also used him for legal reviews to get the benefit of his talents as a lawyer and to let him keep his hand in the practice of law.

Another somewhat sticky situation involved a person of color, Julius J. Hollis. He had detractors, both within the staff and outside it, for his somewhat imperious manner in dealing with people. I always defended him, even with the vice chair of the corporation, who once told me, "Yes, he's all right technically, but you ought to send him to charm school." I had observed during my time as associate counsel that he was not getting enough compensation in salary or bonuses for what he was doing. There were two white people whose responsibilities and performance were comparable to his and they earned significantly more than he did. I pointed this out to Hilder, but he took no action to remedy the disparity. I cannot accuse him of racism because he had put Hollis in charge of two important areas. Still, when Hilder retired, I made certain that Hollis got the pay he deserved. It took a couple of years, but I did it, despite the fact that Hollis always had a kind of negative attitude toward me. Fair is fair.

Although we disagreed about Hollis, Hilder and I agreed on most matters and we developed an organizational philosophy regarding how we evaluated personnel situations and rewarded employees for their contributions. When we took our places in 1974, Hilder, as general counsel, asked me, as associate counsel in charge of personnel and budget, to find out what Frank Kavalege did. Frank was in charge of a very small section called state and local regulations. I quietly pulled files about his office's work and talked to several people about it. I also talked to Kavalege without revealing any ulterior motive. After several weeks of investigation, I came away with the opinion that he was doing a very good job. Hilder and I discussed my conclusion and developed what we called the "Kavalege" principle.

Simply put: It was our solemn duty to see to it that the quietest and remotest lawyer on our staff got the same consideration as the most aggressive, self-promoting lawyer. This was particularly apt in Kavalege's case. I probably saw him only two or three times a year in the ordinary course of business. His office was on a different floor, and he traveled a good bit. He never bombarded us with a lot of memos to make sure we knew what he was doing. He just did his work very well.

185

He never asked for a raise, and he never tried to promote himself. Hilder and I determined that we would do our best to ensure that Kavalege and all of the other people similarly situated on the staff got paid what they deserved.

As associate general counsel I launched a similar campaign on behalf of our secretarial staff. Not surprisingly, there was a huge gap between the kind of money that a great many of the lawyers made—$150,000 to $200,000—and the much lesser amounts made by the secretaries. This became even clearer at bonus time for the lawyers. About 80 or 90 out of 140 or 150 lawyers received generous additions to their more than adequate base salaries. There were no similar payouts for anybody in the lower ranks—younger lawyers or secretaries or file clerks. The less experienced lawyers, of course, could aspire to someday join the upper echelons. The secretaries—most of whom were women—had no such hopes. They were taken for granted, which I believed was wrong because they were really top-flight people—very fast and highly productive.

Ironically, the staunchest opposition I had to improving the secretaries' salaries came from their manager, Barbara Cunningham. She was a fine and smart person, but I thought she had rather archaic ideas about how secretaries should be paid. In particular, I thought the women who came in from the outside and had six, eight, or ten years experience should be paid accordingly. Instead, they started at the bottom of the salary ladder. The automobile companies tended to pay secretaries more than the community in general, so the people who landed jobs at GM did get this benefit. Still, I believed it was unfair not to recognize previous experience. GM would never have thought about hiring lawyers on such a basis. I pushed for change, and Cunningham became very upset and complained. Hilder asked me what the fuss was about and seemed to shrug off the whole thing.

Eventually, I was able to bring more equity to the secretaries' salaries. As general counsel, I also established a career track that led from secretary to legal assistant. I hoped that this would send a message and lead to upgrading the status of these women in the organization. Before I left, a half dozen or more secretaries were able to move up into this slightly higher category, and several even went to law school. I take no credit for their becoming lawyers, but I do think all employers are better off when they encourage employees to reach higher goals.

Years later, I was with a bunch of my favorite people from the legal staff who happened to be women. We were chatting, and one of them, Pat Chasney, reminded me of an incident that happened just after I took over as general counsel. She was in the hospital, and I called to see how she was doing. I told her to stop by and see me when she felt well enough to return to work. She said how surprised she was that I took the time to do that. I was stunned. I did not even remember the incident. But I did appreciate the compliment. I took pride in the fact that I was able to make and keep friends not just among the men but also with the women with whom I had worked in my various jobs.

One key reason for that—a second given of good management—is that it is important to be humane to your employees. One of the young lawyers on GM's staff had been a consistently fine performer until his wife came down with incurable cancer. He took a lot of time off to be with his wife and their six-year-old child. The end of the year came around with talk of bonuses. A colleague on the management staff pointed out that the young lawyer had a bad year and argued that his bonus should be smaller than it had in past years. I disagreed, and he kept his bonus. I did not see it as a matter of sloppy sentimentality; he was a good performer and would have continued to be one had his wife not fallen ill.

A third key part of managing, in my opinion, is finding ways of encouraging young, talented employees while keeping longtime employees fresh by finding them new challenges. That is easier to do in a large corporation because there are so many more opportunities. For example, I had a senior lawyer who was quite skilled at writing. He had been editor of the law review in law school and had continued to write articles while he worked for us, even though that was not part of his job. He was doing a good job in litigation. Nevertheless, I called him in, told him I was happy with his performance, but suggested that he had such a great talent for writing that he might want to consider making a lateral move to head of the appellate division teaching younger lawyers to research and write correctly. He was taken aback, but after a couple of months came and said he wanted to try the new job.

Another lawyer who had been with GM twenty years had clearly peaked at what he was doing, and his job performance was barely adequate. He was also unhappy that younger people were moving past him. He had expressed an interest in computers, and when a huge project in that area arose, I assigned him to it. He worked at the new job several years and seemed quite happy at it. We might have been able to find someone better, but given all the considerations it worked out well for him and for us.

My attempts to reinvigorate older employees were not always successful, but I always felt it was important to try. There is a parallel to this in most organizations. For example, I am sorry when I hear young African Americans say they do not know much about Walter White and Roy Wilkins. Those two men gave so much of their time and talents to running the NAACP. Older folks remember them, but even the NAACP itself has not done enough in establishing permanent memorials to these great men. It does not have the sensitivity to recognize that in honoring the people who contributed in the past, we not only show respect, we also give hope to those who are coming along.

To summarize, in management as in many areas of life, the simplest actions produce the best results. When I became general counsel, I felt that I did not have a full enough grasp of what was going on in the organization. I also believed that we needed more frequent interchanges among the nine of us who headed the legal staff. I initiated a couple of practices. The first was to have an off-site retreat once a year to review our plans and prospects in considerable detail. We also enjoyed some time in the evenings and afternoons getting better acquainted. Those retreats produced a lot of good ideas, especially about administrative changes. I also initiated what I called the "weekly prayer meeting" at which we met for lunch once each week. Each of us would tell about the principle issues that had come up in our particular area of expertise—such as antitrust, tax law, and product liability. This was not only for my benefit. I learned that many of the other people at the table were grateful for the opportunity to hear about the successes and failures in other parts of the staff. My other goal was to train each one of them to be a successor to me because I believe one of the canons of good management is to prepare those who will follow you.

When I hit sixty years old, I decided that I would retire in two years. I was just plain dog tired. I had been working hard all of my life, and I worked awfully hard as general counsel. My career at General Motors had been wonderful because it was so challenging. I literally got to use every ounce of experience I had gleaned in my previous jobs—including all that I knew about people, organizations, government, law, and ethics. Still, I was growing weary, and I was not sure that I could keep the kind of careful surveillance of all the varied activities of the legal staff and be able to supervise the decision-making apparatus. When I went off for the Christmas break between 1982 and 1983, I came back with renewed energy. That lasted for about a month, and then at the end of every day I felt exhausted again.

After some anguish, I went to Chairman Roger Smith and told him that I wanted to retire. He tried to dissuade me. He told me to take three or four months off and relax. I said that would not be fair to the other members of the staff, especially when what I really wanted was to retire early. He advised me to stop working so hard by shifting some of my workload to my subordinates. I thought that was a bad idea because I was afraid that something would get away from me and GM would make a wrong legal decision because I was unable to pay attention. He persuaded me to discuss the situation with former chairman Tom Murphy, who was a good friend of mine.

Murphy and I spoke for about an hour. He tried to figure out if I wanted to leave because I was peeved or really tired. He told me about the many other GM executives who had retired only to find out that they were bored to tears. He wanted to protect me from making a quick, bad decision. I told him I was tired, my health was weakening, and I thought I had better leave. I had no desire to stay around until the day when I realized I was no longer on top of my job and someone else was in control of things. I could not abide that because of who I am and also because of my race. I did not want anyone saying, "Oh yeah, he's a pretty good old guy, but he doesn't know what's going on."

My health was deteriorating. I had been plagued by ulcers since my college days, and they were getting worse. GM's medical director arranged for me to visit a top-flight gastroenterologist at the University of Chicago. I was at the hospital for three and a half days of tests, and he confirmed what the doctors at Ford Hospital had told me: I had colon spasms. But he also concluded that I had an obstruction of my lower bowel. GM's medical director said I was entitled to be placed on disability leave with full pay for one year.

I remained as a vice president of GM, but I decided to resign as general counsel. I discussed my successor with Roger Smith and said the two fellows right behind me had complementary traits. Zalecki was a really bookish lawyer with the ability to see around four or five legal corners. Hartwick was more of a specialist in the personnel labor area and was an excellent administrator. More legal staff members endorsed him than any of the other candidates.

Sometime later, Roger Smith and I talked again, and he asked me what I thought of Elmer W. Johnson, who was a partner in the Chicago law firm of Kirkland & Ellis. I knew Elmer fairly well from his involvement with us at the tail end of the SEC investigations of 1976. I said: "Well, he's a specialist. He's a securities lawyer, and I've got people on the staff trained to succeed me. If you don't like Zalecki and Hartwick, there are four or five others who could run the staff well, who I have trained." This group included Mike Basford, Frank Allen, and a few others who were good lawyers, good organizers, highly respected, and knew the organization even better than I did.

Smith said none of them could replace him as chair; it was clear he thought Johnson could. It turned out otherwise, but that was his thinking at the time. He brought Johnson in as general counsel and also gave him the additional responsibilities of being a group executive in charge of the public affairs staff, which included public relations, government relations, and consumer affairs. He took up residence in the top management side of the fourteenth floor and turned over the day-to-day administration of the legal staff to Zalecki and Hartwick, who were both given the title of vice president. So after I left, the legal staff had three vice presidents. Johnson later brought in Harry Pierce as general counsel. Smith made a mistake because three or four of my assistants were far better acquainted with GM affairs and could have done a much better job than either Johnson or Pierce ended up doing.

Still, I was not surprised by Smith's choice. Roger Smith had many strengths, but in my opinion he was not well suited to be chair of GM. Unlike Murphy, who had a genuine sensitivity to people, a fine grasp of situations, and reacted reasonably to both, Smith used very different methods in dealing with subordinates and had a very different value system. He was, in my opinion, a good number-two guy. I never thought he was equipped to be number one. He operated a lot on hunches and emotions, and he loved to run close to the line. His strong likes and dislikes were based on his instincts. Murphy was concerned that my view of Smith colored my decision to retire, but it did not. I was just ready for a change.

3
Reflections

✦ 10 ✦
Business versus Government

I N MY POSITION as GM's top lawyer, it became clear to me that two of the greatest challenges facing corporate America were the explosion in the amount of litigation and government regulation. Perhaps because of my background in private law and the corporate sector, I was always more tolerant of them than many other corporate executives. I recognized the role that each plays as a check on capitalism, which, despite what some business leaders think, is far from a perfect economic system. At the same time, working at GM and later in my retirement as a member of the boards of Kroger and Detroit Edison, I came to appreciate the need for greater balance.

I became general counsel at a time when GM had never been so legally beleaguered. It faced an onslaught of litigation even though its products were safer and better built than ever. In any given year, my staff handled more than sixteen thousand matters. In one year alone, between 1978 and 1979, GM had a 20 percent increase in the number of cases filed against it, up to nineteen thousand. The largest percentage of legal matters concerned workmen's compensation, followed by product liability and breach of warranty cases. Many of the warranty cases were brought under a relatively new consumer protection statute that allowed treble punitive damages. The sheer volume of claims was not so much the problem as the possible impact that certain individual cases and certain types of cases could have on the reputation of the corporation.

GM was not alone. Other companies faced a similar legal barrage. This change was reflected in the growing size of corporate counsels' offices across the nation. In 1959 GM had fifty-four lawyers on staff.

Twenty years later, I oversaw one hundred fifty lawyers and one hundred seventy-five support employees.

The growing size of corporate legal offices reflected, in large measure, a shift in the kinds of cases they handled. In 1980 the American Bar Association conducted a survey of business lawyers. Those surveyed indicated that the areas of greatest legal need included antitrust (30 percent), government relations (20 percent), litigation (17 percent) and environmental law (10 percent). Decades earlier, government relations and environmental law would probably have ranked very low in importance, if they were included at all. With increased governmental regulation, they became far more important. As a result, lawyers become involved in matters that previously were left to designers, engineers, and managers. For example, when GM comes out with a new model automobile, it must comply with safety, emissions, and fuel economy standards. Designers and engineers must also take product liability into consideration. As a result, designers and engineers consult with lawyers at every stage of developing a new product.

There are many reasons for the litigation explosion. Part of the increase can be attributed to the increased number of lawyers, the publicity given to large verdicts, and the widespread practice of contingency fees under which lawyers rather than getting paid by the hour take a cut of the verdict or settlement costs. But would-be reformers have erred by focusing on the easiest targets: greedy litigants, unscrupulous lawyers, and injudicious judges. In fact, the roots of the problem are far more complex and run much deeper in our history.

The problem stems in large part from our American tradition of relying on the courts to resolve disputes that are better handled elsewhere. One of the glories of the common-law system—that is, law made by judges case by case in written decisions—is its flexibility. So it is natural when our society confronts new challenges of unprecedented difficulty that we turn to the courts. The problem is that by scapegoating a few wrongdoers when something goes horribly wrong, we miss the chance for a larger discussion of public policy on such questions as the environment, taxation, and employment.

This is apparent in many cases that arise from the unintended spillover effects of technology. In the past thirty years, there has been a growing recognition that complicated industrial society, however much it improves the welfare of the populace as a whole, can hurt many innocent people through accidents, failures, and environmental catastrophes. Lawsuits and the courts provide a means of pinning the blame on a few identifiable culprits. In instances where there is deliberate wrongdoing, this is the right course of action. In other situations, where the wrongdoing is the unintended and unpredictable, if inevitable, consequence of a new product or process, it makes little sense.

Another historic reality is our belief that every individual has the right for redress in the courts. Again, there is nothing inherently wrong with this. There are unquestionable rights that every American should enjoy, in addition to life, liberty, and the pursuit of happiness. For example, no employee should face racial or gender discrimination, and no consumer should incur harm because of a company's reckless disregard of safety. At the same time, however, there are many instances in which lawyers, litigants, and the courts have come to confuse rights with entitlements. Not every wrong has a single identifiable cause or malefactor behind it. Nor does every wrong constitute an entitlement that deserves redress. The real, underlying danger to every individual's clamor for specious rights is that we, as a people, end up looking to the law rather than to other people and ourselves for answers. It is a doomed quest because the law is useful as a last resort; it can never provide a substitute for morality or sound social policy.

Another contributing factor to the litigation explosion is the growth of class-action suits. This trend began when the federal rules of civil procedure were changed in the mid-1970s to allow a single plaintiff to begin an action on behalf of thousands of other people who may have similar claims, but who have never heard of the plaintiff or the lawsuit. Class-action suits have their use. It is expeditious to try a group of cases together when the plaintiffs have suffered the same kind and degree of wrong in a single mishap. On the other hand, class-action suits make little sense when lawyers link thousands of plaintiffs with only the most nebulous connections and, in the process, end up reaping enormous legal fees that dwarf the payouts to those who supposedly suffered the greatest harms.

The answer, then, to solving the litigation crisis does not lie with punishing only a handful of wrongdoers. Admittedly, the legal community itself could resurrect some old-fashioned internal discipline against lawyers who file frivolous suits. But that would provide only a partial solution. Instead, our society as a whole must strive to find a balance between righting legitimate wrongs and encouraging frivolous litigation. I agree with many legal theorists who say we must put

195

pressure on courts willing to entertain what were previously considered to be purely social or political questions. Ultimately, the legislative branch is the most important because it is closest to the people. It has much better tools for setting social policies than the courts ever will. That said, the ultimate solution to solving the litigation explosion lies in recognizing that Congress and state legislatures cannot possibly pass laws for every conceivable wrong. Once we recognize that, we will go a long way to solving both the litigation explosion and the problems of government regulation.

At my retirement party, Roger Smith said that one of my most important contributions at GM had been to teach him and other executives "the appropriate role of government," or some words to that effect. Perhaps because I had served as a government regulator and in private industry, I had a larger vision and a greater appreciation of the respective strengths and weaknesses of both sides. I never came to share the animosity that many business executives had about government and government regulation, although I did end up concluding that some reforms were needed.

When I first began working in the corporate sector, I was struck by how executives at GM and other companies assumed that government officials were markedly different than they were. Time and time again I would hear them assail bureaucrats and politicians as lazy and stupid, or both. I always rebutted this by saying that the government folks with whom I worked for ten years labored about as hard as GM folks. If they seemed to be a little wrongheaded when it came to corporate interests, it was more likely because they were following statutory and regulatory requirements rather than because they were stupid or prejudiced against industry.

I always pointed out that it takes a lot of skill to operate successfully both in government and in business. Often there is little difference between leaders of both; they attend the same schools, they work hard and are driven to succeed. Usually, the only difference is in motivation and responsibilities. Otherwise, they function in similar ways. Politicians use feedback, meetings, and voters' letters to feel out public sympathies. At GM we did the same thing through advertising. In both cases, we were running up the proverbial flag to see who would salute. In other words, government officials in many ways function like the heads of nonprofit corporations, except they have more time to debate before taking action and sometimes can decide to take no action at all.

Another thing that struck me about some business executives' hostility to government was their wrongly held belief that regulation was something relatively new and un-American. Nothing could be further from the truth. From the earliest days of our nation, business has had to operate within the framework of laws and regulations. We formally recognized this fact when the Constitution was drafted and gave Congress the power "to regulate commerce with foreign nations and among the several states." Growing populism during the past 130 years fueled this trend. It reflected our nation's strong distrust of large and powerful institutions. Legislatures and courts, especially in this century, have mirrored these sentiments, and accordingly there has been a continuing tendency to shape the rules so as to even up the odds.

Although some critics misunderstand the history of regulation in the United States, they are right that it has gotten out of hand. The federal government responded to the Great Depression of the 1930s by creating many regulatory agencies. That was just the beginning. During the 1950s and 1960s, spurred on by our nation's economic expansion, we came to believe that we had discovered the secret of insuring perpetual economic abundance. We believed we could manage the economy to avoid major business cycles, that our standard of living would improve indefinitely, and that we could declare war on, and triumph over, poverty. Social planners perceived our major challenge to be the fair apportionment and enlightened use of wealth, since the problem of its creation had been solved. Accordingly, we set in motion vast governmental programs and regulatory schemes on the assumption that our wonderful economic engine could sustain the burden. While the economy is booming, such regulations are tolerable. As we learned in the 1970s and 1980s that is not the case in times of recessions and production downturns.

From a philosophical standpoint, there is another problem with the burgeoning number of regulatory agencies. In essence, they have come to constitute a fourth branch of government. Unlike the three branches outlined in our Constitution, these regulatory agencies sometimes function without effective checks and balances.

The first reason for this is the sheer number of agencies. There were times while I was general counsel that it became clear that even the federal government was not sure how many there were. In 1979 President Carter reported to Congress that there were 90 regulatory agencies; a year later the Government Accounting Office stated there were 116.

Compounding this problem is the fact that Congress has created too many regulatory agencies that are assigned essentially one narrow mission. As a result, each agency tends to focus on its own immediate agenda without regard to the concerns of other agencies or other important national goals that could be in conflict.

Another inherent problem is that regulation sometimes seems predicated on the assumption that "government" is a single-faceted entity, created as a perfect surrogate for all Americans with no thoughts, ideas, or partialities of its own. But there is no way to believe that the individuals employed in all of those agencies always make decisions based on some nebulous goal of the "public interest" without allowing their personal preferences or interests to take any part.

Fortunately, there has been a growing awareness that government regulation has built-in imperfections, and this awareness has led to great changes at the federal level—limiting regulation, reorganizing agencies, and so on. But it seems to me that the underlying factors that lead to overregulation still remain.

First, as I mentioned in my discussion of the litigation explosion, is the idea that there has to be some kind of remedy for every perceived wrong in our society. In terms of regulation this translates into the belief that there is some kind of government remedy for every problem.

Second is the belief on the part of some regulators that wrongdoing is usually the result of sinister motives rather than oversight or accident. This attitude became more prominent during my days at GM, when the federal government increasingly relied on criminal law to regulate corporate behavior. Historically, the government mostly used civil penalties to force compliance and relied on criminal sanctions as a last resort to punish flagrant wrongdoing.

During the 1970s, the federal government began aggressively using criminal punishment of corporations and, more threateningly, their employees. This new practice was particularly evident in such areas as securities, overseas payments, taxes, and environmental control. Some state governments, taking their cue from the federal government, launched similar campaigns. This enforcement attitude flourished in an atmosphere created by critics who claimed that corporations have too much economic and social power. Not surprisingly, because these criminal prosecutions were meant to have a deterrent effect, the government focused its attention disproportionately on larger and more visible corporations.

I remember two cases while I was at GM that illustrate this trend. The first involved an investigation by the Environmental Protection Agency (EPA) and the Federal Bureau of Investigation (FBI) into alleged irregularities in the selective enforcement audit of emissions on certain 1978 models of Buicks. A selective enforcement audit is an EPA-supervised check of the emission performance of vehicles currently being assembled to determine if their emissions conform to the levels required. The EPA requires the manufacturer to provide a signed statement indicating that the audit was conducted in accordance with all applicable laws and regulations. One of the requirements is that the vehicles presented to the EPA for selection during the audit be representative of the then-current product. The EPA alleged that the vehicles presented to it for selection were not representative and the statement GM filed was false. What began as a civil investigation abruptly turned into a criminal investigation. The matter was not resolved until GM convinced the EPA and FBI that the matter could be resolved civilly. We then reached a quick settlement. GM became involved in a similar battle with the IRS about whether it could expense machine repair parts during one year or another. What was disturbing about these matters was the government's predisposition to suspect criminal wrongdoing, even when there was little evidence of it.

I could understand, given some of these situations, why my colleagues in the corporate world decry regulation. At the same time, I have always been amused when I hear businesspeople say how much more efficient the private sector and its leaders are than government bureaucrats. They sometimes go on to suggest that business should even take over some government responsibilities. Of course, the obvious flaw with this argument for privatization is that government has a very different purpose from business. Its goal is to do the most good for the greatest number of people, an aim that has little to do with the bottom line that drives so many corporate decisions.

Another reason why such proponents of privatization are wrong is that they fail to admit the obvious: corporations and capitalism in the United States produce immense waste. Often the level of corporate waste is far greater than anything in the public sector. Many projects launched by major corporations fail; a few succeed only because of the financial strength of the organization built up by previous operators over the years. There is another kind of waste reflected when corporations decide that their profits outweigh any considerations of the environment or the social system itself.

The underlying assumption of capitalism, of course, is that people vote with their dollars. The problem is that ultimately that offers little restraint. We are a nation of overkill. Even though I worked for a car company, to me it is the ultimate obscenity to see so many people going and coming from work in automobiles that cost upwards of twenty thousand dollars and more. It is wrong to use all of those resources—the person's and the world's—to create and buy one vehicle that delivers one person to and from work. We use up enormous amounts of petroleum and other resources that could be expended for the common good. It is not just a matter of public transportation. Almost every aspect of our throwaway society is the same. We make things to toss out; we consume like madmen just to throw it all away. We use up forest after forest to produce magazines that do not tell us anything except what kind of mascara some low-grade pop star wears or what kind of clothes some sports figure wears. I am not opposed to advertising per se; it can be useful to inform consumers about valuable products. At the same time, however, our economy spends billions convincing people to buy things they do not need.

In other words, both government and business deserve criticism. They have the same constituents—government calls them voters and business calls them customers—but they are the same Americans. Business's biggest consumer problem is also government's biggest problem—the widespread suspicion of both institutions. It makes it harder for business to sell its products and government to sell its programs. We have witnessed technological miracles, so perhaps it is not surprising that many people wonder why a society that is capable of sending people to the moon cannot build automobiles that never break down or manage communities without crime, unemployment, and social decay. Perfection, of course, can never be reached. There is not enough money, available talent, or simple answers to solve all complex problems. But, I think, both business and government can further their credibility by not promising more than they can deliver and by taking a few steps at improving and showing their concern for the public interest.

I sometimes think that those businesspeople who resist all criticism of business and those government people who can find nothing right about business might do well to keep in mind E. B. White's epigrammatic definition of democracy: "The recurrent suspicion that more than half the people are right more than half the time."

One obvious way to foster improved understanding—and this is partly based on my own experience—would be to have more business-people serve in government. This would accomplish two things. First, government would better understand business. This is especially important in those instances where regulators seem to operate in a utopia far removed from the realities of the marketplace. Second, when the businessperson returns to the private sector, he or she will bring back a better understanding of the necessary and appropriate functions of government.

In any case, the answer lies in striking a balance. Given the complexity of modern society, we must accept, even welcome, a substantial measure of government regulation. But we should be wary of letting it get to the point where it chokes progress, and we must find ways of keeping it rational, accountable, governed always by the spirit of constitutionalism.

Rather than behaving like mortal enemies locked in mortal combat, government leaders and business executives need to recognize that, whatever differences may exist, neither can effectively replace the other. Business is always going to have to live with some government regulation, and government must recognize that most economic decisions in our system will continue to be made in the private sector.

To paraphrase Irving S. Shapiro, the former chair of DuPont (E. I. du Pont de Nemours and Company), business leaders have the responsibility to work with government to achieve public goals, to handle new safety risks carefully, to find ways of introducing new technology without displacing workers and causing larger economic problems, to blend business goals with energy and environmental concerns, and to join other sectors of society in addressing recurring national and international problems. Business cannot stand apart from our great social problems.

The bottom line is that business, more than government and other segments of American society, is in a better position to help solve the challenges we face as a nation. Business has enormous power; it has enormous resources in terms of money and brainpower, and it has the machinery with which to make prompt decisions. It is more adaptable, more flexible, and more receptive to change than government. It also can provide the jobs and the investments that spell permanent improvement in areas where government can offer only stop-gap measures.

For this reason, I have never had patience with social critics who stand outside of business and criticize it. Civil rights leaders were long guilty of this kind of myopia. They failed to appreciate that it is business, not government, that is often in the best position to fulfil the needs and develop the leaders of the African-American community. Although this situation has changed, for many years African-American leaders and other liberals wore their disdain of business as a source of pride. This is a poor strategy. Businesses, after all, are human institutions, capable of doing good or ill. They respond to logic and history and pressure and many things. I think it is far better to populate a company, such as GM, with people who have certain sensitivities and can use them to persuade the company to go in proper directions than to stand outside and do nothing. I would never boast that I changed GM policy single-handedly, but I am immodest enough to suggest that I have had some impact. I prided myself for working at GM, which made substantial progress on many fronts—including minority advancement.

Jobs are the true cornerstones of any effort to bring more minority Americans into the economic system. GM took many steps to promote minority business in the wake of the Detroit riots. Although these statistics are old—they are from a 1980 speech I gave to the National Business League—they give some idea of the huge impact that one company can have.

In 1967 GM developed a program to help meet the needs of minority-owned banks. During 1979 alone it deposited $629 million—about 24 percent of its funds—with these banks. In 1968 the automaker established a minority supplier program to promote and accelerate purchases from minority business. This prompted an active search for minority suppliers, the establishment of realistic objectives to attain greater supplier participation, and provision for managerial and technical support for suppliers who showed promise. The number of minority suppliers and their business with GM grew from $1 million in 1968 to $200 million by 1979.

GM also created a Minority Enterprise Small Business Investment Company (MESBIC) that loaned $3.8 million to 125 minority firms. These loans leveraged an additional $20 million from other lending sources. Under the MESBIC program, a GM employee was assigned to work with each minority entrepreneur to provide technical and managerial assistance in the day-to-day operation of the business.

GM had two programs designed to encourage minority participation in the insurance field. The first involved reinsuring GM Employee Group Life Insurance. By 1980 the company had placed $350 million with four minority-owned firms. The second involved placing GM property damage insurance through minority brokers and agents; this totaled about $4.9 billion by 1980.

All of these programs demonstrate that enlightened business practices can make a profound difference. It is one of the ironies of American life that no matter how many visionary programs they foster or how much social good they spawn, executives at GM and other corporations will never receive the same credit that those in government get for achieving far less. If you flip through the pages of *Who's Who in America,* you will notice that in the biographies of public personages, such as judges, congressmen, governors, and mayors, there is a listing of many honors and distinctions that are accorded to them, including honorary doctorate of law degrees. By contrast, people in the private sector, corporate presidents in particular, receive few of these distinctions.

I always found this discrepancy strange because we are after all a capitalistic society, and it does take great skill to run a successful business. Corporate presidents have enormous responsibilities and wield an enormous impact on the community because of the vast resources that they manage to deploy on behalf of shareholders and employees who receive job security, good pensions, and health care.

I remember one incident involving GM chair James M. Roche. People in the auto industry revered Roche. Some folks even viewed him as a saint of industrial democracy—a man with leadership qualities who showed great courage in handling public and corporate issues. On top of everything else, he was a self-made man. He was born into a poor family in Elgin, Illinois, and overcame poverty to become head of the largest industrial corporation in the world. When I was serving on the board of regents of the University of Michigan, I suggested that the school give Roche an honorary degree. I did not think this was a strange request given Roche's service to Michigan and to the world's business communities. After several weeks, one of the chief academic officers of the university came to me and said there was too much faculty opposition for Roche to get an honorary degree.

I have received eight honorary degrees over the years. Most of these came for my public work, not my service with GM. After my years at GM, I would run into black leaders who asked why I had "disappeared." I found this interesting since I arguably wielded more influence as general counsel of a corporation with 800,000 employees and profits of more than $100 billion than I ever did in my public life.

✦ 11 ✦
Race in Perspective

I N THE LATE 1960s and 1970s the racial situation in the
United States seemed better to me than it ever had. The
nation appeared quite ready to make a lot of changes—
and did. Since then, unfortunately, I think we have gotten stalled, and
in some cases, even moved backwards. Too often, our national dia-
logue on race has devolved into a screaming match suffused with emotion and based on faulty assumptions and unrealistic expectations. We
have ceded the debate to extremists on both sides. Once useful social
policies—such as affirmative action—have become locked in a rhetorical and political time warp. As a tragic result, we are now considering
getting rid of such programs rather than adapting and improving
them to meet changed conditions. What is needed, now more than
ever, is for well-meaning citizens—both white and black—to reclaim
the moral middle ground so we can again begin to move forward.

There are many reasons for our current malaise. To begin with,
the American attention span is not very long, and our tolerance for
intractable problems is low. When we cannot solve problems quickly
or easily, we tend to turn our backs on them. In this vein, many whites
have dealt with the nation's racial problems by simply denying that
they exist—as if by not recognizing them they will simply disappear.

Many blacks, on the other hand, talk as if there has been little or
no progress. This is not only patently false, it also infuriates those—
whites and blacks—who have worked so hard for improvement. More
important, the belief that nothing has changed becomes a self-fulfill-
ing prophecy and an excuse for accepting failure.

Both of these errant white and black views stem from the lack of
a larger, historical perspective. We should begin by being realistic. The

fact that racism is the most difficult of all problems in American culture is evidenced by the simple, stark fact that it predates the founding of the republic itself. Racial problems have been and always will be complex. They defy easy, quick solutions.

At the same time, we have made great strides. We have survived the Civil War, the early peak years of the Ku Klux Klan, the Jim Crow laws under which I grew up, and the riots that rocked the cities during the 1960s. Admittedly, we still face problems of unemployment, inner-city turmoil, and other inequities. Still, I get frustrated when I listen to the pessimists. I get especially angry when I hear them attack the United States—as if somehow our nation's racial problems are unique. A brief review of the morning's headlines amply proves that we are not alone. Just look at events in eastern Europe, the Middle East, and Africa.

Set against the world stage, I believe, the United States has done a remarkably good job of dealing with diversity. Our nation is a wildly improbable combination of more than 250 million individuals representing virtually every racial, cultural, and national element of the human race. It is a vast complex made up of a spectacular variety of groups pursuing—sometimes at cross-purposes—their own economic, social, and religious interests. It is a forever evolving community whose mores, governing principles, and change-powered economy discourage rigid class structures, hereditary elites, or similar forms of social cement that have held together other societies. It is not merely remarkable that a nation of such positively incongruous composition has endured and thrived for two centuries. It is unprecedented and it is incredible.

If we measure nations and societies by the way they allow each person the freedom to aspire to great heights, to move freely, to speak and worship freely, and to go as far as his or her abilities will take them, then we will have to admit that the United States is far ahead of most.

Compared to six months or six years ago, there may have been little improvement. But in the past fifty years, change has been amazing. Ask any of us who are my age. Compared with when I was growing up, it is a new world.

I attended segregated schools in Memphis, and I remember a time when black folks were lynched for just trying to vote. To many people nowadays these little swatches of history may seem light years away, but there are many of us who saw them happen, read about them, and in some cases lived them. Few people who lived through those awful things will say that no progress has been made. In terms of the legal structure, there are no laws left on the books anywhere that deliberately discriminate against blacks. Blacks have educational and employment opportunities in both the public and private sectors unheard of fifty years ago.

It is not just a matter of personal experience. Signs of change abound. In government there have been decisions like *Brown v. the Board of Education* and legislative enactments such as the Civil Rights and Voting Rights Acts. In higher education alone, perhaps the most significant advance has been under way for more than four decades. The University of Michigan succeeded in raising the number of black students to 10 percent during the five years that I served on its board of regents in the late 1960s and early 1970s. Harvard Law School, which may have had two or three blacks in the 1940s or 1950s, had more than one hundred when I was visiting there in the 1980s. In business and industry, either voluntarily or under the persuasion of law, many more jobs are available, and increasing numbers are of high quality.

This is not intended to let anybody off the hook for what remains to be done, but it is a simple recognition that we are winning the struggle, not losing it. It is a failure of leadership not to recognize positive, as well as negative, phenomena. The captain of the ship has the same responsibility to report the calm seas as he has to report the rocky shoals and approaching storms. Although the latter is done with perhaps greater frequency and certainly greater urgency, the need is there and the duty is there to report the favorable so that passengers and crew will have a standard by which to judge.

We should be hearing, more and more, that in this country with so much flexibility and freedom of choice and of movement, changes most often bring opportunities, especially for those who see them and are prepared to take advantage of them.

The rhetoric of "we're losing, we'll never make it" is terribly self-defeating. Many of us feel we have not come far enough. I do not think we have. But to use that as a basis for feeling we have made no progress, that nothing will ever happen, inculcates in younger minds more than a defeatist attitude, it develops a defeated attitude. The progress we have made is definite, it is measurable, it cannot be refuted. We have made tremendous gains; we must have the confidence to accomplish even more.

The seeds of what we have achieved provide a good foundation for future improvement. Now instead of sitting on our laurels claiming no further work needs to be done or claiming nothing has changed, we should take stock, leave what works in place, and change what has become outmoded.

This kind of approach could get us moving on several fronts. One that comes to mind is affirmative action. The good kind, which I have always advocated and helped implement as a corporate executive and as the first African-American trustee at the University of Michigan, provides equal opportunity to the means of achieving success. Unfortunately, that has evolved into something that I find more questionable.

A lot of people have forgotten that affirmative action began long before the 1960s. It started at the beginning of World War II when President Franklin D. Roosevelt issued an executive order forbidding

Smith was a strong believer in public service. Among his civic posts was serving as the first African-American trustee at the University of Michigan. He is pictured here with Dr. Robert C. Weaver and University of Michigan president Robben W. Fleming.

employment discrimination by companies supplying war material to the government. In 1948 President Harry S. Truman ordered equal treatment for all military personnel, effectively ending the segregation of the armed services. Even before an aide to President John F. Kennedy first coined the phrase "affirmative action" to describe a federal program of requiring government contractors to recruit and hire blacks, it had been used in a number of countries. Even a section in the United Nations Charter allowed for "special measures for the sole purpose of securing adequate advancements of certain racial or ethnic groups."

I point this out by way of showing that affirmative action programs began as a way of addressing long-standing social injustices that could not have been eradicated by any other means. That was still true in 1968, when I joined the board of regents at the University of Michigan during the height of student protests. The university gained notoriety for its unrest, in part because its best-known student leader, Tom Hayden, went on to achieve national fame.

It was not a time or an era in which people were tolerant of those seeking common ground—in terms of race or any other issue. I ended up growing frustrated with both sides. In 1968, after meeting with student leaders, I urged my fellow regents and the university's administrators to accept faculty and student input on such questions as increasing students' role in decision making, problems of African-American students, whether the Reserved Officers Training Corps (ROTC) should exist on campus, and whether the university should engage in classified research. I thought it was a matter of simple fairness that those affected by the board of regents' decisions should have some say. It was also a matter of common sense. By addressing hot-button issues, I argued that we could avoid providing the lunatic fringe with causes to exploit. I was overruled by my fellow board members, and protests shut down the campus.

Not surprisingly, as the only black member of the board of regents, I focused many of my efforts on increasing the numbers and improving the lot of African-American students on campus. When I joined the board of regents, the University of Michigan had a shockingly low number of black students—about four hundred out of a total enrollment of approximately thirty thousand. It also offered no black studies courses. During the spring semester of 1970, both white and African-American members of the Black Action Movement (BAM) staged protests and disrupted campus life. Among other requests, they demanded that the university increase its black enrollment to 10 percent and institute an Afro-American studies curriculum.

Although I shared their larger goals, I did not agree with their tactics or many of their specific requests. For example, I sat on a committee to establish an Afro-American studies program in May of 1969. During one roundtable discussion, a student proposed organization of an interdisciplinary studies program to deal with problems of black people's existence in a hostile society. My response to him, and I still believe it is apt, was: "Do you want a black psychological crutch or do you want to probe the historical and cultural situation dispassionately to see what really happened and why?" I argued that I could see the value of research that could result in productive advances by studying the black experience in the greater context of American history and society. After all, the United States has never been monolithic. You only have to look at the influx and assimilation of Catholics, Irish, Germans, Jews, Italians, Arabs, Hispanics, Africans, and other ethnic groups to appreciate that. All of these groups had problems to overcome in order to assimilate. A useful approach to history appreciates the fact that the African-American experience is unique, but it is still the experience of only one minority group among many.

Perhaps the most pressing problem, about which we all agreed, was the need to increase African-American enrollment. In those early years, I became somewhat of a traffic cop fielding letters from black students complaining that they had not been admitted and administrators explaining their reasoning. As I explained to everyone concerned, I had great doubts about any policy that placed nonachievers in a competitive situation with students who had high academic qualifications. This was often traumatic for students who never realistically had a chance to succeed. Some folks who questioned my hard-line approach pointed out that a large number of marginal admittees to various schools were able to do the required work. In my mind that did not prove my approach wrong, it merely suggested that methods of measuring ability and achievement needed some modification to more accurately reflect the qualifications of applicants.

Within five or six years, the University of Michigan did increase black enrollment by three thousand—roughly approximating 10 percent of the student population. I took pride in that, but I urged the board of regents and university president R. W. Fleming to go further. In a memo to them in April 1969, I urged that the university adopt a policy that went beyond race to include all disadvantaged students. I argued that the matter of black admissions should be regarded as only the first leg up on a general policy of affirmative action admissions with respect to the "disadvantaged" of whatever race, color, or creed. The ultimate goal I hoped for was that this broad group of deserving students would comprise 15 to 20 percent of the student body.

I suggested that "disadvantaged" be defined as: "Any applicant without regard to race, creed, or color who has demonstrated potential so that admission to the University would be with a high probability of success, but who, however, does not meet standard admissions criteria for the reason that his ethnic, geographic, or other origins have tended to produce a student whose achievement is substantially below potential."

I argued then, and I believe now, that such a broad-based policy was needed because it was morally and legally fair, it would have enhanced the university's image, and it would have avoided a backlash from angry whites, Hispanics, Asians, and Native Americans. The backlash I predicted then has come about, not just at the University of Michigan but across the nation.

Another ingredient in the tragedy of affirmative action—and I say this as someone who has visited and spoken at many college and university campuses—is the way in which so many students who have been the beneficiaries of it have no sense of history. In the main, they seem to feel that admission to these schools is their birthright. They do not see that this birthright—if that is how it should be viewed—was earned by other blacks, their parents, their aunts and uncles, their grandparents, and all the people who came before and suffered from discrimination.

In other words, they have lost sight of what matters. They have lost sight of the question of whether or not they should have a special entitlement. They seem not to ask what they owe in return. The saddest thing of all to me is that so many believe they should be able to come in with lower grades, to graduate with lower grades, then go on to get the same kinds of jobs as higher-achieving students. To me the whole question of whether there is cultural bias in standardized tests is so much Mickey Mouse nonsense. These tests are standardized just so everyone—native whites, African Americans, Jews, Asians, and immigrants—are able to use the language effectively in writing and speaking.

The alarm bells have been sounding for some time. Affirmative action—as it is presently used—should not go on forever, and African

Americans should be the first to admit it. The flip side is that many whites have also misconstrued affirmative action with the twisted American attitude of "what's in it for me?" They claim we can abandon it altogether, even though there is still a definite need, just as there is for veterans' preferences.

This view in white society is nurtured by a commonly held misperception that when human rights, including those based on affirmative action, are exercised according to the law, the majority gives something away and is bestowing some special indulgence on the minority. This is not so. When we allow talent to soar without arbitrary restrictions based upon gender, race, or anything else, we not only allow individual fulfillment, but the society is made better because each person is allowed to contribute his or her maximum. We have made progress, but there is much yet to be done.

I have always disliked those who say the only reason that corporate America helps blacks is because of government pressure. Undoubtedly that is true at some corporations, but there are many more companies that recognize the value in what minority businessmen have to offer clients. In other words, they recognize, as one business leader said, that "civil rights is good business." When GM began actively recruiting blacks, one executive told me: "If we shut out capable people because of their color, their sex, their religion, or their national origin, we are hurting those people, we are breaking the law, and we are hurting ourselves as well."

One reason our society has failed to reexamine affirmative action and similar programs is because of the civil rights movement's historic reliance on white guilt. One of the things that has bothered me for years is the insistence by so many black leaders and would-be leaders that virtually every failing of the African-American group is attributable to racism.

In 1967, when GM assigned me to speak to civic groups about the race riots, I was struck by how many black folks tried to pin all of the blame on white racism, and how many whites accepted the guilt. The nation's race problems, then and now, are far more complicated than that.

The guilt of white liberals and the social paranoia on the part of many blacks struck me as a social psychopathic reaction far more dangerous in its potential results than the social ills themselves. It becomes a dodge and a convenient scapegoat for every kind of human failing we have, individually and collectively. It is a failure to be truthful, to be honest with oneself, to look in the mirror and ask in the Biblical words: "Is it I, Lord?" It reminds me of that expression: "We have met the enemy and it is us." If we cannot be candid, honest, accurate, and sincere, about both our faults and our virtues, our conclusions and our actions are likely to be emotional and irrational. All of the soul-searching for group answers can only result in a stultifying uniformity of individuals into a kind of mass-produced goodness, rather than the removal of artificial barriers to personal achievement. In other words, the ultimate goal should be to reaffirm heterogeneity and individuality.

In 1968, when the National Advisory Commission on Civil Disorders came up with the conclusion that white racism lay at the foundation of racial strife, my immediate question was: Where do we go from here? While whites are working at overcoming their racism, what are Negroes supposed to do in the meantime? I thought at the time this was a narrow approach. It implied that blacks should simply take the position that the problem is purely a matter of ridding the country of racism. In the first place, this was not very likely to happen, and second, it was not likely to happen in the foreseeable future. To pursue such thinking, even subconsciously, was to give the problem the aspect of a guardian and ward relationship, which is despicable and demeaning, and deprecatory as well.

There is no doubt that many problems are attributable to historic racism. Certainly the legacy is there in terms of generation after generation of deprivation, first in slavery and then in the segregation that followed. Despite all that can and has been said about that, for us to dwell upon injury only induces a kind of paranoia that makes us hypersensitive to the minutest slight and conditions us to think we have nothing to do with the solution and are merely helpless victims. Legitimate blame should be carefully analyzed, but we can also face our own failings, not so much of race, but as an ethnic and social group. Once we face the facts, good and bad, our solutions will less likely be symbolic and nonproductive, but realistic, self-generative, and productive.

When I was working with New Detroit, Inc.—the organization established to rebuild the city after the riots—it became clear to me that most of the white members were doers while most of the blacks were protestors. I thought the whole thing was doomed to failure without more black business leaders and professionals on the committee. After all, to be successful, we needed not just folks who knew the problems but also those who could solve them.

It has always puzzled me why African Americans, who have been so close to one of the most dynamic societies and economies in the history of mankind, have not picked up more pointers on how to be self-sustaining by simply watching other people function, including a lot of immigrants who come here not knowing the language and culture.

I always take offense when I hear black leaders, especially the younger ones, who point to a particular social ill, then claim that it is simply the product of three hundred years of slavery and discrimination. Take, for example, the problems of performance in the Detroit public schools. The system is overwhelmingly run by black people— the school board, the principals, the teachers, and the students. Granted, the funding is not equal to schools in the white suburbs. Still, I attended schools that received lower funding in neighborhoods just as poor, in a school system far more racist, and I received a good education. Clearly, the problems go beyond a simple matter of racism.

I think a scrupulously honest and objective analysis of the various factors that produce extremely high crime rates, extremely low school attendance and performance, and other kinds of problems would result in a modification of the conclusions as to what our problems really are. They are undoubtedly mixed, with a large percentage falling on individual shoulders. Give outside forces like segregation and discrimination their proper weight, but also give internal things— lethargy and failure to organize, for example—their proper place in the analysis, and we will come up with better solutions and better results.

I think the sooner we realize that it is not always racism or not largely racism that holds us back in so many areas, the sooner we are going to be able to pull ourselves out of the muck and mire and perform on a par with everybody else. Nobody is going to save us but us.

My sons and I have discussed at various times this business of racism, and I think we have concluded that people are affected by many emotions other than racial prejudice: fear, greed, selfishness, lust, envy, and so on. It is a mistake to assign racism as the motivation for a hostile act just because someone is white. My rule of thumb is to look at all the possibilities for conflict, and if none of them apply, then and only then assume it is racism. I never begin by jumping to that conclusion. It is unfair, and at a more practical level, it is not likely to help in analyzing or resolving the situation.

The flip side of blaming discrimination for all ills is the ridiculous notion held by some blacks that being white somehow solves all problems. They ignore the fact that whites, like blacks and everyone else, can be born poor or born into families with little energy, brains, or imagination. They, too, can run into misfortunes such as bad health or other disasters.

When racism undercuts sympathy and empathy for anyone in real trouble—whether they are white, black, brown or whatever—it is dead wrong. One of the basic requirements that each of us should strive for is to nurture that warm human strain that makes us sympathize with people of all nations and all nationalities. As I used to tell my sons, "You are kin to all the other four billion people on earth, and although some of them won't recognize it, it's a fact." Living on this small planet, we are somehow remotely involved with the destiny of everybody else, and we all have to be thoughtful.

I know some people may think that I am very hard on my fellow African Americans. Well, I am really not. I have known and have had great fondness for the hundreds of people I have met over the years who have had real struggles, who have faced difficulties and great problems trying to get an education, and who have, relying on their own abilities and energies, pulled themselves up and have done remarkably well despite the handicaps they have had to overcome.

I admit I am very hard on black leaders who do not know anything but the politics of protest. They spend so much time blaming external forces that it never occurs to them to see what we can do for ourselves. In a speech I first made twenty years ago, I said what African Americans need is a "Department of the Interior." We already have a well-developed "Department of the Exterior"—spearheaded by such national groups as the NAACP and the Urban League and many local and regional organizations that examine outside problems such as segregation and discrimination. The "Department of the Interior," by contrast, is represented by very few organizations.

One pioneer "of the interior" who should be a model for other blacks across the nation is Sybil C. Mobley, the dean of the School of Business and Industry at Florida A&M University. She has made a noble effort to establish a business culture among young black people. This kind of thinking needs to be multiplied tremendously to improve the commercial arena for African Americans.

Even if we could develop organizations to promote the "Department of the Interior," I am not sure how well they would get along with existing groups. One of the tragedies of civil rights leadership has been its great divides. I base this on my own experiences with the two leading civil rights groups in the nation—the NAACP and the Urban League.

Going back to at least midcentury, there has been a cleavage between the two. The Urban League was founded in 1911 to assist Negroes, many of whom were just off the farm, to cope with the problems of life in cities. Its staff was recruited from the ranks of social workers, and they established contacts with the business community to make small breakthroughs in hiring. The League also had a history of successfully enlisting the aid of whites for fund-raising and studies. The NAACP was more of a mass-based organization. Its approach was the essential one of public protest, coupled with legal attacks on discrimination.

I have worked with both groups. As a youth in Nashville, I was active in the NAACP and continued working as its legal advisor in Flint. While in Flint, I also joined the Urban League and served on its national board when Vernon Jordan was its president.

The difference between the two was like east and west and never the twain shall meet. This always seemed patently absurd to me. After all, there could be ten national organizations working on various facets of racial problems, and there would still be enough for everyone to do. The Urban League worked well within the system, the NAACP outside of it. Together they could have made a powerful team. I always wished they had followed the example of Jewish activist groups—each pursuing what they did best but joining in federation for the greater good.

The divide has been so pronounced in the black community that leaders have been called either Urban League or NAACP types. I found this personally distressing. I have known Ben Hooks, former president of the NAACP, since we were in high school together in Memphis. When he was still serving as president, we would have dinner and lunch together in Washington. He would call me several times to solicit money, and I would send a thousand dollars at a time. He would also discuss his problems with infighting on the NAACP's board. Yet he never asked me to go on the national board, which I would have done if asked. I was sorry not to have served because I believe I could have made a real contribution by pushing for action in new directions.

I can only conclude that I was regarded as an Urban League rather than a good, reliable NAACP type.

Several years ago, when Julius Chambers took over the NAACP Legal Education Defense Fund, he came to Detroit to see me. I agreed to serve on his board, but I never heard back from him. I was also frozen out at the local level. The biggest NAACP fund-raiser in Detroit is the annual Freedom Fund Dinner. For many years, it was probably the largest civil rights dinner in the country. It raised lots of money and was attended by thousands of people. I had been cochair of one of the dinners, but in recent years I have not been invited to help. I can only conclude that people recognized that I would not have agreed with simplistic chants about racism, and I would have disagreed when folks trotted out the same old rhetoric that had been used twenty-five and thirty years ago, as if nothing had changed. Again, I think I could have contributed, if asked, by pushing the local organization to expand its horizons.

Over the years, I also became disenchanted with the Urban League's failure to grow with the times. We did not go nearly far enough in trying to understand either our membership or the larger society. I suggested one remedy might be for the Urban League to consult with some of the best public relations minds on Madison Avenue to determine how best to promote our services. Fellow board members dismissed the idea.

A problem shared by the Urban League, the NAACP, and the United Negro College Fund has been their heavy reliance on corporate donations. Leaders of these groups acted as if these donations were some kind of entitlement. Of course, there are philanthropies that have this kind of charitable impulse. But, as I tried to tell Ben Hooks once, corporations do not give money just for the love of it. They expect some kind of quid pro quo—an easing of tensions, support in some area or another, or input into an organization.

I argued to Hooks and Jordan that they either had to recognize this fact or work harder to pursue support from African Americans. They always maintained that there was not enough money in the black community. I just do not believe that. There are more than twenty-five million of us, and I read someplace that our incomes now approximate those of the entire population of Canada. I do admit, however, that it takes a long time to change old attitudes, and we need to work on that.

Another area in which the traditional civil rights groups have been weak is in their failure to promote African-American business expansion. Largely because of the history of black Americans, we have somehow managed to excel in providing our nation with some of its best teachers and some of its best preachers. To a lesser extent, some of the most capable professional people—doctors, dentists, even lawyers—have been African Americans. But, traditionally, black America has not produced its share of well-trained business leaders.

That has, of course, been changing. When I was growing up, the phrase "black business" brought to mind a very limited picture of a mom-and-pop service organization, generally located in a black neighborhood, serving only the local black community. Generally "mom and pop" had little or no business training or knowledge—except what they picked up from the school of hard knocks. They ran their business out of their back pockets, and too often they did not survive for long.

To be sure, there are still many black folks in small businesses, but they have learned that it takes more than desire and eighteen-hour days to succeed in business. We have also learned that it takes more than a corner store with your name on the window and a few family members if we want to take full advantage of the most our economic system has to offer.

Our grandparents had little control over their personal destinies. Our parents could influence their lives to a degree, but too often simple economic survival required all their energies. Today, we are infinitely more fortunate; not only do we have the opportunity to shape our lives pretty much as we wish, but we have the opportunity to guide the next generation along a path that can bring even greater rewards. Black businessmen have to do a better job of encouraging young blacks to enter business. And blacks who enter corporate America, rather than starting their own businesses, have to be more able and willing to compete.

I remember one article I read a long time ago in the *Pittsburgh Courier* blaming racism for why there were few black executives in corporate America. I would certainly never claim that racism does not exist in businesses today, but in my experience over the years it has become a far smaller factor in decisions about hiring, training, promotion, and pay.

I gave a speech about this to the Los Angeles Chapter of the National Black MBA Association in 1979. What I said then still holds true. I suggested that it is time for all of us to set racism to one side.

If you do not get the job you want, or the promotion, or the raise, do not automatically think that you are the victim of racism. Instead, think about where you might have come up short in the competitive arena. Make a real attempt to evaluate yourself as a professional, not as a black professional. Perhaps that can help you to identify the personal or professional shortcomings that you have. But you will neither identify nor be able to change those faults if you continually fall back on the easier rationale of racism.

We have been seeking equality, and we have gained a great measure of it. Now we should be prepared to compete, personally and professionally on that basis. All of us have the opportunity to succeed, regardless of how we individually define the word. In any definition, success is not handed to anyone. As with any worthwhile goal, we must pursue it with every resource we have.

I never have believed in the philosophy that it is more important who you know than what you know. Of course, all things being equal it is better to know people in positions of power than not to know them, but few people in positions of authority will suffer the embarrassment of appointing incompetents only to see them fail miserably. Corporations are always on the lookout for well-educated, intelligent, hardworking self-starters.

Over the years a number of young black people have asked me to tell them how to succeed in the corporate world. I remind them that it is not easy for anyone, irrespective of race or sex, to succeed in a highly competitive environment. To be sure, there is still great unevenness in African-American progress up the corporate ladder, but if I were just starting out in my career, I would be more worried about measuring up than whether there would be a position waiting for me.

One reason I have come to have faith in business as a means of racial progress is the realization that some of our most difficult problems continue to revolve around poverty and joblessness. There is no doubt in my mind that since the great groundswell of programs during the 1960s, the poor have been steadily losing their patrons.

In part, this is because we have relied too heavily on the public sector in dealing with the seemingly intractable troubles of the poor. Some temporary governmental help may be necessary, but it is essentially a job for the private sector. As I told an Urban League gathering in Indianapolis more than a decade ago, if every black businessman would adopt one youth and help him or her find a job and keep a job, it would be a good start.

219

In this regard, I believe all of us who have been successful have an obligation to help those who follow. When I retired from GM, I received several offers to join Detroit's largest white law firms. Instead, I opted for less money and decided to become "of counsel" to the black commercial law firm set up by David Lewis, Richard White, and Eric Clay, known as Lewis, White & Clay. (It is now Lewis & Munday). They offered me a partnership, but I declined it, in part, because I wanted a break from the day-to-day practice of law. So I chose to be "of counsel," a designation that has many different meanings depending on the particular lawyers and law firm. My role was to serve as a senior lawyer, acting primarily behind the scenes, to offer advice about litigation, legal strategy, and the growth of the firm.

There was a wonderful irony in my working for Lewis, White & Clay. In 1972, when I was still at GM, David Lewis sought my advice about setting up a commercial law firm of color. There had not really been much progress on that front; most African-American civil firms at that time still focused on the personalized business of law: divorces, personal bankruptcies, domestic relations, and contingency work. I did not see how David and his prospective partners, who were young lawyers, could establish the business clientele needed to sustain a commercial law firm. I advised them to join larger white law firms, establish their reputations, and only then strike out on their own.

I took great satisfaction in the fact that my advice proved wrong. The firm was able to get a toehold in corporate business. Richard White represented a small health maintenance organization that had just started in Detroit. It grew to become one of the firm's most important clients. Aetna Casualty hired the firm to handle personal injury defense work. And the newly elected mayor Coleman Young hired the firm to work on a number of municipal law matters.

By the time I joined in 1984, Lewis, White & Clay had twenty-five lawyers and enjoyed the distinction of being one of the largest and best minority firms in the country. The lawyers were much younger than I was, but I had great respect for them. They showed vision, worked hard, and accomplished much.

Success had created a dilemma: whether or not the firm should go "mainstream." I remember one strategic planning retreat in which we discussed whether the firm should shed its self-designation as one of the largest minority firms in the country and commit itself to racially integrate. It was clear that the majority of the partners enjoyed the distinction of being a successful minority firm. I, on the other hand, recommended that the firm should shed the designation. Few people in Detroit would forget the firm's beginning. And I viewed its unique status in the same light as my accomplishments as a "first." The important thing was not who was first but what they did with the opportunity.

No immediate decision on the firm's designation was ever made because there was no need to make one. It would not, after all, have had any effect on our character or day-to-day operations. However, David Lewis has said that my advice has sunk in over time and helped the firm recognize the importance of diversity, especially in terms of public relations. These days, Lewis & Munday bills itself as a diverse law firm founded by African Americans.

Putting all the rhetoric aside, all social relations, including business relations, boil down to the fact that we are all human first. Our race, gender, and backgrounds make us unique, but our humanity is the more fundamental reality. With that in mind, I think we should all aim to bring back civility to our interactions. Over the years, I have been privy to the unknowing comments or the unknowing actions of people in one group who think I belong to the other. As a result, I have experienced racism from both sides. It is not a pleasant thing, but it is a fact. I am past the point where it makes me personally uncomfortable, but it does sadden me.

On planes people will begin talking about a topic that turns to race. If I am engaged in a long conversation with someone who does not recognize that I am black, I usually find some way—trying not to be offensive—to identify myself. Very often that changes the tenor of the conversation, and sometimes it has even occasioned apologies—especially from whites.

As I have gotten older, I have faced similar bad treatment from blacks—especially young ones—who assume I am white. This is a relatively new problem for me in Michigan. Among people of my generation, I have always been clearly identified as black, especially during the years I was in public office. But being out of public life for so long, I now find myself often being identified as white. I find this strange because despite the light color of my skin, I am not what one would typically consider "white looking." Nevertheless, I have noticed that some young blacks who regard me as white do so with great hostility. I receive worse treatment in service stations. Some will slam doors in my face or hurry on elevators ahead of me. I call it a kind of aggressive unfriendliness. I look at such behavior as a miscalculation—a way of incurring animosity or hatred where there was none before because blacks miscalculate how white people feel about them. These youngsters point fingers and say things that are unwarranted. They earn enemies we do not need.

On the other hand, as I have pointed out, whites also have an obligation to overcome racism and recognize that diversity is our national strength. In this period of drift and self doubt, we should remember that we are all Americans, and, as such, we are a beacon of hope for the rest of the world. Many years ago, I gave a commencement speech at a law school and a young Nigerian student came up and engaged me in an earnest discussion about the role of American business in South Africa, which was still governed by apartheid. After a while I asked him why he expected more of Americans than Europeans or Asians, and he looked at me with genuine astonishment and said, "Why, America is the greatest nation on earth because it has the highest regard for human rights."

For those who are tempted to lose hope, I invoke a quote that I used to use in the 1960s when I was often asked to speak about racial questions. It appeared in a Jewish theological seminary publication, and it seems as apt now as it did then. "The night is never wholly dark, and no night is endless. As each of us learn, in our own times of trouble and darkness, the light is never far. Certainly, there is much that is dark and wrong in the world today and in ourselves— meanness, anguish, brutality, greed, frustration, despair. Yet there is order and goodness in the world and in ourselves: love, courage, sacrifice, creativity, growth, renewal and concern. We have been given the power and responsibility to live our life as if the scales of what is right and wrong in the world were exactly balanced and our actions change this balance. To learn how to live this way is not easy. But enriched by the insights of the past, and strengthened by one another . . . we are not alone. And the light is never far."

✦ 12 ✦
Success and Failures, Likes and Dislikes, Family and Faith

I HAVE NEVER been one to blow my own horn. It is not that
I am particularly holy or righteous. I just like to keep
things in perspective. Obviously, I am proud of the good
things I have done, and I appreciate the praise that I have received
over the years, especially when I think it is warranted. I have more
mixed feelings about compliments that I do not think I have earned.

When I was still a member of the Michigan Supreme Court, a
newspaper reporter called me "heroic" because of what I accomplished as an African American. I never saw any great degree of hero-
ism in what I did. In fact, like most of us, my success was in large part
an accident of history. I came of age at the right time, and I was grateful for the opportunities that I have had. Anybody who has been allowed to do everything I did—to be chair of the Michigan Public
Service Commission, auditor general, a supreme court justice, and
general counsel for GM—would have to be grateful. Those kinds of
opportunities are rare—for whites or African Americans or anyone
else. I am only glad that I was able to justify peoples' confidence in me
by discharging my responsibilities well.

I think a lot of people have the wrong idea about what constitutes
success. For one thing, it has nothing to do with how much money
you earn or amass. Some of the most successful people I have known,
including my mother and my Scoutmaster, Charles Chatman, did not
have much money. Yet they were far more successful human beings
than many of the folks I have met who ran Fortune 500 companies.

Perhaps because of the way I grew up, I never had much trouble keeping money in perspective. As a child, millionaires seemed to me as distant as the stars. When I realized that I had amassed my first $1 million, it startled me. Then I recognized that it was the least interesting fact about me. My first instinct was to try and figure out how to preserve it for my wife, children, grandchildren, and my brother. After I made sure they were taken care of, I thought briefly about ways to spend the rest. I say briefly because I have never been very good at spending money. I live in a modest apartment and drive a modest car. What I am good at is giving money away. It is not something to brag about; it just seems to come naturally. I have always tried to help people I know, and because of my memories of growing up poor, I send money to help children's causes around the world.

I realize that my views about money may be rather unusual for someone who spent many years working for the world's largest industrial corporation. Even during my years at General Motors, I never believed that it was right for top corporate officials to overpay themselves. For example, I thought it was outrageous when GM gave Roger Smith an annual pension of $1.1 million. I especially dislike the idea, which is held by some executives, that it is all right to squeeze employees while they pay themselves outlandish bonuses.

To me, success is ultimately just a matter of doing well with what you have been given. I remember an evening I spent with Stan Musial in the 1960s. The St. Louis Cardinals great had attended a conference about fair housing at which I was a speaker. We were seat mates, and after the event ended, he asked David Lawrence, who was then mayor of Pittsburgh, and me if we wanted to accompany him to Sportsman Park to watch the Cardinals play the Pirates. At that time, Musial was vice president of the Cardinals organization. The three of us sat in the president's box, just above home plate. After a short while, Lawrence left us to sit in the broadcast booth with the Pittsburgh commentators. So I had a chance for a long talk with Musial.

We compared notes about growing up in poverty during the depression. Musial was raised in a very poor Polish family in Donora, a blue-collar industrial town outside of Pittsburgh. He remembered that his family survived by eating a lot of cabbage. Musial was not a big man, but he was wiry. As baseball fans may remember, he had a unique stance, crouching deep in the batter's box. He explained that he did that to compensate for his lack of size; by unwinding from the crouch, he was able to get more power.

Despite his humble origins and his size, Musial became one of baseball's most famous hitters. He batted over .300 season after season. I asked him how he could maintain such consistency at hitting, which some commentators claim is the most challenging feat in all of professional sports. He explained the ins and outs of baseball—the alleys, the fielding, and so on. I did not understand most of it. But, he said, "The most important thing was I just tried not to hit bad balls."

I think that is a good philosophy for all of us. It signifies that success has more to do with common sense and good values than anything else. In many speaking engagements over the years, especially at African-American colleges and business fraternities, I was invariably asked what it took to succeed in business. I always disabused my questioners of the implication that success means having "pull" or connections. Undoubtedly, they help some folks get a foot on the rung of the ladder, but it seldom helps anyone get much further.

I always began these speeches by addressing the question of just what success means. I do not think any of us can afford the luxury of saying we are or were successful simply because we happen to hold or happened to hold a certain job. What matters is what we contributed while we held those positions. The most successful men I have known in my life have been Charles Chatman, Dudley Mallory, Governor G. Mennen Williams, and GM chair Tom Murphy. Like all successful people, they shared the same attributes. I like to call these the seven "C's" of success: competence, character, commitment, confidence, cooperation, concern, and competitiveness.

There is no substitute for competence. No matter who we are, no matter what we do, no matter what else we can offer, we must be able and anxious to handle our present work competently. The emphasis here is on *present* work. We all know people who view today's job as simply a stepping-stone to a bigger one. Too often, in their zeal to move on, they look upon their present assignment as one that can be glossed over. They overburden themselves with fantasies of the next job or the next big promotion and forget that it is the present that is most important. Their approach does a disservice to the business, the individual, and the people with whom they work. And for those cynics who think that "pull" and "bull" are the ingredients of success, I offer absolutely no hope.

As my law partner and mentor, Mr. Mallory, used to say: "Cover the ground on which you stand." Whatever your task at the moment, give it everything you can. Do your job well, then give it that extra step. Do your job fully and completely; do it better than anyone else ever could. Or as my brother and my high school football coach used to say, "Don't hold your job, do your job."

Few of us, if any of us, know what directions our lives will take tomorrow. So it is futile to live for the future. When I was pushing a broom in Nashville, feeding elephants at a circus in Chester, Pennsylvania, or swinging a sledgehammer in a Philadelphia foundry, I had no idea where my life would lead. When I decided to study law, I had no idea I would become chair of the MPSC. When I was sitting on the Michigan Supreme Court, a job with General Motors was the last thing in my mind. We would all be better off if we lived in the present, did the best job we could each day, and let the results of our efforts determine the shape of tomorrow.

In every job there are tasks that are little more than daily drudgery. At GM I reported to a group of senior executives who expected me to be conversant with everything going on, every day, in GM's legal staff. The only way to deal with it was to read and understand everything that came across my desk, from every lawyer on the staff, regardless of whether I ever had to get personally involved. I never particularly enjoyed the chore, and I never figured out a way to make it interesting. I just had to do it. We all have tasks that are little more than daily drudgery. And we must do these things well. They count, they are important, and they often play as great a part in our careers as the more significant projects.

Another trait of all successful people is character. Our character sustains us. It is what enables us to make the decisions that will best meet our goals. Character reinforces our sense of right and wrong, and, in the end, it is what makes us all individuals. It is not the same as personality, which is a more superficial concept, just as education and learning are superficial concepts compared to wisdom.

When we can do our jobs adequately, we have learned. When we take that extra step, when we give more than what is minimally required, when we see the goal of our individual task as part of the goal of the organization, when we work toward the improvement of others, then we have acquired a measure of wisdom. Character stems from wisdom; both must be refined and both are necessary for any measure of success, however defined.

After competence and character, the next significant attribute is commitment. It is the spark that turns us on and lights us up to achieve our fullest potential. We all understand commitment in love, but successful people also have a strong emotional attachment to their professions, their callings in life, their work, whatever it might be. It fuels their efforts and cements their loyalties. It is what keeps us up at night and gets us up early in the morning in pursuit of excellence.

The next trait is confidence. Never hide that ability, either from others or from yourself. If you have no faith in your ability to do your job, then you are likely to take the approach of the proverbial door-to-door salesman who greeted every customer with, "I don't suppose there is any chance you would like to buy some brushes today, is there?" Know that you can accomplish what you set out to do. Never forget it, and never let anyone else forget it. Perhaps even more important, never help anyone else develop a lack of confidence. Nothing is more defeating than the feeling, "I won't be able to make it."

The next "C" is cooperation. I know of no individual who exists independently of others. I am quite certain nobody could exist that way, and none of us would want to, even if we could. We all, in every way, are part of a team. The team may be family, friends, coworkers, or those who do not even know us but depend on us. Everything we do, every day, depends on a team effort.

In the car industry, for example, the team includes miners who bring iron out of the ground, the steelworker who transforms the raw material into a sheet of metal, the press operator who turns the metal sheet into an automobile fender, the assemblyman who installs the fender on the auto body, the truck driver who transports the automobile to the showroom, the salesman who sells the car, and the customer who buys the product. Along the way, there are hundreds of thousands of individuals who have equally important roles in the team. A less than adequate performance by any one of them adversely affects the product.

Another of the personal attributes that is important to success is concern. I do not know of a single individual I admire who has ever lost, or repressed, concern for others. The finest people I know, without exception, have devoted a considerable portion of their talents and efforts to making their society a better place in which to live.

The last on my list is competitiveness. You must be ready and willing to compete in your personal and professional life, and to compete on an equal basis with everybody. This is especially true for women and African Americans. Equality is what the battle has been all about for hundreds of years. We have more equality today than we have ever had, and we had all better be ready to take full advantage of it.

227

In addition to these traits shared by all successful people, we all
have unique talents that make us special. I have always taken pride in
my ability to analyze current events. I have a knack for understanding
and predicting trends in the law, in politics, and in governmental actions. Sometimes, as in the case of affirmative action, I have found
myself five, ten, or fifteen years ahead of my time. This trait has served
me well in all walks of life because it has allowed me to act as a catalyst
for bringing issues into the open that otherwise would have remained
undiscussed.

Another trait that has served me well is my commitment to public
service. Holding high office has always meant more to me than just
developing a larger résumé, or feeling important, or earning a good

Otis Smith is shown here with his brother, Hamilton Smith, at an American
Bar Association reception in New York City in the mid-1980s.

living. I consider public office to be a public trust of the first magnitude. Service to God's people of whatever race or class is, in my opinion, second only to serving God. This is what service in government means to me. It is service to the total community; it is doing for people those things they cannot do for themselves, or cannot do so well. It is totally different in concept from the car business, or the grocery business, or the clothing business, not that these are not useful callings. It is just that making the laws and regulations under which people must live calls upon us "to do justice," which has been described since ancient times as mankind's highest civil calling.

That is why in my long public career I have spent far more effort in part-time, nonpaying government positions than I spent during my ten years on the public payroll. I am proud to say that five Michigan governors appointed me to positions in state government, some paying, most nonpaying, never at my request. G. Mennen Williams appointed me to the Michigan Public Service Commission and the auditor generalship. John B. Swainson appointed me to the supreme court. George Romney appointed me to the University of Michigan's Board of Regents. Bill Milliken wanted to appoint me to head the state Department of Labor, but I just could not see returning to Lansing at that point. However, I did agree to serve with his Commission on Educational Reform in 1968, on the Board of Regents of Oakland University in the 1970s, and the State Civil Service Commission. Jim Blanchard also appointed me to a couple of committees. Of the five governors, three were Democrats and two were Republicans. Chief Justice Warren E. Burger appointed me to serve as a member of the Federal Commission on Executive Legislation and Judicial Salaries. I also served on various commissions and boards under several presidents, including Jack Kennedy, Lyndon Johnson, Jimmy Carter, and Ronald Reagan.

I am not going to list all of these, but if you were to ask me "what do you think you are doing on all of the boards, commissions, and advisory groups for over thirty years?" I would have answered that I thought I was helping to fine-tune the machinery of this republic. In other words, making it function a little better. Again, I take no special pride in having served. I believe we all have the responsibility to make our community and the world just a little bit better by applying our intelligence and judgment and energy to particular problems.

That said, I have always been careful to avoid getting appointments where I would have been pulling somebody's chestnuts out of the fire. Former Detroit mayor Coleman Young conscripted me to serve as chair of the Committee on Wages of his budget revitalization committee in 1980 and 1981. He did it not by contacting me directly but by calling GM chair Roger Smith to see if I would be available. I thought it was a bad way of going about getting my services, but in view of the city's fiscal crisis, I agreed to serve. It turned out that the committee was not the hot potato I feared it would become. Still, I have always tried to avoid getting drawn into such politicized situations. I turned down two appointments from Governor Jim Blanchard for this reason. One concerned welfare reform, about which I did not have any expertise, and the other was a task force to review a negative report by the state auditor general about management of the Michigan Employment Security Commission.

In connection with that job, the head of the Department of Labor tried to persuade me that I was the ideal person to head the task force because of my reputation. Whenever I hear that kind of pitch, I always duck. Although I admit I may have credibility in the community, I also know that credibility can dissolve very quickly. In this situation, the only possible reason for convening a task force was political. The man who had just left management of the MESC was African American, and his wife was a federal judge. I thought the whole idea of the task force was kind of flimsy. The auditor general's report was either valid or it was not. If it was wrong, then the governor should have said so. If it was right, then the governor should have stood behind it. There was no need for a task force.

I turned down a similar assignment involving the Detroit Police Department. When allegations first surfaced that Kenneth Weiner, a deputy civilian police chief, and William L. Hart, the police chief, had pilfered money from a fund set up for special investigations, an assistant to Mayor Coleman Young contacted me to investigate the matter. I refused. I did not tell him, but I thought to myself: "How in the devil could I conduct an investigation of the police department without subpoena power? I do not belong to the department. They are not accountable to me. They could run rings around me. They could hide things. They could lie to me." I decided there was little I could do. Ultimately, the U.S. attorney's office handled the investigation.

I offer these experiences and thoughts to prove the adage that even in public and charitable service, it is important to keep a strong sense of values. If you do, you will keep your good reputation. I have always been proud that, among the citizens of Michigan and the people who know me, I have a reputation as an honest man. I value that and have always worked hard to see that nothing tarnishes it.

My strong sense of values probably explains why I never sought a divorce—even when I realized that Mavis and I could no longer live together. I suppose if I have any sense of failure in my life, it concerns my family. I am not sure I can evaluate my marriage and my life with my children with any objectivity. In general, I will say that it has been a great sadness to me that things did not turn out as I wished when I was a young man, dreaming about the ideal marriage, the loving close family, the cooperative parents, and the successful, aspiring children. I do not fault myself entirely. A lot of it is just happenstance—the inheritances that both parents bring to marriage in terms of expectations, genes, and everything else. Regrettably, Mavis and I had such differences that it made our marriage very difficult.

I cannot help but think that if I had been a little bit more intuitive about things, or a little bit more analytical about what I was getting Mavis and me into, I might have opted for a different path. If I had married someone else who had more of my kind of upbringing—Old Southern, striving, and ambitious—things might have turned out differently. Maybe the children would have been more successful academically and professionally. Maybe we would have had a stormy time anyway. The fact is that it happened the way it did, and I am still struggling with how best to help my wife and my four sons.

Mavis and I were always different. It became clear to me soon after we married that she was not comfortable around my kinfolk. My mother, my Aunt Maggie, and all of my cousins were talkative, whereas Mavis was quiet. My mother did the best she could with the situation and never tried to drive a wedge between us. The most she would say about Mavis or her relatives, who were from Jamaica, would be something to the effect that "Those West Indies people are a little funny."

My mother and the other women in my family were all highly skilled at cooking and homemaking, which Mavis was not. It was embarrassing for them that our house was always a mess, and they finally stopped coming to see us. We never had friends over for dinner because it was just too much for Mavis, and we did not go out because Mavis was not comfortable with strangers and we could never reciprocate. I bowed out of a lot of social engagements over the years but rationalized our lack of socializing by saying it left me with more time to concentrate on my work.

I hoped when we moved from Flint to Lansing that it would be easier for Mavis. I figured it would be a relief for her not having to deal with all of my relatives. But things just got worse. I was under a lot of pressure at work, and I was not able to cope with troubles at home. When we moved to Detroit, I hoped that Mavis would be happy to return to her hometown and live near her brothers. But our life did not improve. Mavis was angry with me much of the time, and there were weeks and months of silence. By the time I urged that we go to counseling, it was too late. She could not see the need for it since we had gone on for years without finding ways to resolve our differences. In 1974, I left the pressure cooker of trying to cope with the situation and took an apartment in downtown Detroit.

It was very disappointing to me and one of the sadder things about my life. I would have loved to have had the closeness of a happy marriage, but I just did not know how to pull it off. I am certain that had I understood family life better and brought more in the way of understanding to her, I might have been able to work around her ideas and inclinations. I finally moved out as a way of saving my sanity. During the years of our separation, we have had long soul-searching talks, with the idea that we might go back together. As a result, I have become strongly convinced that she did the very best that she could with a house full of kids and a husband who was out of the home most of the time. I am not angry with her, but I am sorry that our life together did not turn out better.

I feel much the same way about my sons. Like a lot of men in my generation, I just got swept up in my work. The jobs required so much time that I was not in the best position to monitor my kids closely. Of course, a lot of kids survive because of a strong mother. But Mavis and I never saw eye-to-eye about how to raise children. Her idea was to let them alone to develop without requiring too much from them. I would have demanded a lot more.

I wanted them all to be achievers, and I just expected that they would all go to college and some would go on to professional schools. I did not try to make lawyers out of any of them because they never expressed any interest in it. I also did not demand that they attend political or civic functions with me because, after they became teenagers, I did not think I had the right to drag them along. I never really wanted them to be any particular thing except well trained and comfortably situated in their own careers.

In retrospect, I wish I had pulled them along. But I was always skeptical of parents who tried to force their kids into doing things. I felt my role was to expose them to different things, so they could find what they liked and were good at and then could develop into their potential. I used to tell them all the time, "If you guys want to go to graduate school to become a Harvard Ph.D., I'll borrow on my life insurance and do anything and everything necessary to put you through."

Steve was the only one who finished college. I'll never forget one conversation we had when I asked him what he would study. He said, "Business. That's what you want me to do, isn't it?" I figure he assumed that because I was then working at GM. I asked him about his love of music. His eyes grew wide, and he said, "You mean I can study music?" I said it was fine with me. He worked tenaciously and got his degree. I was so excited that I bought him a car, hoping it would be an incentive to his older brothers. It was not.

I was disappointed that the other three did not go to college, but it does not mean that I am disappointed with them as human beings. They are very nice young men. Each one is different. But they are all pleasant to be around and reasonably alert and generally reliable. I am thankful that Steven, Ray, Anthony, and Vincent are all gentlemen and that we are all fond of one another.

On the whole I have enjoyed being a father. I used to get a big bang out of coming home when they were little. Even though I was busy at work, I never minded doing the grocery shopping or washing diapers. I would have loved to have had at least one daughter, but having sons was a lot of fun. As they got older, we would play in the snow in the winter and play ball in warm weather. We traveled a bit together, piling into the station wagon and taking our bikes for rides in the country. Once we went up North to stay at Mennen Williams's cottage. On a scale of one to ten, I would rank myself about eight as a father. Even Mavis would admit that I always made time to be with my sons.

Despite my reservations about the Vietnam War, I felt strongly that young men should not run away from military service. I felt if they had moral ambivalence about the war, they should refuse induction and do their jail time. I did not like the idea of wealthy young men staying in school getting deferments based on taking courses in which they had no interest. I also did not like the idea of people going to Canada to escape induction. If people could just evade the government's call for service, then how could we ever raise an army to fight the country's enemies? In retrospect, this thinking led me to one of the stupidest mistakes I ever made. My oldest two sons, Vince and Ray, registered for the draft, and I said, "You know if you run and hide, as far as I am concerned you will no longer be my sons." They were very quiet. I do not think either one had strong feelings about the war, and neither ended up getting called for action. I am especially grateful for that considering the great futility and stupidity of that war. In light of what was revealed later, I would never again maintain that ordinary citizens do not have the right to subject the government and its leaders to great scrutiny. Our leaders can and do make mistakes, and it is up to us to be ever vigilant not only about our liberties but also about the kinds of engagements in which the leadership of our country gets us involved.

When I left GM in 1983, Mavis and I began talking about trying to get back together. We looked at twelve or fourteen houses together. We could not agree on one we liked. She might have compromised, but I was set on finding the ideal place. In the back of my mind, I probably was having reservations about a reconciliation. The more time we spent together, the more I realized that we would be doing the wrong thing trying to pick up our marriage. I think she agreed. We have been pleasant and civil to each other, but I do not think either one of us has thought seriously of changing our situation.

I have no doubt that the Catholic Church's analysis of matrimony is correct. When marriage functions, it is the ideal relationship. It satisfies virtually every human need when the parties are well-paired, love each other, have similar backgrounds, similar aspirations, the ability to work together, weep together, and laugh together. People who are contemplating marriage should be taught how to pick a mate and then get the skills they need to start off properly. If we were taught properly, there would be a lot fewer divorces.

In any case, I hate coming from a broken home and I hate even worse being a participant in one. I regret it horribly. But I am okay. When I put everything in perspective, I realize that we could have done a lot worse. All of us could have. I think we did the best we could.

I have been reflecting more about these things lately because of my poor health. My ulcers, a source of pain throughout my life, have become worse lately. I have also been diagnosed with prostate cancer. I am not really morbid about it. I do not go around thinking about my health problems all of the time, although I recognize that the older I get, the more wearing my poor health is. It is something that people without chronic illnesses probably do not understand. Still, there are a lot of people who have worse things wrong with them, so I try not to complain too much.

Still, I realize that my life is winding down. And, as I get older, I take more pleasure in simple things. I like walking trails through the woods. I like well-maintained parks with plenty of lush, green grass. I like sailing in a sturdy boat in a moderately brisk breeze of about eight knots. I love the beautiful blue-green waters of the Great Lakes. I have always liked playing games with my sons—football, baseball, basketball, and tennis. I do not get to do much of that anymore, but I still enjoy watching children at play. I enjoy melodic jazz music. And there is something very special about a big piece of blueberry pie.

My dislikes have also become more firmly entrenched. I do not like people who are loud and rude. I do not like people who prejudge others, especially by race or nationality. I do not like the way discourteous people in service jobs are rough and crude to the people they are supposed to help. I do not like people in the media who trivialize political campaigns by covering them like horse races and, in the process, hurt democracy. By the same token, I do not like politicians who consider finessing the truth to be a worthy skill. In the process, they betray the public trust.

Most of all, I dislike the dogmatism that has come to pervade so much of our public life. We must all learn to live with tentative truths because we can never really know the final truth about anything. I have operated that way most of my life. I do not have a need for absolute certainty. Society would be a lot better off if everyone could realize that the best we can ever have is reasonable certainty.

For example, politics has taken on a bitterness that can only undermine our political life. Generally put, Republicans look at problems from the standpoint of capital and management while Democrats look at issues from the viewpoint of the proverbial "common man." I would not want to see a world where either one predominates. If you treat workers fairly, for example, they can buy goods that spur the economy. In the same vein, if you keep giving money to rich people, they will just buy bigger yachts and more homes in Europe or the West. On the other hand, if government impedes business, there will not be enough jobs for everyone. Both parties, and the liberals and conservatives they represent, play a useful role.

I suppose one reason why politics has become so divisive is religion. My specific views of religion have changed over the years. I was brought up in a religious family, although I cannot say that I have always been religious. I am one of those people whom the epic poem describes best: The hound of heaven is always looking for my soul, and I always seem to be resisting. I am not an institutional church person as I perhaps ought to be. I tried to be a good Catholic, but when my wife and I had four sons, I appreciated her argument that we abandon the Church's teaching against contraception.

I suppose it would be wonderful if everyone in the world were to accept Christianity as the one true faith and then proceed to practice it with utter abandon. International and domestic tensions would soon evaporate, leaving the Heaven on Earth that we always discuss. But this has never been a real hope. Christian nations have led the world in nationalism and war for a thousand years. Christianity has developed several hundred subdivisions, all with claims of truth. During the early 1960s, I attended a meeting in Memphis where I heard about a program sponsored by the "Catholic Committee Against Integration," or some such name. I picked up a newspaper and saw an ad placed by a restaurant owner, complete with Biblical quotations purportedly supporting his policy of segregation. The problem has always been how do we "draw all men unto Him" when we cannot agree what we want to draw men to?

In spite of my reservations about organized religions, I have always believed that an all-powerful being set this universe in motion. It is an orderly system that is obviously the result of extraordinary intelligence, far beyond the capacity of man. I am not sure whether there has been or ever will be a heaven. I have doubts about the specifics of any doctrine. Yet, I think deep in the wellspring of our being is the desire to ascribe to something that is wholly pure and powerful and sound. This may not be the God as Christians, Muslims, Jews or any other religious faith perceive, but there is obviously a very powerful spiritual force that has pervaded over centuries, among all kinds of people in all kinds of different places. I guess I believe with the Baha'is that there is a substantial amount of truth, if you want to call it that, in all of the major prophets, in all faiths, of all times, who have tried to give us their vision of what God is like.

In a related vein, in part because I have been nominally a Roman Catholic for so many years, I have been wary of discussions that describe God as masculine. The church uses that as an excuse to conclude that there is no place for women in its hierarchy. I find that difficult to swallow. I cannot believe that a just God, whoever He or

She is, would assign half of the human race to a lower spiritual status than the other half.

For this reason and out of a simple sense of fairness, I have never had any problem with women going as high as their abilities—physical, mental, emotional—will take them. Over the years, I heard some men say that women were too emotional to hold high positions. That is ridiculous. Some men are highly emotional, while some women—such as former British prime minister Margaret Thatcher—are cool customers.

The so-called division of the sexes points up one human tendency that has always been my pet peeve, people's tendency to draw divides among people. I never have liked it, whether it involves the sexes or the races. That having been said, I admit that coming together is not always the easiest thing to do. But I will share one final story to show that it is worth attempting.

I cite my own family. Perhaps because he was older and knew our father better, my brother was more interested initially in our white relatives than I was. During one trip to Memphis, he went to visit one of our white cousins. My father did not have any other children besides Hamilton and me, but he was close to his sisters' children. In any case, my brother went to visit our cousin, who was named Samuel Williamson after our father.

My brother did not want to impose, so he merely talked in general terms about my father. He said he had always wanted to meet the man named for Samuel Williamson, because he had come to know the first Samuel Williamson while working as a headwaiter at the Claridge Hotel. My brother embellished this fiction by saying that they had discussed the value of education. He then went on to name several members of the family and some of my father's business associates.

Our cousin Sam asked my brother a few questions. A few days later, he called my brother, said we were cousins, and suggested that we get together. At first, I was not very enthusiastic at the suggestion, but my brother insisted that it was important to him.

We ended up having dinner, and since then we have had many talks about my father and our very different lives growing up on separate sides of Memphis's racial divide. We have learned quite a bit about our family's background and more details about our father's personality. We had a family reunion of sorts in St. Louis with Sam, his sister Anna, and other relatives. It turned into a grand get-together. Later, when Sam was having a difficult time, I invited him to join my brother and me in Washington for a few days of sightseeing. It was the first time that my cousin met my brother's family. It was not high drama, but it was interesting. My cousin is a dyed-in-the-wool southerner, but he was not at all upset to meet his African-American relatives. Since then, a sincere bond of family has developed, and we have communicated on a regular basis. This is what America is all about.

Afterword

Otis Milton Smith died of cancer on June 29, 1994. Hundreds of friends honored him in a memorial service at Bethel A.M.E. Church in Detroit. He is buried at the River Rest Cemetery in Flint, Michigan.

Acknowledgments

This book is based largely on memoirs that Otis Milton Smith dictated in the three years before his death. I have condensed and edited that material, then supplemented it with speeches, interviews, and newspaper accounts by and about Otis Smith contained in his papers at the Bentley Historical Library at the University of Michigan.

At the Bentley, Francis Blouin, Nancy Bartlett, and their staff members were very helpful. Rosemary Nelms at the *Memphis Commercial Appeal,* David Larzelere at the *Flint Journal,* and Pat Zacharias at the *Detroit News* took time out from their busy jobs as library directors to research information, find pictures, and check names.

Jo Jones efficiently transcribed the memoirs. Margaret Edwards, John D. Silvera, Frederick C. Branch, Edward Littlejohn, Dores Mc-Cree, David Baker Lewis, Mavis Smith, and Raymond Smith kindly offered me their insights about and memories of Otis Smith. My father, David Fox Stolberg, proved again to be an insightful reader and editor. As always, he has been a constant source of encouragement. James Edwards and Patrick Murray were wonderful hosts for my many trips to Michigan.

Finally, this book would not have been possible without Hamilton Smith, who fits the bill of a doting big brother. He came up with the idea for this project, prodded Otis to dictate his memoirs, then labored diligently to see the book through to publication. He has been an invaluable resource and inspiration.

Mary M. Stolberg

Index

Titles in the Great Lakes Books Series

Freshwater Fury: Yarns and Reminiscences of the Greatest Storm in Inland Navigation, by Frank Barcus, 1986 (reprint)

Call It North Country: The Story of Upper Michigan, by John Bartlow Martin, 1986 (reprint)

The Land of the Crooked Tree, by U. P. Hedrick, 1986 (reprint)

Michigan Place Names, by Walter Romig, 1986 (reprint)

Luke Karamazov, by Conrad Hilberry, 1987

The Late, Great Lakes: An Environmental History, by William Ashworth, 1987 (reprint)

Great Pages of Michigan History from the Detroit Free Press, 1987

Waiting for the Morning Train: An American Boyhood, by Bruce Catton, 1987 (reprint)

Michigan Voices: Our State's History in the Words of the People Who Lived It, compiled and edited by Joe Grimm, 1987

Danny and the Boys, Being Some Legends of Hungry Hollow, by Robert Traver, 1987 (reprint)

Hanging On, or How to Get through a Depression and Enjoy Life, by Edmund G. Love, 1987 (reprint)

The Situation in Flushing, by Edmund G. Love, 1987 (reprint)

A Small Bequest, by Edmund G. Love, 1987 (reprint)

The Saginaw Paul Bunyan, by James Stevens, 1987 (reprint)

The Ambassador Bridge: A Monument to Progress, by Philip P. Mason, 1988

Let the Drum Beat: A History of the Detroit Light Guard, by Stanley D. Solvick, 1988

An Afternoon in Waterloo Park, by Gerald Dumas, 1988 (reprint)

Contemporary Michigan Poetry: Poems from the Third Coast, edited by Michael Delp, Conrad Hilberry and Herbert Scott, 1988

Over the Graves of Horses, by Michael Delp, 1988

Wolf in Sheep's Clothing: The Search for a Child Killer, by Tommy McIntyre, 1988

Copper-Toed Boots, by Marguerite de Angeli, 1989 (reprint)

Detroit Images: Photographs of the Renaissance City, edited by John J. Bukowczyk and Douglas Aikenhead, with Peter Slavcheff, 1989

Cobb Would Have Caught It: The Golden Age of Baseball in Detroit, by Richard Bak, 1991

Michigan in Literature, by Clarence Andrews, 1992

Under the Influence of Water: Poems, Essays, and Stories, by Michael Delp, 1992

The Country Kitchen, by Della T. Lutes, 1992 (reprint)

The Making of a Mining District: Keweenaw Native Copper 1500–1870, by David J. Krause, 1992

Kids Catalog of Michigan Adventures, by Ellyce Field, 1993

Henry's Lieutenants, by Ford R. Bryan, 1993

Historic Highway Bridges of Michigan, by Charles K. Hyde, 1993

Lake Erie and Lake St. Clair Handbook, by Stanley J. Bolsenga and Charles E. Herndendorf, 1993

Queen of the Lakes, by Mark Thompson, 1994

Iron Fleet: The Great Lakes in World War II, by George J. Joachim, 1994

Turkey Stearnes and the Detroit Stars: The Negro Leagues in Detroit, 1919–1933, by Richard Bak, 1994

Pontiac and the Indian Uprising, by Howard H. Peckham, 1994 (reprint)

Charting the Inland Seas: A History of the U.S. Lake Survey, by Arthur M. Woodford, 1994 (reprint)

Ojibwa Narratives of Charles and Charlotte Kawbawgam and Jacques LePique, 1893–1895. Recorded with Notes by Homer H. Kidder, edited by Arthur P. Bourgeois, 1994, co-published with the Marquette County Historical Society

Strangers and Sojourners: A History of Michigan's Keweenaw Peninsula, by Arthur W. Thurner, 1994

Win Some, Lose Some: G. Mennen Williams and the New Democrats, by Helen Washburn Berthelot, 1995

Sarkis, by Gordon and Elizabeth Orear, 1995

The Northern Lights: Lighthouses of the Upper Great Lakes, by Charles K. Hyde, 1995 (reprint)

Kids Catalog of Michigan Adventures, second edition, by Ellyce Field, 1995

Rumrunning and the Roaring Twenties: Prohibition on the Michigan-Ontario Waterway, by Philip P. Mason, 1995